COMPARING COMMUNICATION SYSTEMS

Emphasizing the perspective of ordinary users, this book compares the uses of the internet in three centers of the global economy and world politics: China, Europe, and the United States. It examines the internet as the current center-piece of communication systems encompassing interpersonal communication, mass communication, and social networking.

The internet is unique as a medium in that it hosts both "old" media and "new" media. As such, it also integrates the prototypes of one-to-one (interpersonal) and one-to-many (broadcast) along with many-to-many (social media) and many-to-one (surveillance) communication. This book considers how all these media and communicative practices are embedded in social structures, cultural traditions, and historical legacies of place. Comparing conditions in China, Europe, and the United States, the chapters provide an overview of the distinctive regulatory regimes framing the internet and its local uses, the place of the internet in everyday life in each setting, and how the internet serves as a resource for political, economic, and cultural actions and interactions.

Linking comparative analysis of media and social systems with ethnographic studies of internet usage on the ground, this book will be of particular interest to students and scholars working in global media, intercultural communication, and internet studies.

Klaus Bruhn Jensen, Professor, Department of Communication, University of Copenhagen, Denmark. Publications include *A Theory of Communication and Justice* (Routledge, 2021) and *Media Convergence: The Three Degrees of Network, Mass, and Interpersonal Communication*, 2nd ed. (Routledge, 2022).

Rasmus Helles, Associate Professor, Department of Communication, University of Copenhagen, Denmark. His work has appeared in *New Media & Society*, *Surveillance & Society*, the *International Journal of Communication*, and the *European Journal of Communication*.

"The Peoples' Internet project embodies all that is admirable about excellent research. Presenting data from seven countries across three continents, its scale is matched by its theoretical heft, methodological innovation, and analytical rigour. The rich insights we can plumb from this ambitious study will fortify our understanding of how communication is evolving in an intensely connected yet deeply fractious world. The authors deftly explore the contestation between structure and agency, the tussle between commercial imperatives and social good, and the challenge of alienation within community."

Sun Sun Lim, *Professor, Singapore University of Technology and Design*

"Jensen and Helles do the brave work of imagining the internet as a global information infrastructure that serves us all in ways that we understand and want. The internet envelops us and frames our engagements with reality, it provides us with forms of action and interaction, and it can exacerbate or help overcome our cognitive biases. Jensen and Helles are critical but not fatalistic in their theorizing – an internet that helps us produce, maintain, repair and transform reality is still possible."

Philip N. Howard, *Professor, Oxford Internet Institute*

"This is an exceptional book. Placing communicative practice at the center, it weaves the material, the institutional, and the cultural to provide an empirically based comparison of communication systems. Its methodological sophistication, international scope, and theoretical richness make it a unique and remarkable contribution to the study of contemporary communication."

Fernando Bermejo, *Faculty Associate, Berkman Klein Center for Internet & Society, Harvard University*

"What does the internet do to us – the people – and how do we use it across different regions of the world? How does it affect our social life, our identity, and our ability to engage in society? These are some of the important questions that this book explores. Based on diverse empirical data from Europe, the US, and China, the book provides important new insights into people's everyday communication as well as the local regulation that shapes such practices across different regional contexts. Congratulations to the Peoples' Internet project for helping us understand how the internet's material, social, and economic infrastructures interact with communicative practices on the ground."

Rikke Frank Jørgensen, *Senior Researcher, Danish Institute for Human Rights*

COMPARING COMMUNICATION SYSTEMS

The Internets of China, Europe, and the United States

Edited by Klaus Bruhn Jensen and Rasmus Helles

Routledge
Taylor & Francis Group

LONDON AND NEW YORK

Cover image: Rawpixel/Getty Images

First published 2023
by Routledge
4 Park Square, Milton Park, Abingdon, Oxon OX14 4RN

and by Routledge
605 Third Avenue, New York, NY 10158

Routledge is an imprint of the Taylor & Francis Group, an informa business

British Library Cataloguing-in-Publication Data
A catalogue record for this book is available from the British Library

Library of Congress Cataloging-in-Publication Data
Names: Jensen, Klaus Bruhn, editor. | Helles, Rasmus, editor.
Title: Comparing communication systems : the internets of China, Europe, and the United States / edited by Klaus Bruhn Jensen and Rasmus Helles.
Description: 1 Edition. | New York, NY : Routledge, 2023. | Includes bibliographical references and index.
Identifiers: LCCN 2022021999 (print) | LCCN 2022022000 (ebook) | ISBN 9780367522339 (hardback) | ISBN 9780367522346 (paperback) | ISBN 9781003057055 (ebook)
Subjects: LCSH: Internet--China. | Communication--China. | Internet--Europe. | Communication--Europe. | Internet--United States. | Communication--United States.
Classification: LCC HM851 .C6564 2023 (print) | LCC HM851 (ebook) | DDC 302.23/1--dc23/eng/20220728
LC record available at https://lccn.loc.gov/2022021999
LC ebook record available at https://lccn.loc.gov/2022022000

ISBN: 978-0-367-52233-9 (hbk)
ISBN: 978-0-367-52234-6 (pbk)
ISBN: 978-1-003-05705-5 (ebk)

DOI: 10.4324/9781003057055

Typeset in Bembo
by Deanta Global Publishing Services, Chennai, India

CONTENTS

ILLUSTRATIONS

Figures

Tables

CONTRIBUTORS

Piermarco Aroldi is Professor of Sociology of Culture and Communication in the School of Education at the Università Cattolica del Sacro Cuore in Piacenza and Milan, Italy, where he coordinates the master's program in Media Education and is Head of OssCom, its Research Centre on Media and Communication. His research interests lie in the areas of audience studies and media experience, especially television and online media; media and children; media literacy; and media and generations.

Julia Behre is a student assistant at the Leibniz Institute for Media Research at Hans-Bredow-Institut and a master's degree student in Journalism and Communication Studies at the University of Hamburg, Germany. Her research interests are news media usage and public disconnection.

Verena K. Brändle is Senior Research Fellow at the University of Vienna, Austria, and Visiting Fellow at the European University Institute, Fiesole, Italy. She received her PhD from the University of Copenhagen, Denmark, where she also worked as a postdoc. Her research interests include the democratic implications of social media, migration studies, and governance studies. Recent research has appeared in *Social Movement Studies* and in the co-authored volume *Solidarity in the Media and Public Contention over Refugees in Europe* (Routledge, 2021).

John Downey is Professor of Comparative Media Analysis at Loughborough University, UK. From 2016 to 2019, he was Director of the Centre for Research in Communication and Culture, and from 2019 to 2021 Head of the Department. He has written extensively about digital media, political communication, and journalism, as well as research methodology. His current research project on Indian political communication is funded by the Arts and Humanities Research Council in the UK. He is currently Vice President of the European Communication Research and Education Association.

Uwe Hasebrink is Director of the Leibniz Institute for Media Research at Hans-Bredow-Institut and Professor of Empirical Communication Research at the University of Hamburg, Germany. His main research fields are media use and media policy.

Rasmus Helles is Associate Professor in the Department of Communication, University of Copenhagen, Denmark. His research focuses on digital media studies and media regulation, with a special emphasis on quantitative and qualitative methodologies. His publications have appeared in *New Media & Society*, *Surveillance & Society*, the *International Journal of Communication*, and the *European Journal of Communication*, and he has co-edited three special issues of international peer-reviewed journals.

Sascha Hölig is Senior Researcher at the Leibniz Institute for Media Research at Hans-Bredow-Institut, Hamburg, Germany. His main research interests lie in the areas of news media usage, research methods, and science communication.

Klaus Bruhn Jensen is Professor in the Department of Communication, University of Copenhagen, Denmark. His research and teaching emphasize communication theory, empirical research methodologies, and the history of media and communication. Recent publications include the *International Encyclopedia of Communication Theory and Philosophy* (Wiley-Blackwell, 2016, 4 vols and online), *A Handbook of Media and Communication Research: Qualitative and Quantitative Methodologies* (Routledge, 3rd ed., 2021), *A Theory of Communication of Justice* (Routledge, 2021), and *Media Convergence: The Three Degrees of Network, Mass, and Interpersonal Communication* (Routledge, 2nd ed., 2022). He is a recipient of the Royal Danish Order of Dannebrog, an elected member of Academia Europaea, Life Member for Service of the Association of Internet Researchers, and a Fellow of the International Communicology Institute.

Signe Sophus Lai is a tenure-track Assistant Professor in the Department of Communication, University of Copenhagen, Denmark. Her work is situated at the intersection of infrastructure studies, critical data studies, and the political economy of communication, focusing on the societal implications of digital infrastructures, datafication, and emergent business models. Her research has been published in *New Media & Society*, the *International Journal of Communication*, *Big Data & Society*, and *Media, Culture & Society*.

Adrian Leguina is Lecturer in Quantitative Social Science in the School of Social Sciences and Humanities, Loughborough University, UK. His interests lie at the intersection of the sociology of cultural consumption, media and communications, and stratification and social statistics. Adrian's research has been funded by UK Research and Innovation and has been published in the *British Journal of Sociology*, the *Journal of Consumer Culture*, and *New Media & Society*. He is Board Member of the European Sociological Association's Sociology of Consumption research network and co-convenor of the British Sociological Association's Consumption Study Group.

Jun Liu is Associate Professor in the Department of Communication, University of Copenhagen, Denmark. His research covering political sociology and communication technologies has been published in sociological, political-scientific, communication, and computer science journals such as *New Media & Society*, the *Journal of the Association for Information Science and Technology*, and the *European Journal of Sociology*. He is the recipient of awards from the American Political Science Association and the International Communication Association. His latest monograph is *Shifting Dynamics of Contention in the Digital Age* (Oxford University Press, 2020).

Stine Lomborg is Associate Professor in the Department of Communication, University of Copenhagen, Denmark. Her current research focuses on datafied living, exposing digital tracking infrastructures, and exploring people's communicative practices and engagement with tracking data. She is the author of *Social Media – Social Genres* (Routledge, 2014). Her work has been published in *New Media & Society*, the *European Journal of Communication*, *Big Data & Society*, *The Information Society*, *Information, Communication & Society*, and *Convergence*.

Jacob Ørmen is a tenure-track Assistant Professor in the Department of Communication, University of Copenhagen, Denmark. He studies user engagement, digital economy, and research methods. He co-edited the volume *News across Media* (2016) and has contributed chapters to *A Handbook of Media and Communication Research* (3rd ed., Routledge, 2021), *The Routledge Handbook of Developments in Digital Journalism Studies* (2018), and *The Routledge Companion to Social Media and Politics* (2016). His work has also been published in *New Media & Society*, the *European Journal of Communication*, *Digital Journalism*, *Journalism Studies*, *Mobile Media & Communication*, the *International Journal of Press/Politics*, and the *International Journal of Communication*.

Jesper Pagh is a postdoc in the Department of Communication, University of Copenhagen, Denmark. His PhD dissertation examined internet use and communicative practices in everyday contexts in the United States. His current research is part of the project "Don't take it personal – privacy and information in an algorithmic age." Research interests also include internet regulation and qualitative methodologies.

Francesca Pasquali is Professor of the Sociology of Cultural and Communicative Processes at the Department of Letters, Philosophy, and Communication, University of Bergamo, Italy. Her research interests lie in the field of sociology of communication and culture, with a particular focus on the relationship between digital platforms and legacy media; digital platforms and the mediatization of everyday life; and digital communication and media participation. Her publications include *Fenomenologia dei social network: Presenza, relazioni e consumi mediali degli italiani online* (Guerini e Associati, 2017).

Fiona Huijie Zeng Skovhøj received her PhD from the University of Copenhagen, Denmark. During her PhD studies, she was a visiting scholar at the Chinese Academy of Social Sciences (CASS) and Fudan University in China, continuing as a postdoctoral researcher in the Peoples' Internet project. Her research interests include digital communication, censorship, everyday uses of the internet, and digital transformations in China.

Chris Chao Su is Assistant Professor of Emerging Media Studies at the College of Communication, Boston University, Massachusetts, focusing on media audiences online, social media analytics, and mobile media use and consumption. His work has been published in the *Journal of Communication, Journalism and Mass Communication Quarterly*, *New Media & Society*, *Computers in Human Behavior*, and the *International Journal of Communication*.

Nicoletta Vittadini is Associate Professor of the Sociology of Cultural and Communicative Processes at the Catholic University in Milan, Italy, where she directs the master's program in Digital Communications Specialist and is Deputy Director of the master's program in Journalism. Her main research theme is communication through social media in economic and institutional perspectives. Her latest book publication is *Social Media Studies. I social media alle soglie della maturità* (Franco Angeli, 2018).

Baohua Zhou is Professor in the School of Journalism, Research Fellow of the Center for Information and Communication Studies, and Director of the data mining and computational communication research group at Fudan University, China. His research focuses on new media and society, media effects, public opinion, and computational social science. His work has been published in *New Media & Society*, the *International Journal of Communication*, the *Chinese Journal of Communication*, the *Asian Journal of Communication*, and other leading journals in China.

PREFACE

This book is the product of a project spanning three continents and joining scholars across geographic and disciplinary boundaries. The Peoples' Internet (PIN) project, hosted by the University of Copenhagen, Denmark, has taken stock of the internet as a global communication infrastructure whose future hangs in the balance in the 2020s. In addition to comparing and contrasting the distinctive *internets* of China, Europe, and the United States in their present form, along with their place in the wider communication systems of each world region, we take up some of the contested choices currently facing publics and policy makers around the world. In trying to make sense of what the internet is, but also what it could be and, perhaps, ought to become, we have been privileged to work with an intellectually curious and committed group of international colleagues. It is their collective efforts that inform the findings and insights we share in the chapters ahead.

Special thanks are due to special people, who helped along both the PIN project and this publication. From the first steps of conceiving and planning the project, James G. Webster of Northwestern University, USA, played an essential part in conceptualizing its comparative and multi-method framework. We are grateful for Jim's continuing support throughout the different stages of the project.

As we note in the Methodological Appendix in Chapter 8, a complex endeavor such as the PIN project will encounter practical as well as theoretical challenges. When our original partner in the People's Republic of China proved unable to continue the collaboration, Baohua Zhou of Fudan University kindly joined the PIN team and gave generously of his time in overseeing surveys and other aspects of the project in China. Meanwhile, in the United States, another logistical issue presented itself. Harsh Taneja, along with Jim Webster, contributed to early conversations about the PIN project, and the plan had been for Harsh, joined by Angela Wu, to have a leading role in analyzing web traffic data from a US-based service provider. Unfortunately, as we explain in Chapter 8, it proved impossible to secure the relevant data access, which would have provided one more vantage point from which to assess global internet use. We remain thankful for Harsh and Angela's contributions to the development of the PIN project.

The PIN Scientific Advisory Board offered incisive comments and important suggestions as we planned and implemented the various components of the project. Many thanks are due to Fernando Bermejo of the Berkman Klein Center for Internet & Society at Harvard University; Phil Howard of the Oxford Internet Institute; Rikke Frank Jørgensen of the Danish Institute for Human Rights; Sun Sun Lim of the Singapore University of Technology and Design; and Lee Rainie of the Pew Research Center in Washington, D.C.

Last but not least, we thank the Carlsberg Foundation for its generous funding of the Peoples' Internet project through its Semper Ardens program, grant CF16-001.

Klaus Bruhn Jensen and Rasmus Helles
Copenhagen, August 2022

1

FROM MEDIA SYSTEMS TO COMMUNICATION SYSTEMS

Klaus Bruhn Jensen and Rasmus Helles

The internet and beyond

The internet stands as the global communications infrastructure of the twenty-first century, half a century after its 1969 military origins in the ARPANET (Abbate, 1999), and a quarter century after its 1991 opening to the public at large in the form of the World Wide Web (Berners-Lee, 1999). More than a medium as traditionally understood, the internet is an economic means of production and distribution, a vehicle of national and international political governance, and a cultural forum of human expression and social interaction crisscrossing private and public spheres (Habermas, 1989/1962). As such, the internet has challenged the field of media and communication research to revisit the definition and delimitation of its object of study. Founded in the era of mass media and mass communication (Park & Pooley, 2008; Simonson, Peck, Craig, & Jackson, 2013), the field has commonly centered on *media* systems, specifically in comparative studies of the institutions that carry news and public debate feeding into diverse forms of political democracy in different nations and regions of the world (Hallin & Mancini, 2004, 2012). The internet has served as a reminder that communication flows in many other genres and through multiple networks, for instrumental as well as reflective purposes, as people – and peoples around the world – live their lives and make their own histories. Departing from a study of internet use in three regions of the contemporary world – China, Europe, and the United States – this volume presents a framework for comparative studies of *communication* systems, at a time when a worldwide and society-wide process of digitalization is reconfiguring the technological, institutional, and discursive conditions of human communication.

We take the ordinary human beings who communicate – day to day and generation to generation – as a normative reference point. Communication systems

DOI: 10.4324/9781003057055-1

can and should be examined and evaluated in terms of the ways in which, and the degrees to which, they enable individuals and groups to send and receive, act and react, in their various roles as citizens and consumers, workers and entrepreneurs, members of families and communities, locally as well as globally. From the outset, publics, audiences, and users occupied key roles in utopian and dystopian accounts of what the internet is, ought to be, and could become. Whereas early interventions would highlight its expressive and empowering potentials (e.g., Jenkins, 2006; Rheingold, 1994), more recent assessments have cast internet users as subject to both state and commercial surveillance as a standard operating procedure (e.g., Woolley & Howard, 2019; Zuboff, 2019). The internet, thus, returns the field of media and communication research to its two foundational questions: What do media *do to* people – and what do people *do with* media? (Katz, 1959). What is the nature and scope of the interchange between media as communicative resources and people as communicative agents? What are the implications of their widely distributed and highly differentiated encounters, across place and time, for the maintenance and transformation of relationships and identities, societies and cultures? In the classic terminology of social theory, what is the role of communication in mediating human agency and social structure (Giddens, 1984)?

To outline a framework for the comparative study of communication systems, this opening chapter first maps the interdisciplinary landscape in which we situate our analyses and arguments. We model the configurations of material technologies, political economies, and cultural traditions that intersect in contemporary communication systems, and we characterize the relationship of communication systems with other systems in the basic structure of society, from families and local communities to national political democracies and global economic markets. The middle section of the chapter specifies the empirical research questions that inform our analyses of communicative practices on the ground in each of the three regional contexts. We reemphasize the complementarity of multiple methods for describing differences and similarities across social and cultural contexts: Population surveys, ethnographic fieldwork, and big-data analyses of internet infrastructures, supplemented by documentary evidence and policy studies of the global diffusion of communication technologies and their local regulation by nation-states. The chapter, lastly, anticipates some of the normative debates that follow from, and are informed by, comparative perspectives on communication systems around the world, ending with a preview of the other chapters in the book.

Communications and determinations

Communication is a material, a social, as well as a discursive phenomenon, as suggested by three remarkably similar communication models and classics that derive from engineering (Shannon & Weaver, 1949), the social sciences (Lasswell, 1948), and the humanities (Jakobson, 1960), respectively. From vocal cords and sound waves to broadcast antennas and bit streams, matter is a necessary condition for communication to serve a remarkable range of human ends and social interests. Communication, further, accomplishes the socialization of individuals and the structuration of societies over time. And, as modes of representation and interaction, it is communication in signs and symbols that lends meaning to all human doings and beings. As bodies and minds, humans are both necessary and sufficient conditions for communication to unfold – for most of human history, we were the only media around. But, for centuries and millennia, we have gradually extended ourselves (McLuhan, 1964) in technologies that have enabled rich and diverse communications across space as well as time. And, in recent decades, several generations of artificial intelligence have contributed to a further blurring of the lines between humans, machines, and other constituents of reality in a process that is still ongoing (Gunkel, 2020), summed up so far in the idea of an internet of things (ITU, 2005).

Figure 1.1 lays out three categories of material, social, and discursive conditions that have circumscribed – enabled and constrained – communicative practices over the *longues durées* of history (Braudel, 1980). The figure offers a thumbnail representation of the elements of a communication system. While some earlier work has reserved the terminology of communication systems for digital variants (Flensburg & Lai, 2020), we approach communication systems as the entire ensemble of media of representation and interaction in a given historical time and cultural place. *Material technologies*, first, have reconfigured a wide variety of private and public communicative practices. Indeed, the very idea of 'public' communication emerged along with the introduction, first, of printing and, subsequently, broadcasting during the modern period of history (Habermas, 1989/1962). While recognizing the complexities of the long process in which a sequence of technologies has been embedded in different societies and diverse cultures, has gradually gained momentum (Hughes, 1983), and has come to be a taken-for-granted (Ling, 2012) constituent of everyday life, we begin from the

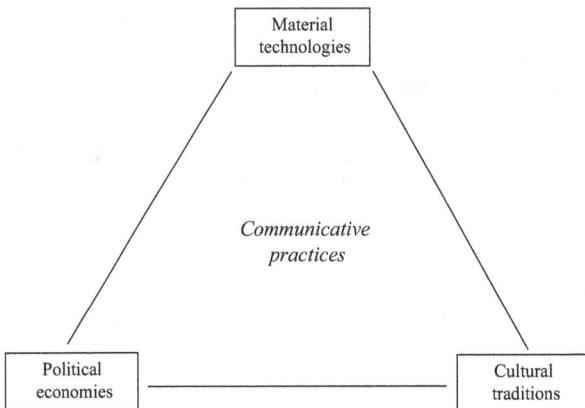

FIGURE 1.1 The three aspects of communication systems

understanding that certain forms of communication were impossible – inconceivable and impracticable – before the availability of either writing, printing, broadcasting, or computing as material goods. Matter matters.

Political economies, equally, delimit certain forms of communication as either likely or unlikely, possible and impossible. Media and communicative practices are among the material as well as immaterial goods that economic markets produce and circulate, and which institutions of political governance regulate. Rights of information and communication have been associated historically with the coming of print media and, later, broadcast radio and television, but have been curtailed, more or less routinely and ruthlessly, by religious and political authorities throughout the six centuries since Johannes Gensfleisch zur Laden zum Gutenberg introduced metal types to print more Bibles (Briggs, Burke, & Ytreberg, 2020). We turn in Chapter 2 to the distinctive regulatory regimes in contemporary mainland China, in five European nations, and in the United States to characterize their different windows of opportunity for human action and social interaction.

We add *cultural traditions* as a third conditioning factor of human communication. While commonly conceived less as a determinant than as a long-term outcome of communication, we go on to unpack culture as a consequential component of how communication systems differ and develop. Communication scholars, along with anthropologists and historians, have adopted Raymond Williams' (1975/1958) insight that cultures constitute whole ways of life. Culture, literally, is cultivated and handed over, as suggested by the Latin root of tradition (*tradere*), person to person and throughout generations. Culture is both a process and a set of products with a manifest and continued presence, forms as well as contents, from alphabets and conceptual frameworks to discursive conventions of conversational interaction and genres of fact and fiction – all of which articulate what philosophers (Divers, 2002) and literary theorists (Ryan, 1991) have referred to as possible worlds: The places and times in which people do things together, with words and with the many other material and immaterial resources of communication currently at our disposal. At once input to and output from innumerable concrete events and experiences of communication, cultural traditions belong alongside material and institutional circumstances as determinants of communication writ large.

In responding to the vexed question of determination, we stand on the shoulders of Stuart Hall. In a bold conceptual move, Hall (1983) embraced the general idea of determination, but challenged the received understanding of the concept, for example, within the tradition of cultural studies of which he was a founder. Despite enthusiastic recognition of the creative and potentially oppositional nature of culture, a premise of critical cultural studies has been that, in the *final* instance, the economic basis of society determines its ideological superstructure: When all is said and done, money talks. Hall proposed speaking, instead, of determination in the *first* instance: The economy, along with other social institutions and infrastructures, including the historically available technologies, set certain outer limits to what it is possible for individuals to achieve and collectives to accomplish – what they can do and be (Nussbaum, 2011; Sen, 1999), alone and together. But neither economic markets nor technological infrastructures can predict the specific forms and contents of the communicative practices that take shape and take hold. In sum, communication is subject to several *kinds* and variable *degrees* of determination that call for theoretical specification and empirical examination in order to interpret and explain the actual communicative practices that unfold around the globe.

Figure 1.2 elaborates on the dynamic relationship between communicative practices and their several conditioning factors. If material technologies, political economies, and cultural traditions *circumscribe* communicative practices, these practices, in turn, *inscribe* different understandings of and engagements with reality – new technologies as they become part of everyday life; people's working lives, consumer preferences, and leisure activities; and the historical worldviews, values, and norms that lend meaning and orientation to everyday lives and plans throughout life. We place communicative practices as the center of interest for the study of communication systems (the outer arrows linking the three corners of the triangle in Figure 1.2 duly note the many other interactions between technologies, social institutions, and cultures, beyond the ones centered in and mediated through communication). We, further, approach the three corners of the model as different, but equal analytical perspectives; the placement of material technologies at the top here does not suggest any primacy. If this were a three-dimensional model rather than a printed or static screen page, you might twist, turn, and observe it repeatedly from many different angles to prioritize diverse insights. The different graphic notations for each arrow within the triangle, finally, emphasize that each conditioning factor operates according to characteristic mechanisms. For example, the availability (or not) of high-speed internet connections represents a different sort of mechanism than freedom of expression (or its suppression), which again is different from culturally distinctive norms of whether or not to interact with (some) other people, online and (or) offline.

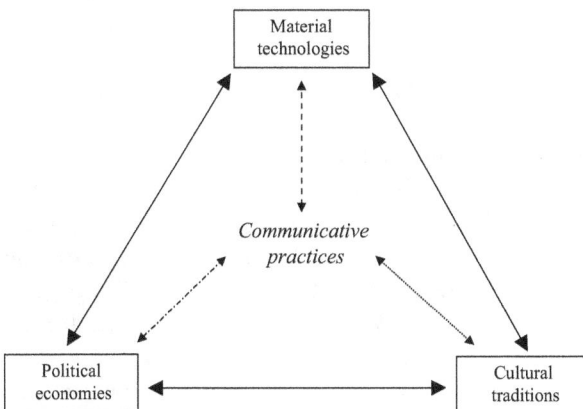

FIGURE 1.2 The triple determination of communicative practices

Empirical studies explore how these different determinants, jointly, result in specific communicative practices through a process that Sigmund Freud (1911/1900) had referred to as *overdetermination*: Just as the happenings of an ordinary day will mix and merge with long gone (and perhaps repressed) experiences in the contents and forms of a person's dreams, so diverse technological, institutional, and discursive mechanisms interact to produce certain predominant forms of communication. As illustration, consider the three-way determination of the internet. As a generic *technology*, the internet has lent itself to a unique variety of public and private uses, reproducing and recombining all previous media of representation and interaction on a single material platform of hardware and software, and adding several new ones. But some representations and interactions are more common and consequential than others, in some places and times. Embedded in *political economies*, the internet, as mentioned, originated as an initiative of the US military in the shape of the ARPANET in 1969, but was reconfigured in institutional terms, first as a research network (NSFNET) in 1985, and as a commercially operated common carrier in 1995 (Abbate, 1999). What might have remained a closed command-and-control system was transformed, via a specialized sectoral infrastructure, into a general-purpose public medium, still subject to different national and regional regulatory regimes – which motivates the reference to *internets* in the plural in the title of this book (see also O'Hara & Hall, 2018). *Cultural traditions*, further, articulate superficially similar online communicative practices in distinctive repertoires of signs and symbols, sometimes with fundamentally different meanings and implications. As we elaborate in Chapter 4, networking with Facebook 'friends' represents a rather different set of social actions – even a different form of sociality – than the cultivation of *guanxi* or interpersonal relations on WeChat and other Chinese social media.

Historical prototypes of communication

By way of introduction, we briefly note the place of the internet and of current media and communication environments as such in longer historical trajectories. Table 1.1 relates three prototypes of human communication – one-to-one, one-to-many, and many-to-many – to three categories of media technologies and institutions that have enabled and circumscribed communicative practices in different historical periods and cultural settings. While we refer to these prototypes throughout the book, Table 1.1 serves to recognize, from the outset, the range of communicative practices that enter into contemporary communication systems, along with their historical origins and transformations, and their repeated and recursive remediation (Bolter & Grusin, 1999). Face-to-face interaction (frequently including references to additional written, printed, or audiovisual discourses) remains both an implicit model for other kinds of communication and an essential ingredient of any and all communication systems, anywhere and anytime. (For purposes of the present overview, we bracket writing and manuscript cultures – see further Jensen, 2022). Print and subsequent

TABLE 1.1 Communicative practices across media types

Communicative practices	Media types		
	Embodied media	Analog media	Digital media
One-to-one	PROTOTYPE Face-to-face conversation, hand-written letters, and records	Telegraph, telephone, fax	Email, text message, instant messaging, IP telephony
One-to-many	Manuscript, theater, painting, sculpture, architecture, musical composition	PROTOTYPE Book, newspaper, magazine, broadcasting, audio and video recording	Web 1.0/webpage, download, streaming (mass) media
Many-to-many	Cave painting, gaming, graffiti, notice board, agora, marketplace, stadium	Community media, public-access radio and television, telephone chat services	PROTOTYPE Web 2.0/wiki, file-sharing site, online chat, massively multiplayer online gaming, social network site, blog, auction site

analog media and, recently, digital media have all introduced novel varieties of human communication. All along, new media have restated and reworked earlier communicative practices; they also, to varying degrees, have been antedated or anticipated by older media and communicative practices; from theater to broadcasting to streaming; and from the agora to public-access radio and television to the online discussion forum. Whereas our primary purpose, in this volume, is to compare communication systems across space (nations and regions of the world representing diverse social systems and cultural traditions), the historical perspective serves as a reminder of changes as well as continuities across time of how people say and do things with media.

Complementing the classic communication models already noted (Jakobson, 1960; Lasswell, 1948; Shannon & Weaver, 1949), we take inspiration from medium theory (Meyrowitz, 1994) and the wider research tradition of media ecology (Strate, 2016). A key contribution of this family of approaches has been to conceptualize media – beyond contacts, channels, and codes – as *environments* that envelop individuals and collectives, conditioning how they relate both to their natural circumstances and to received social and cultural conventions. Far from endorsing technological determinism, and in line with Hall's (1983) account of determination in the first instance, medium theory makes the simple, but essential point that societies with access to writing systems, printing presses, telegraphy and telephony, broadcasting, and digital networks – none, some, or all of these – have been different in kind. This perspective seems especially important, not only to begin to assess the historical scale and systematic scope of digitalization, but also to specify, for comparative purposes, the parameters that are subject to change or continuity, with many intermediate gradations. So far, several candidate terminologies for encapsulating the present age have been advanced, from the information society (Porat, 1977) and the control society (Beniger, 1986) to the network society (Castells, 1996) and the surveillance society (Zuboff, 2019), all of which center on human communication in signs and symbols as both a condition and a constituent of social coordination. (On the question of surveillance, we return in Chapter 6 to a fourth prototype of communication – many-to-one or into the system (Jensen & Helles, 2017) – to examine different variants of surveillance as a standard operating procedure of digital media.) For now, we reemphasize the importance of refocusing research on communication systems rather than media systems, if the field of media and communication research is to deliver timely and relevant contributions to an interdisciplinary understanding of the contemporary world and its potential future trajectories.

Along with the conception of media of communication as environments enveloping people and framing their engagements of reality, medium theory suggests a second premise for the study of communication systems: More than a way of representing reality – to one person, a few, or many others – communication is a form of human action and social interaction that literally makes a difference. In the terminology of another founder of cultural studies, communication serves to produce, maintain, repair, and transform reality as a shared point of reference and an arena of collaboration as well as conflict (Carey, 1989b/1975: 23). It is this premise that we foreground by placing communicative *practices* at the center of Figures 1.1 and 1.2.

In a longer and broader interdisciplinary perspective, we take as a premise a key insight of twentieth-century philosophy, namely that humans do things with words (Austin, 1962), and they play games (for real) in and through language and other modes of communication (Wittgenstein, 1953). In comparison, the broad mainstream of media and communication research has tended to reproduce a common-sensical understanding of communication as the transmission or sharing of information. Communication is that, and more.

First, to communicate is to act, in a context and for a purpose. Whenever I say something to someone, I do something to and with that someone. Second, human actions are communications in and of themselves. Regardless of my intentions or preconscious inclinations, others will associate meaning with the behaviors, however casual and contingent, that I constantly engage in. Third, communication anticipates action. Communication is a vehicle of recursive and self-reflective agency, introducing additional links between what was said, what could have been said, and what ought to be said in the future. It is, above all, the understanding of human communication as performative that breaks the boundaries of media systems as traditionally understood, and of media studies as most commonly practiced. Communication systems afford the concrete, practical vehicles of community and culture – necessary conditions of arts and sciences, markets and states, a good life (*eudaimonia*), and local and global coexistence. Cultures constitute, at once, representations and resources: *Representations* of what is, but also what could be and what ought to be, and instrumental as well as reflective *resources* orienting interactions about what should (not) be done.

Cultures of communication

The understanding of communication and culture as mutually constitutive is a shared legacy of contemporary social and human sciences, even if communicative conceptions of society and culture have remained minority positions in disciplines such as sociology and anthropology. The seminal work of James W. Carey (1989a) merged multiple strands of this legacy, outlining an approach to communication as a cultural ritual in which humans come together to reflect and deliberate on the natural and social circumstances they share. It is in this perspective that communication presents itself as "a symbolic process whereby reality is produced, maintained, repaired, and transformed" (p. 23). As production, maintenance, and repair are carried out, over and over again, the long-term and accumulated outcome is a transformed reality: A revised understanding of what is or ought to be the case, and what could and should be done, by the individual and by the collective.

Whereas these formulations might seem to privilege the cultural traditions in Figures 1.1 and 1.2 – the process of trading (*tradere*) and disseminating information and ideas – Carey (1989a) took on board both the material technologies that carry traditions and the institutions that make up political economies. On the one hand, regarding society as an institutional framework, he returned to philosophical pragmatism in the words of John Dewey to clarify two different, interrelated aspects of communication: "Society exists not only by transmission, by communication, but it may fairly be said to exist in transmission, in communication" (cited in Carey, 1989b/1975: 13f.). Communication is not external, but internal to, and constitutive of, society. Communication makes a difference *both* through specific effects on the attitudes and behaviors of media audiences and other communicators, *and* throughout innumerable ordinary and extraordinary interactions involving individuals as well as institutions. *In* communication, people jointly produce, maintain, and repair reality and their own identities; *by* communication, they are further able, to variable degrees, to transform reality, to participate in the ongoing structuration of society. Chapter 5 elaborates on the things that people do with media and by communication, as citizens, consumers, and more, circumscribed by material and institutional structures and inscribed in cultural traditions.

On the other hand, Carey (1989a) integrated insights from medium theory as part of a long and broad historical perspective on the changing conditions of human communication. With specific reference to the telegraph, he noted that this technology marked the "decisive separation of 'transportation' and 'communication'" (p. 213). Not only could people now have virtual contact across space in real time, but they could also act at a distance. The telegraph "allowed communication to control physical processes actively" (p. 203), with railroad signals as one early example. Shifting technologies have been associated with generic forms of culture, for example, written culture (Powell, 2009) and print culture (Eisenstein, 1979). With specific inspiration from Carey's model of communication, Horace Newcomb and Paul Hirsch (1983) outlined an agenda for studying television as the central, shared cultural forum of the second half of the twentieth century. In contrast to a common view of television as a transmitter and source, it could be seen as a repository and resource: A forum to which agendas and issues are brought and negotiated in a process of communal meaning-making.

Extending Carey's (1989a) perspective from the telegraph through television to the internet, we approach the internet as a new category of cultural forum (Jensen & Helles, 2011) and a centerpiece of contemporary communication systems. Not only does the internet combine and complement one-to-one and one-to-many prototypes of communication with many-to-many communication as instantiated most evidently, so far, by social media (but also by, for example, online gaming and Wikipedia). The internet, further, has enabled an immense variety of public and private uses of communication, from finding a new job to finding a life partner, filing tax returns, and engaging in public debate about appropriate levels of local, national, or global taxation. In all of these respects, the internet has brought home the performative nature of human communication: Saying something means doing something. The internet produces, maintains, repairs, and transforms reality across most domains of public and private life, in and by distinctive prototypes of communication. At the same time, the internet coexists with a long line of historical media, including humans as media in and of themselves, as elements of communication systems and carriers of cultures of communication. To sum up, communication systems can be seen to host cultures of communication – defined as distinctive combinations and configurations of communicative practices – which can be expected to vary across social segments, nations, and world regions (even if neither communication systems nor cultures of communication may map neatly onto received national cultures or sociodemographic hierarchies). And, in a future perspective, communication systems likely will be reconfigured, repeatedly so, as the internet – and an emerging internet of things – saturates more corners of society and parts of the world. It is the current state of this changing social and cultural landscape that we propose to examine empirically in this volume.

Communication systems and other systems

Communication systems intersect with other systems of social interaction, as suggested by Figure 1.1, with implications for necessarily selective and partial empirical studies. Our findings are based on data from seven countries, which were chosen to include measures of both geographic and systemic diversity, with reference to most different (three continents) and most similar (five European countries) criteria of selection. Most basically and in geographic terms, the project spans three regions of the world: Asia (China), Europe (Denmark, Germany, Italy, Hungary, and the United Kingdom), and North America (the United States). These regions, further, have different historical and cultural backgrounds, and represent distinctive ways of organizing a state: A federal republic (the United States), sovereign nation-states within a federalist framework (the five European Union countries), and a socialist one-party state with deep civilizational roots (China). And, in the early twenty-first century, the three regions represent economic and geopolitical centers of the world, with alternative outlooks on how each other, and the rest of the world, ought to develop in the future.

For an overview, Table 1.2 first describes the sample countries at a glance (see further Leguina & Downey, 2021). Drawing on official statistics from the World Bank and other international agencies, Table 1.2 brings out a number of broadly familiar characteristics of the seven countries and three regions, which serve to place our analyses of communication systems and communicative practices in context and perspective. For instance, whereas low-income per capita in China goes together with high inequality, in the United States high income per capita coincides with high inequality. In the European setting, in comparison, high-to-medium income per capita translates into low inequality for the citizens of some countries (Denmark, Germany, Hungary), but medium inequality for others (Italy, the United Kingdom). The quality of political democracy, similarly, varies, notably with two European countries occupying only a medium level of democracy (Hungary, Italy). Educational attainment at age 15 begins to address questions of how well so-called information or knowledge societies may be faring in practice. Table 1.2, finally, includes basic indicators of media freedom and internet use, both of which call for elaboration for present purposes.

Table 1.3, accordingly, adds detail regarding media systems and internet infra-structures in the seven countries. First of all, the classic framework of media

TABLE 1.2 Country sample by standard social indicators

Country	Income per capita	Inequality	Education attainment at age 15	Media freedom	Democracy	Internet use
China	Low	High	High	Low	Low	Low
Denmark	High	Low	High	High	High	High
Germany	High	Low	High	High	High	High
Hungary	Medium	Low	Low	Medium	Medium	Medium
Italy	High	Medium	Low	Medium	Medium	Medium
United Kingdom	High	Medium	Medium	High	High	High
United States	High	High	Low	High	High	High

Source: Leguina and Downey (2021: 1829)

TABLE 1.3 Country sample by media systems and internet infrastructures

Country	Media system[1]	Internet penetration (%)[2]	Digital Economy and Society Index (DESI)[3]
Denmark (Europe)	Northern	97.32	Highest
United Kingdom (Europe)	Central	94.90	High
Germany (Europe)	Central	89.74	Middle
United States (North America)	Western	87.27	Middle
Hungary (Europe)	Eastern	76.07	Low
Italy (Europe)	Southern	74.39	Low
China (Asia)	Authoritarian	54.30	Lowest

[1] Brüggemann et al. (2014), Castro Herrero et al. (2017), and MacKinnon (2011)
[2] ITU (2019)
[3] For China and the United States, data are from 2017 (European Commission, 2018, 2019)

systems theory (Hallin & Mancini, 2004) has been refined by Brüggemann et al. (2014) and by Castro Herrero et al. (2017). Media systems theory, however, has focused rather narrowly on legacy or traditional media organizations (news and journalism, in particular), giving comparatively little attention to the ongoing digitalization of social infrastructures around the world (or to the world beyond Europe and North America). In addition to noting basic internet penetration, we therefore refer to the Digital Economy and Society Index (DESI), which was developed by the European Commission (2019), and ranks countries by several parameters in addition to the possibilities for citizens to go online (broadband and mobile access): Internet user skills, citizens' use of online services, business digitalization and e-commerce, and the quality of digital public services. Taken together, the media systems perspective and the digital index capture a range of opportunities for accessing information, communicating with others, and inter-acting with important institutions in society.

The model developed by Brüggemann et al. (2014) identified four types of media systems: Northern, Central, Southern, and Western. As part of this typology, Denmark instantiates a *Northern* system, defined by "highly professional journalism, an inclusive press market, powerful public broadcasting, and gener-ous press subsidies" (p. 1056). The Northern type provides favorable conditions for a diversity of media forms and contents, including public-service, subsidized, and private media organizations. Moreover, Denmark is one of the most digital-ized countries in the world in terms of broadband and mobile internet cover-age, government investment in infrastructures and services, as well as very high internet penetration rates in the general population.

The *Central* type, represented here by Germany and the United Kingdom, covers countries with "strong public broadcasting, strict ownership regula-tion, and low press subsidies" (Brüggemann et al., 2014: 1056). Such coun-tries marry funding for national and federal public-service media with a substantial free-market sector. Online, the United Kingdom ranks high on all DESI parameters, in particular regarding the variety of internet services that people use. While Germany is otherwise similar to the United Kingdom, the strong position of public-service media here is not matched by a digitalized public sector: Few Germans, for example, interact with the state through the internet on a regular basis.

The United States epitomizes the *Western* or regulated-market type, defined by limited support for public-service media and few opportunities to obtain public funding for communication services, but with strict regulation of ownership (Brüggemann et al., 2014: 1056). Americans are, in general, well connected to the internet, and have access to good online public services, but only command a moderate level of digital skills.

Italy and Hungary, while exhibiting several similarities, represent two different types of media systems. Italy belongs to the *Southern* type, which is characterized by a combination of the "highest degree of political parallelism with the least professional journalism and the least inclusive press market" (Brüggemann et al., 2014: 1056) ("political parallelism" refers to close relations between political parties and the press, which tends to limit the role of journalism as a watchdog or fourth estate). Building on and complementing the model by Brüggemann et al. (2014), a later study examined countries in central and eastern Europe (Castro Herrero et al., 2017), concluding that Hungary is exemplary of an *Eastern* model of media systems, typified by high levels of political parallelism, low investment in national media content, and a small audience for public-service media. In both the Southern and Eastern systems, in short, the media environment is rather heavily politicized, public-service media have a weak position, and there is limited funding available for independent publishers. In the digital domain, as well, both Italy and Hungary score low on the DESI index, mainly because of poor public online services (especially in Hungary), limited use of online services generally, and internet skill levels below the EU average.

The People's Republic of China presents an especially challenging case for media systems theory, which was originally developed for, and has primarily been applied to, Western contexts (Zhao, 2012). Other research, however, has examined the role of state and market in providing media and communication services to the Chinese population. In essence, the Chinese model is unique in its combination of a one-party political system with a market-based media sector. Because of the one-party system (in contrast to multiparty democracies), there is a manifest correspondence between the party line and the editorial line or, in Hallin and Mancini's (2004) terms, a high degree of "party-press parallelism" (Zhao, 2012: 152). Nevertheless, beyond official state channels, media in China are, in general, privately owned or publicly listed, and compete both domestically and internationally in the market for audience attention and interaction (Stockmann, 2013).

Also when it comes to governance of the internet, China stands out. On the one hand, the Chinese state generally restricts access to the internet (through the so-called 'great firewall' filtering system), and it places specific limits on many aspects of online communication (through automatic as well as human censorship systems). In combination with deliberate and sustained attempts at hiding information and influencing public opinion, the state thus runs an effective regime of "porous censorship" (Roberts, 2018). On the other hand, China allows for a certain measure of free speech online. Studies have documented that censors, in fact, allow a large proportion of the critical comments posted by citizens to stay up, as long as they do not contain calls for collective action in opposition to the party (King, Pan, & Roberts, 2014). This monitoring of the citizenry "functions as a thermostat" (Schroeder, 2018: 54) for the party to gauge, and influence, public opinion. In all, these censorship and surveillance regimes represent a type of internet governance apart, which Rebecca MacKinnon (2011) has dubbed "networked authoritarianism." In the present context, we refer to the Chinese model as an *Authoritarian* media system.

In the DESI index (European Commission, 2018), China generally scores low on all parameters (on a par with European countries such as Bulgaria and Romania). It should be noted that, in the data that this volume relies on, the latest available point of comparison between the EU countries and China (as well as the United States) is 2016. The rapid development of digital infrastructures in China does call for caution in interpreting data and findings. Not least the diffusion of mobile internet connections has brought a large share of the rural population of China online in just a few years (CNNIC, 2019). Still, the DESI index offers a characterization of the Chinese internet and its uses by a public that is less tech-savvy than what has sometimes appeared from Western media accounts.

In summary, the communication systems that we compare represent a sample of countries in which internet use has by now become widespread (covering more than 50% of national populations); which, simultaneously, exhibit substantial differences in terms of the geographic (urban to rural) and demographic (high to low education and income) diffusion and use of the internet; and which comprise distinctive legacies of media systems and, most generally, of the social systems that are in place for funding, operating, and governing the availability of information and the access to communication, online as well as offline. To register the diversity of such communication systems in a comprehensive, yet empirically manageable manner, we rely on several different methods and compare their deliverables as part of a multi-method research design.

Comparing communications, comparing methods

The Peoples' Internet project makes up the third step of a research program that has sought to make sense – theoretically, empirically, and methodologically – of the ongoing digital transformation of the institutions and infrastructures of communication, departing from the question of what people do with media (Katz, 1959) and, in doing so, "what the devil they think they are up to" (Geertz, 1974:

29). In the first step, we developed the model and methodology for examining communication in patterns of one-to-one, one-to-many, and many-to-many, and applied these in a national or local pilot project of sorts (Jensen & Helles, 2011). We next widened the perspective to consider variations of internet use and other communicative practices across nine European countries (Belgium, Croatia, Denmark, Germany, Hungary, Israel, Italy, Poland, and Portugal) (Helles, Ørmen, Radil, & Jensen, 2015). The present study, then, goes global or, to be precise, regional to further explore ongoing changes and continuities of the universal human practice of communication.

The analyses ahead address four main research questions (RQ):

- RQ1: What are the characteristic configurations of one-to-one, one-to-many, and many-to-many communicative practices in mainland China, Europe, and the United States? (Chapter 3)
- RQ2: How do people in different national settings and sociodemographic segments build and maintain social networks, personal identities, and imagined communities in and by communication? (Chapter 4)
- RQ3: To what degree, and in which ways, do communicative practices contribute to the production and (unequal) distribution of capitals (material and immaterial resources), locally and globally? (Chapter 5)
- RQ4: What are the characteristic configurations of many-to-one communication (systematic online tracking of communicative practices) in mainland China, Europe, and the United States? (Chapter 6)

Before turning to each of these questions in turn, in Chapter 2 we offer additional descriptions of the complexities of technological infrastructures and political economies in each of the three regions of the study, preparing additional premises for the interpretation of how and why people do what they do with media. Following the conclusion in Chapter 7, which pulls together empirical findings, discusses theoretical insights, and presents normative implications, Chapter 8 constitutes a methodological appendix which, in addition to providing technical details, reflects candidly on some of the challenges and dilemmas facing future comparative studies of communication systems.

Prepared and supported by literature reviews and complemented, in Chapter 2, by document and indicator studies of national policies and regulatory frameworks, the study combined three main empirical approaches:

- representative surveys of the online population in China, Denmark, Germany, Hungary, Italy, the United Kingdom, and the United States
- ethnographic fieldwork in China, Denmark, and the United States
- big-data analyses of online third-party tracker services.

Figure 1.3 lays out the methodological architecture that integrates these different sources of evidence across several levels and steps of analysis and inference.

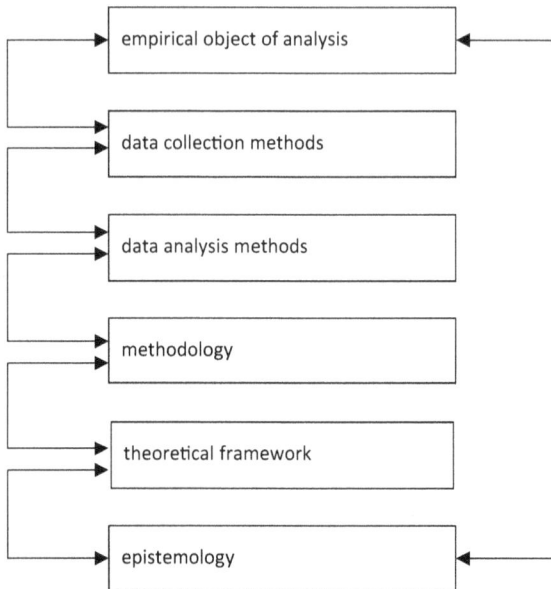

FIGURE 1.3 Six levels of empirical research

The primary *empirical objects of analysis* are the communicative practices that people engage in across a broad range of media and genres, in public and private contexts, online and offline, including traditional or legacy media as well as face-to-face interaction. We asked, variously, about the type, frequency, and duration of different communicative practices; we asked for people's views on the relevance and quality of selected media and communication services; and we asked them to consider the place of media uses and communicative practices in the context of their own lives and as points of access to wider worlds. To include communicative practices that move below the typical bandwidth of human communication, and thus may go unnoticed, we further identified the presence and patterning of tracking software on websites, which has become a constitutive feature of online communication infrastructures, and which have attracted considerable public attention recently (and which invite theory development as instances of what Gregory Bateson (1972) had referred to as meta-communication (Jensen, 2013)). And, to contextualize communicative practices historically and culturally, we draw on literatures about information and communication technologies, political economies, and cultural traditions, in part through secondary analyses of consolidated statistical evidence from national and international agencies.

The *data collection methods*, as noted, included population surveys, in-depth fieldwork, and harvesting online trackers. As such, we drew on found as well as made data (Jensen, 2012): While survey and qualitative interview responses are *made* to address the research questions at hand, trackers, records of informants' smartphone use, and policy documents are *found*, typically generated for other ends, and retrieved without any direct intervention by researchers. Some forms of found digital data provide welcome means of going beyond self-reported accounts of media uses and communicative practices (Salganik, 2018), for example, through web traffic measurements, which have established the fundamental importance of geography, culture, and language for localized uses of the internet (Taneja & Webster, 2016). For many research questions, however, surveys remain an indispensable instrument, including for comparative purposes across national borders, but also to cover separate media and communication systems which, as sources of data, remain incompatible. The availability of data is also limited, in some cases, by forbidding fees; in other cases, data may simply be inaccessible because of their proprietary nature, for commercial reasons. In order to tap the breadth and depth of contemporary communicative practices, we relied on triangulation (Denzin, 1970), combining several methods of data collection in parallel, rather than treating one method as pilot and another as primary. We approach various data forms – qualitative and quantitative, found and made – as different, but equal contributions to answering our research questions.

Data analysis methods follow, in part, from the nature of the data being collected. Surveys invite a variety of quantitative, statistical techniques; fieldwork data call for qualitative, more or less open-ended forms of coding to recognize what communication is and does – what it means. In both cases, visualization in various formats offers, at once, means of analysis and presentation. For the survey component, we introduced the technique of latent cluster analysis to arrive at types of media users and communicators, which, in a second step, could be compared across countries and sociodemographic segments. For fieldwork in the three regions, the same systematic of qualitative interviewing combined with informant diaries facilitated the identification of comparable, yet distinctive communicative practices. And, for the tracker aspect, we turned to analytical techniques that largely derive from computer science, and which only recently have been transferred to communication studies as part of a consolidation of digital methods in this field (Helles, 2021; R. Rogers, 2019).

Distinguishing between methods and *methodology*, we define the latter as a theoretically informed plan of action in relation to a particular empirical domain of social and scientific interest. If methods are techniques, methodologies can be understood as technologies of research. Methodologies map theoretical macrocosms onto necessarily selective empirical microcosms. Methodology, thus, is key to the selection and combination of specific methods of data collection and analysis in order to address particular conceptual and practical issues. It is at this level that the distinctions between qualitative, quantitative, and multi-method research designs belong. We emphasize the relevance and importance of combining several methods in comparative research projects; we particularly note the potential of multi-method studies for identifying the levels at which, and the forms in which, social and cultural difference and similarity manifest themselves.

Theoretical frameworks constitute configurations of concepts that lend coherence, meaning, and relevance to particular patterns of empirical findings. Theories can be thought of as cognitive and interactional frames (Goffman, 1974; Lakoff & Johnson, 1980) that enable or afford (Gibson, 1979) certain interpretations and explanations, while discouraging others. Theories are qualitative, to the extent that they offer one preferred configuration of ideas and information, even while subsuming diverse kinds of quantitative and qualitative evidence. In this opening chapter, we have introduced a broad conceptual landscape, populated by grand theories and models of historical and cultural change and continuity, bounded by material and immaterial limits to what communication is, could be, and might become, as instantiated by medium theory and Stuart Hall's (1983) idea of determination in the first instance. We go on, in the overview of chapters below and in the rest of the book, to draw on several additional theoretical traditions from the human and social sciences to specify how communication systems work, as observed from multiple disciplinary and interdisciplinary perspectives.

Theoretical frameworks are substantive or domain-specific – they apply to particular portions of reality, in this case human communication as circumscribed by material technologies, social institutions, and cultural traditions. The choice of theoretical frameworks is motivated and substantiated by metatheory, theory of science, or *epistemology*: Premises concerning what kinds of knowledge can be arrived at, and how, by which sorts of analysis and inference. Epistemology, further, holds two sets of implications regarding the kinds of things researchers do with media and people. On the one hand, epistemologies imply *ontologies*: Premises regarding the nature of the reality that research may hope to encounter and represent. The arrow in Figure 1.3 linking epistemology to the objects of analysis suggests this ontological commitment. As elaborated in the Methodological Appendix (Chapter 8), we depart from the tradition of critical realism (Archer, Bhaskar, Collier, Lawson, & Norrie, 1998), approaching empirical data as evidence of *experiences* of communicative practices that bear witness to specific *events* (e.g., getting news updates (or not), being included in (or excluded from) particular social networks, exercising (only) certain forms of political and economic agency), which, in a third step, may be explained by material, institutional, or discursive *mechanisms*, or combinations thereof. On the other hand, epistemologies imply *knowledge interests* (Habermas, 1971/1968): Premises as to why a certain kind of knowledge ought to be produced in the first place. Critical realism, for one, is realist in that it seeks to identify material and institutional boundaries to the good life and social justice, and critical in that it proposes to question and shift such boundaries.

Whereas human communication is a prime candidate for culturally comparative research, comparative perspectives have commonly been assigned to sub-specializations such as intercultural communication studies (Kim, 2018), rather than being recognized as a general source of reflexivity about necessarily localized communicative practices. In one sense, all human and social sciences are comparative:

> After we designate researchers who compare across time (historians) and across space (geographers), researchers who compare communications content (content analysts), organizations (organizational sociologists), institutions (macrosociologists), countries (international relations specialists), cultures (ethnologists), and languages (linguists), and researchers who compare individuals in terms of gender, race, social class, age, education, and religion, what remains?
>
> *(Beniger, 1992: 35)*

What remains, in media and communication research, is a shift of focus from media systems toward communication systems and, more broadly, a building of bridges across the de facto divide that has separated communication research into two subdisciplines of mass and interpersonal communication studies, respectively (E. M. Rogers, 1999). Digitalization represents a historical opportunity and an empirical context for accomplishing both of these things. People do things with media one-to-one and one-to-many, but also many-to-many and in multiple steps that make a difference, here and now and over time, for the societies of which people are citizens and the cultures in which they participate. This book is a contribution to understanding communication systems as works in progress, in theory as in practice.

The chapters of the volume

The chapters of the volume proceed from an overview of communication infrastructures and regulatory regimes, through detailed analyses of the things people do with media and the communicative practices they thus engage in, to a synthesis of empirical findings, a review of perspectives for theory development, and a discussion of normative implications for the national and international regulation of communication systems. Throughout, we combine the different sources of evidence outlined in this introductory chapter to produce a comprehensive, detailed account of the current state of communication systems across the three regions of the study. Our aim is to offer a rich, yet readable statement, to strike a balance between pointed characterizations and supporting details. Much of the documentation is given in tables and models, and while we invite readers to explore the nuances of numbers and visualizations, the text has been formulated to facilitate the presentation – communication – of a central narrative and focused arguments. Along the way, we refer to supplementary publications from the Peoples' Internet project, in addition to the Methodological Appendix in Chapter 8, and to important work by many other scholars.

What people do with media, is conditioned by what states and markets already did to media (and to people). Chapter 2 first details infrastructural and related structuring conditions that make China, Europe, and the United States distinctive communication systems, despite important and interesting overlaps. Building on national and international statistics and indicators, the chapter develops models that capture and represent the technological, political, and economic dimensions of communication systems for comparative purposes. The theoretical background to the models comes from two literatures, in particular: Research on the social diffusion of technological innovations (E. M. Rogers, 2003) and studies of the media systems that traditionally have been the carriers of news and public debate within national public spheres (Hallin & Mancini, 2004). It is these systems that are being, if not replaced, manifestly reconfigured in response to digitalization. In a longer and broader perspective, communication systems are subject to the tectonic forces of state and market, in historically variable political economies, as addressed from Adam Smith via Karl Marx to recent interventions highlighting the constitutive role of communication – whether directly as in the case of Shoshana Zuboff (2019), who addressed bit trails as a productive force heralding an era of surveillance capitalism, or indirectly as in the case of Thomas Piketty (2020), who considered the dance of capital and ideology over the centuries, as mediated by communication. As infrastructures for human doings and beings, communication systems make available lessons from the past, resources for acting in the present, and perspectives on possible and preferable futures, for the individual and for the collective.

Chapter 3 goes on to outline the contours of predominant communicative practices, in China, Europe, and the United States and for different sociodemographic segments, in the context of the characteristic media and communication environments of each region. We develop an understanding of such environments as menus from which individuals and groups will create their own diets, with reference to a concept of *repertoires*: Research of the past few decades has responded to increasingly complex media environments by examining people's distinctive selections and combinations of various media and genres for different private and public ends; here, we add *communication* repertoires as an analytical category to accommodate the full range of media uses and communicative prototypes in contemporary communication systems. Prioritizing a quantitative overview, the chapter identifies different typologies or styles of media use and communication, and explores their prevalence across national settings and social segments, complementing the overview with qualitative perspectives on how expats and internal migrants navigate and orient themselves in several social and cultural worlds, here and there, in and by communication. With specific reference to an ongoing transformation of analog into digital media and communication environments, we introduce an understanding of computers and, broadly speaking, digital systems as *meta-media* (Kay & Goldberg, 1999/1977), which reproduce or simulate (all) earlier media forms while adding and integrating new forms. It seems an open question, at the time of writing, whether and how meta-media may eventually replace what has been thought of, for the last two centuries (Peters, 1999), as media. Chapter 3 offers a baseline on the state of communication systems at the beginning of the 2020s.

Chapter 4 deepens the account of communication systems with particular reference to the constitutive role of communication in articulating and maintaining human communities, large and small, locally and globally. Communication technologies have extended what had remained, for most of evolutionary and historical time, the basic medium: Humans engaging in face-to-face interaction. We begin from the insight that humans and technologies have comparable if different *affordances* (Gibson, 1979) for communication. We go on to explore the media and communication repertoires that people draw on for the ties that bind, more or less intensively, across space and time. Identifying quantitative patterns of contact as well as qualitative criteria of when and why (not) to make contact with (some) others, we ask, most fundamentally, how communication contributes to sociality and, by the same token, the maintenance of personal identities. Sociality is *scalable* (Miller et al., 2016), from intimate relations to imagined communities (Anderson, 1991). We further address both the specific question of how sociality is enacted – communicated – across a presumed online–offline divide, and the more general question of how different cultures and civilizations administer sociality in signs and symbols. In the end, what people do with media, and with each other, accumulates as remarkably persistent and meaningful structures – cultures.

In Chapter 5, we return to the question of how communication mediates agency and structure, shifting the emphasis from the processes and networks of social interaction toward their products, the *capitals* – material and immaterial resources – that individuals are in a position to access and accumulate, before, during, and after communication. To that end, we turn to the seminal work of Pierre Bourdieu (1984/1979) on different varieties of capital, their translation back and forth, and their circulation as part of the distribution of privilege and power within and across different social fields. Recent research has identified an additional variant of *digital* capital, which serves a bridging role between other capitals, and which may extend and exacerbate classic inequalities. Again combining quantitative survey evidence with qualitative fieldwork data, we characterize both the distribution of capitals in the very different social systems of the three regions of the study, and the strategies and tactics that people mobilize to make it through their daily chores, as well as pursuing more long-term plans in life. In this regard, digitalization presents, at once, opportunities and challenges. Compared to earlier media forms, digital media in general and the internet in particular enable human actions and social interactions at a distance (Mansell & Ang, 2015). Accordingly, we ask, in the most mundane terms possible, what people do with media, within embodied contexts of use, but also embedded in virtual realities beyond the here and the now. The internet has highlighted the point that, more than serving as a *representation of* the world, communication constitutes a *resource* for acting *in* and *on* the world.

Chapter 6 extends the understanding of communication as action, from the side of ordinary users to the side of organizations and institutions operating as economic and political agents, examining what digital intermediaries and, in turn, the clients who buy and rework their data, *do to* the users of communication systems. Identifying and categorizing third-party software on websites in the countries of the three regions, the analyses serve to track the trackers, so as to describe and explain forms of contact and control that have not traditionally been considered communication, but which have become key components of digital infrastructures. Beyond the moments of contact, such many-to-one communications play into a complex marketplace of attention (Webster, 2014), with implications for patterns of one-to-one, one-to-many, and many-to-many communication, as well. It is not only that (more or less) personal data are monetized in less than transparent steps and sequences; data can be and are "weaponized" (Frankopan, 2019: 41) by institutional agents, as vividly suggested by Edward Snowden's 2013 revelations of US government surveillance of its own citizens and by China's 'great firewall' and its system of networked authoritarianism (MacKinnon, 2011). In this respect at least, an early motto of critical media studies still holds true: The center of media studies lies (ought to lie) outside of the media (Negt, 1973: iv). In order to assess the implications of contemporary communication systems, it is essential to analyze not only the generic communicative practices they circumscribe, but also *their* intersections with other systems overseen and influenced by diverse local and global institutions and interests. Communication systems are just that: Systemic conditions of who can say what to whom, and the difference these conditions make for human existence and social coexistence.

The conclusion in Chapter 7 summarizes the empirical findings, discusses their theoretical implications, and addresses some of the normative issues that follow from a comparative analysis of contemporary communication systems. Under an empirical heading, we reconsider the current state of one-to-many mass *communication* (not to be confused with the commercial viability of classic mass *media*), the global and locally specific aspects of one-to-one interpersonal communication, and the relative prominence in media and communication repertoires of many-to-many interactions, which have been widely thought of as competitors, even alternatives to the other two prototypes, in research and in public debate. As a contribution to theory development, and to interdisciplinary dialogue with other fields of inquiry about contemporary societies and cultures, we revisit the models presented in this introductory chapter, with particular reference to the relative determination of communicative practices by technological, institutional, and discursive conditions, and to the intersection of communication systems with other social systems and infrastructures. A normative outlook on the future, finally, ties in with ongoing conversations and contestations, again in research as in public debate, about communication systems as a centerpiece of information, control, network, or surveillance societies still to come (Jensen, 2021). It is timely and appropriate that citizens around the world should communicate in detail and at length about systems that they will depend on for the foreseeable future.

The Methodological Appendix in Chapter 8 provides additional detail for interested readers and researchers on three main topics. First, we include information on samples, analytical procedures, and other methodological aspects of the surveys, the three cases of fieldwork, and the tracker studies. Second, the appendix elaborates on critical realism and the complementarity of different methods as part of this framework, including consideration of the critical potential and knowledge interest (Habermas, 1971/1968) of multi-method comparative research. Third, we offer some practical lessons for research and policy from a project spanning three continents, seven nation-states, and a range of political economies and cultural traditions. Finally, we recognize and reflect on the question of what can and cannot (and sometimes ought not to) be known about communication systems and their users through the currently available conceptual and methodological repertoires of media and communication studies – which circumscribe and inscribe researchers' outlooks on the world.

2

THE COMMUNICATIVE STATE OF STATES

Verena K. Brändle, Rasmus Helles, and Klaus Bruhn Jensen

Communicating like a state

In an analysis of "how certain schemes to improve the human condition have failed," James C. Scott (1998) identified distinctive ways of "seeing like a state" – of observing people, places, and resources in order to plan ahead and anticipate beneficial outcomes for citizens. In a subsequent intervention, Marion Fourcade and Kieran Healy (2017) outlined complementary ways of "seeing like a market" – of assessing the value of people and other units of interest, as enhanced and appropriated through digital tracking and measurement. Representing and balancing the perspectives of states and markets, while still centered in the modern nation-state, contemporary communication systems afford ways of monitoring society and the world at large, from above in the perspective of the powers that be, but also from below and to all sides by individuals and communities – what Lee Rainie and Barry Wellman (2012) summed up as processes of surveillance, sousveillance, and coveillance. Grounded in long histories and deep cultural traditions, communication systems articulate distinctive ideas of what a state is, could be, and ought to be; how a state should engage its own people as well as other peoples and states; and how it should enable individuals and groups to relate to each other, locally and globally, in and by communication. This chapter offers a brief overview of communication systems around the world, situating the three regions and seven countries of the Peoples' Internet (PIN) study on a technological and institutional map of the world. As outlined in Chapter 1, distinctive configurations of material technologies and political economies, in each case, circumscribe – enable and constrain – who can say what to whom, within and beyond national boundaries.

The first section reviews and relates two key strands of previous research on communication systems as technological and institutional structures. On the one hand, studies of the *diffusion of innovations* (Rogers, 1962) have examined the

DOI: 10.4324/9781003057055-2

processes through which different categories of technologies have been implemented and adopted, to variable degrees depending on material circumstances, providing one measure of the unequal conditions of communication across nation-states and world regions. Consonant with medium theory as introduced in Chapter 1, diffusion research has provided more fine-grained analyses of how technologies come to be embedded in economic and other human interactions from micro to macro levels of social organization. The diffusion of innovations, including most recently the digital computer as both device and infrastructure, must be assessed in the context of wider local and global political economies with long and conflicted histories.

On the other hand, as also previewed in Chapter 1, media have traditionally been studied as a distinctive kind of systems grounded in political philosophies – *media systems* (Hallin & Mancini, 2004, 2017, 2012) – with important links to other social systems, notably the political systems regulating material production and cultural interchange. In this regard, research on digital forms of communication is still getting its bearings, as suggested by the title of one intervention, *The Hybrid Media System* (Chadwick, 2013), registering the reconfiguration of analog and digital media that is ongoing and open-ended. Whereas this volume focuses on the uses and users of media, the present chapter outlines the geopolitical background to communication systems as infrastructures shaped by and, simultaneously, shaping politics and economy. Between them, the literatures on technology diffusion and media systems chart the territory in which a new category of communication systems is emerging as we speak and write.

The middle section of the chapter presents the data sets and analytical approaches employed here to arrive at an overview of current global infrastructures of communication. The interpretation of findings on their uses and users, as well as an evaluation of their implications for social participation and human quality of life, depends crucially on contexts. Noting the limited and localized nature of available baseline information, we describe the multiple sources of evidence that are needed to begin a study of communication systems, typically from international organizations devoted to political and economic cooperation involving science, technology, and trade. These data sets are consolidated here and examined through multidimensional modeling to arrive at characterizations of the three regions and seven countries of the PIN project against the background of a wider selection of nation-states. Because of the provenance of the data, they bear witness to ways of "seeing like a state" and "seeing like a market" as well as a degree of media-centrism, in view of the priority historically given to the press as the vehicle and arena of public (mass) communication. By joining complementary data and models, we seek to contribute to the necessary labor ahead in mapping communication systems.

The third section presents the findings from the empirical analyses and considers their implications for further research and policy debate. A principal component analysis (PCA) served to identify two main dimensions differentiating the communication systems of countries and regions. Figures with visualizations provide overview and reference points for dialogue in and with the field of practice. While the first dimension comprised indicators of participation, recognition, and inclusion – democracies versus autocracies – the second dimension brought out the fundamental resource divides separating different world regions, when it comes to communication infrastructures as well as the additional infrastructures on which communicative practices depend. In combination, the two dimensions constitute a spectrum of quantitative and qualitative capacities and opportunities for communication. We first provide a mapping of a sample of 80 countries on these two dimensions and next elaborate on the seven countries and three world regions of the PIN project. In addition to constituting a ground for assessing the findings concerning users and uses in the following chapters, the present chapter points to avenues for further studies of communication systems in other world regions. The final section of the chapter sums up the current state of communication systems, noting, as well, ongoing geopolitical contestations of what communication systems could be and ought to become.

The local embedding of global technologies

The political economy of technology diffusion

All technologically mediated communication depends crucially on material and immaterial resources – wealth and knowledge. To serve a diversity of personal and communal ends, communication technologies have to be diffused – they must become materially *available* and discursively *accessible* for substantial populations, whether local communities or national publics. Availability, first, presupposes the invention and development of a particular technology, and its dissemination and relative affordability throughout a given historical and cultural context. Accessibility, next, hinges on potential users recognizing its relevance and potential applications, in addition to substantial groups having or acquiring the necessary cognitive and cultural competences. With technologies and competences in place, individuals and collectives may accumulate further wealth and knowledge.

From the outset, the tradition of diffusion research (Rogers, 1962, 2003) had a strong family resemblance with another tradition within the field of media and communication research as it was taking shape in the decades following 1945, namely, development communication (Lerner, 1958; Schramm, 1964). In both traditions, technologies and practices of communication were understood as instruments of social progress broadly speaking, not least in what came to be referred to, variously, as 'the developing world' and 'the Third World,' caught between and courted until the 1990s by the other two worlds of East and West. Whereas media and communication studies have largely left these terminologies behind, recognizing the conflicted histories and intercultural communications currently relating the Global North and Global South (Kim, 2018), it remains evidently true that the diffusion of communication technologies and communicative competences constitute necessary (if far from sufficient) conditions of individual self-realization and collective self-determination – means for more people to lead better lives.

Diffusion research, far from centering on media, developed as an interdisciplinary field of inquiry, with applications ranging from agriculture and industry to healthcare and education (Rogers, 2003). An innovation derives from information that is perceived as new and relevant in a particular context, and the innovation is diffused less as specific artifacts than as principles and procedures that reorient actions, whether on the material environment or as social interactions, increasingly from the local to the global level. The field of media and communication research suggests the point: The emergence and consolidation of printing presses, broadcasting stations, and digital networks depended on ideas, competences, and resources enabling their construction and implementation, and their wider diffusion was interwoven with practices of communication predominant in historical and cultural contexts. Innovations, in short, can be understood as affordances (Gibson, 1979; Hsieh, 2012; Hutchby, 2001) – potentials that humans realize in interaction with their natural and cultural environments. Innovations constitute interfaces with reality, identified by inventors and entrepreneurs, and subsequently appreciated by users in their various roles as citizens, consumers, and members of communities and cultures, with long-term consequences for the understanding of self and society.

Innovations afford more innovation: The printing press, for one, supported the local invention and global dissemination of broadcasting and computing as common technologies and institutions. In this regard, media represent a distinctive category of innovation, a set of generic technologies for representing and communicating about things that communities and cultures, large and small, might decide to do together. As resources for imagining and enacting alternative ways of life, communication technologies constitute engines of innovation. All historical societies, then, have been information societies, to the extent that economies, polities, sciences, arts, and everyday lives have been characterized by particular modes of access to information and means of communication (Finnemann, 1999). It is this circumstance of social life and of the human condition writ large that was reemphasized by digital technologies from the mid-twentieth century and into the twenty-first century.

The idea of a society revolving around information and communication has been a long time coming. In thumbnail review, the modern turn of science and scholarship had subordinated theory to practice, and had redefined practice as productive activities rebuilding the natural environment for human and social ends (Lobkowicz, 1967). In consequence, industrial and other material production assumed a scale and a scope that presented growing problems of social coordination, accelerating throughout the nineteenth century and into the twentieth century. Matter was getting out of control, and had to be in-formed by immaterial means – through innovation by information. Summed up as a *control revolution* (Beniger, 1986), solutions were devised gradually from the last decades of the nineteenth century, relying on systems of bureaucratization and rationalization, and deploying technologies such as telegraphy, telephony, and punch-card processing. After 1945, a consensus emerged that industrial society had transitioned into an *information society* (Bell, 1973; Porat, 1977), in which, quantitatively, a majority of the workforce is employed in information and other service occupations, while, qualitatively, information has become a key means of production in its own right (and an increasingly profitable consumer product) and, hence, a strategic element of private business as well as public governance. The contemporary world has also been characterized, more grandly, as an information age in which both local and global social interaction is structured along network principles (Castells, 1996–1998).

In retrospect, world history interpreted through the lens of human communication holds two lessons for the study of contemporary communication systems. First, the diffusion of information and communication technologies has witnessed an all too familiar, decidedly unequal process, interwoven with economic, political, and cultural trajectories. Like other technologies, information and communication technologies constitute means of production yielding significantly different outcomes for the haves and the have-nots, nationally and internationally. Across the long historical haul, the industrial revolution that picked up steam from the eighteenth century had resulted in what historians term *the great divergence* (Pomeranz, 2000) of the West from the rest: A period of unprecedented economic growth producing more goods for more people, but largely in and for the Global North. Following multiple steps of decolonization and stages of globalization, the development of the internet as a global digital infrastructure certainly has facilitated economic and other social development in the Global South (e.g., Myovella, Karaçuka, & Haucap, 2019). In a volume titled *The Great Convergence*, Richard Baldwin (2016) mapped how, from the 1990s, information and communication technologies entailed a new global division of labor, as know-how was exported to low-wage countries to expand the high-tech production there of material goods. Baldwin was also careful to note, however, that such technological convergence still entailed economic divergence and continued inequalities: "Just six developing nations − […] (China, Korea, India, Poland, Indonesia, and Thailand) − accounted for almost all of the G7's decline" (the G7 being the United States, Germany, Japan, France, Britain, Canada, and Italy) (p. 3).

The second lesson of communication history follows from the generic nature of communication technologies, which lend themselves to a great variety of economic and cultural, public and private uses. As infrastructures, they pervade both work and leisure, and enable the production of profits as well as arts. An early focus of research and public debate on the internet was the *digital divide* between those with and without opportunities to use such an essential infrastructure, originally in a national perspective (NTIA, 1995). Soon, regional and global perspectives were added to the social equation, and digital divides were articulated in the plural: There is a first-level divide of basic access or not, but also a second-level divide regarding differential skills of comprehending and utilizing the information on offer, and a third-level divide focusing on the (lack of) outcomes of internet use in the form of economic, political, and cultural participation (e.g., Scheerder, van Deursen, & van Dijk, 2017). Further research has included attention to the systemic nature of communication infrastructures. Their versatility helps to explain their strategic position both as objects of investment and as public services, which tends to produce market concentration as political authorities have preferred to limit regulatory measures in order to secure investment in comprehensive national infrastructures for citizens (Flew, 2021).

The outcome, by the 2020s, was a globalized, if segregated, infrastructure comprising, in the West, the so-called Big Five (Alphabet, Amazon, Apple, Facebook, Microsoft) and the BAT or Big Three of China (Baidu, Alibaba, Tencent). This development has been summed up as *platformization*, with a few quasi-monopolies guiding the flows of information and communicative practices across key institutions and sectors of society (Gillespie, 2010; van Dijck, Poell, & de Waal, 2018). More than information intermediaries, these corporations in effect operate as stakeholders in the regulation of a critical social infrastructure, as prominently as national governments and international agencies, if still in collaboration with communities representing technical expertise and civil society. A further terminology of *infrastructuralization* has been suggested to capture this shift in the status of platforms, from private profit-seeking companies to hybrid entities at the intersection of multi-sided markets, nation-states, and civil societies spanning the local and the global (Plantin, Lagoze, Edwards, & Sandvig, 2018). And, beyond the platforms so familiar to users as front offices, the back offices of communication infrastructures include less familiar alliances blurring classic market-state and local-global boundaries. While the content and code layers of the internet are controlled by private, typically US-based companies, its material infrastructure is owned by multinational consortia with states as co-investors cultivating national interests, from economic growth to cybersecurity (Winseck, 2017).

The present conjuncture recalls Larry Lessig's (1999, 2006) succinct summary: *Code is law*. Internet architecture enables and constrains human actions and social interactions, online and increasingly offline, as well. Platforms and consortia constitute collaborators, but also competitors in their dealings with the political authorities that traditionally have regulated both commerce and communication, nationally and internationally. Responding to the diffusion of digital communication technologies, governments have variously sought to define the terms on which information is exchanged and communicative practices conducted, with long-term structural implications for how profit, privilege, and power will be negotiated and distributed on and through the internet. In this strategic domain, classic issues concerning freedoms of information and communication as well as national security and personal privacy have taken on renewed relevance. At the time of writing, countries around the world are struggling, with each other and with platforms and consortia, to reconfigure regulatory regimes to serve their own interests and, at best, to deliver a common international and cross-cultural good for the coming decades.

Regulatory regimes reconfigured

Communication has historically stimulated political and ethical reflection on the appropriate ways of regulating its discursive forms, social institutions, and technological bases, from the Socratic dialogue as a potential avenue toward the true and the good, via Enlightenment ideals of public reason, to political and other social sciences addressing communication technologies as a key condition and constituent of human flourishing (*eudaimonia*) in modernity. The engagement of the field of media and communication with the grand normative issues at stake was accelerated in the shadow of the Cold War, as different models of the good society and the good life of citizens confronted each other. The classic publication (Siebert, Peterson, & Schramm, 1956) identified four positions with particular reference to the press: Authoritarian theory (associated with a medieval cosmology), totalitarian theory (ascribed to the Soviet Union and its Eastern bloc), libertarian theory (a classic free-market position), and social-responsibility theory (an understanding of the press and other media as public trustees in an era of market concentration and conglomeration). Subsequent developments surrounding media in the Global South and additional media facilitating public participation – from community radio to the internet – prompted the formulation of two additional positions (McQuail, 1983; McQuail & Deuze, 2020): Development communication, as previously noted, and democratic participant theory. Although media and communication research has continued to develop and debate normative theories (Christians, Glasser, McQuail, Nordenstreng, & White, 2009; Jensen, 2021), the several social-scientific, interpretive, and critical mainstreams of the field have emphasized theoretical interpretations of, rather than practical interventions into and reforms of, media and communicative practices as they currently exist (Craig, 1989, 2018).

A revival of normative research agendas was marked by the publication of Dan Hallin and Paolo Mancini's *Comparing Media Systems* (Hallin & Mancini, 2004). In this widely influential analysis of the relationship between national political systems and media systems, the authors distinguished three models, departing from conditions in Europe and North America: A "liberal" market-based model (grounded in the United States and the United Kingdom); a "democratic corporatist" or social democratic welfare model (prevalent in Northern Europe); and a "polarized pluralist" model with a more antagonistic political system and a stronger state influence on media (characteristic of Southern Europe). Introducing additional empirical evidence, a follow-up study identified not three, but four categories of media systems (Brüggemann, Engesser, Büchel, Humprecht, & Castro, 2014), while still observing the world from a northwestern position. Responding to calls for studies and perspectives beyond the Western world, a volume by Hallin and Mancini (2012) recognized the importance of more inclusive comparisons of media systems around the world. But, despite attempts at devising alternative typologies (e.g., Blum, 2005), research has tended to stay focused on the specific media systems of particular (sets of) countries, for example, the Baltic nations as cultural formations predating Soviet state and media supremacy (Høyer, Lauk, & Vihalemm, 1993; Vihalemm, 2002), or the BRICS countries (Brazil, Russia, India, China, South Africa) as economic as well as cultural agents in global arenas (Nordenstreng & Thussu, 2015).

As outlined in Chapter 1, the present volume seeks to contribute to the consolidation of comparative studies of communication systems, beyond media systems as traditionally conceived and with reference to shared parameters of material technologies, political economies, and cultural traditions. We write at a time when governments around the world are still developing (more or less) local regimes for regulating a global internet (Mueller, 2017). With an open-architecture internet, operated by private corporations, governments face distinctive challenges of how, in practice, to enable and constrain the communicative practices of citizens, companies, and other interests in society. We further recognize that national initiatives in regulating international communication infrastructures are not new, but have been part and parcel of the administration of empire and the conduct of war (e.g., Tworek, 2019; Winseck, 2017). There are important path dependencies of a political, economic, as well as cultural nature to consider when interpreting the present and potential future trajectories of internet regulation in different world regions.

It should be added that we do not explore, in the present volume, the details of *internet governance* (Kurbalija, 2016), which has established itself as a domain of research and practice involving a multitude of stakeholders including governments, commercial operators, and civil-society organizations. When it comes to the actual communicative practices of citizens and consumers in the context of everyday life, as emphasized in this volume, national governments remain the primary agents preparing the conditions under which users encounter technologies, platforms, contents, and devices, subject to variable measures of censorship, surveillance, price control, and other regulation broadly speaking. Accordingly, in the following sections, we rely on a variety of national indicators to gauge the nature and quality of the communication systems on offer. In the case of internet censorship, for instance, a complex set of technological, institutional, and cultural factors determine who gains access (or not) to contested information (Ververis, Marguel, & Fabian, 2020). In order to contextualize findings from the Peoples' Internet project, we depart from an extensive mapping of the technologies diffused throughout, and the regulatory regimes within, 80 countries in total, and we go on to detail distinctive features of the communication systems of China, the United States, and the five European countries in our sample.

Data lost, found, and re-made

Like communication technologies and communicative competences, empirical data bearing on who is, in fact, in a position to say something to a few, many, or masses of others, are unequally distributed across the globe. In some cases, data are simply unavailable – missing infrastructures of research entail missing variables and values, in this and other domains of inquiry. In other cases, relevant information and implications must be inferred from data collected for different purposes. In order to produce a robust, if preliminary, mapping of the basic communication infrastructures of the world, we relied on two analytical strategies. On the one hand, we pursued *secondary data analysis* (Goodwin, 2012) of selected sources of data for technology diffusion and national regulation. The sources included international organizations such as the United Nations, the International Telecommunication Union, the World Bank, and the World Economic Forum, supplemented by organizations such as Freedom House and the Varieties of Democracy project, which monitors and measures the state of democracy in different countries according to consolidated indicators (https://www.v-dem.net, accessed on August 15, 2022). On the other hand, we relied on *multidimensional modeling* in the form of principal component analysis (PCA) (Jolliffe & Cadima, 2016) of the available data sets so as to integrate measures into synthetic descriptions of the state of communication systems. The resulting models provide summary characterizations of the technological and institutional factors circumscribing communicative practices on the ground.

In accordance with the premise of *determination in the first instance* (Hall, 1983) as advanced in Chapter 1, we adopted a "position of 'soft determinism' in which technology designers and policy makers make decisions that provide capacities for and impose constraints on users" (Howard, 2010: 16–17). This position leaves open for comparative and contrastive empirical analysis diverse questions of the intercultural and institutional convergence or divergence of communicative practices, as digitalization works out its effects in different nations and regions. Our selection of data sources emphasized evidence on the two aspects of technology diffusion and regulatory regimes: National infrastructures and patterns of regulation.

The complete data set comprised 35 variables for a total of 80 countries of the world. A variety of countries and variables were excluded from the analysis because of missing values for a number of the indicators of interest. As quality control, the set of countries excluded from the analysis was inspected for evident bias, for example, whether countries from particular world regions were systematically overrepresented; a similar check was performed on variables with many missing values. No such patterns could be detected, even if countries with many missing values for communication infrastructure variables also appeared likely to have weak infrastructures overall. In a world of 195 countries, the present sample suggests the fundamental challenge of securing data for more comparative studies of the communication systems of the world.

The 35 variables covered standard indicators of national infrastructures, supplemented by measures reflecting the best available estimates of factors enabling or constraining communicative practices, for example, from the Varieties of Democracy/Digital Society Project. To illustrate, one variable registered responses to the question: "Independent of whether it actually does so in practice, does the government have the technical capacity to actively shut down domestic access to the Internet if it decided to?" (Coppedge et al., 2019). To one side, indicators of technology diffusion included factors such as the number of broadband connections per 100,000 inhabitants and the cost of a postpaid mobile subscription relative to average income in the country in question. Additional infrastructural indicators measured gender gaps in broadband access and the percentage of rural populations with access to electricity (and hence, digital communication services). To the other side, indicators of regulatory regimes considered traditional measures of press freedom and of freedom of information and communication generally. To register the intended scope and actual efficiency of regulation, the indicators also counted questions such as "What type of content is covered in the legal framework to regulate Internet?" and "Does the government have sufficient staff and resources to regulate internet content in accordance with existing law?" (Coppedge et al., 2019). (A full list of the variables included in the analysis is available from the authors. The 80 countries are listed in relation to Figure 2.1.)

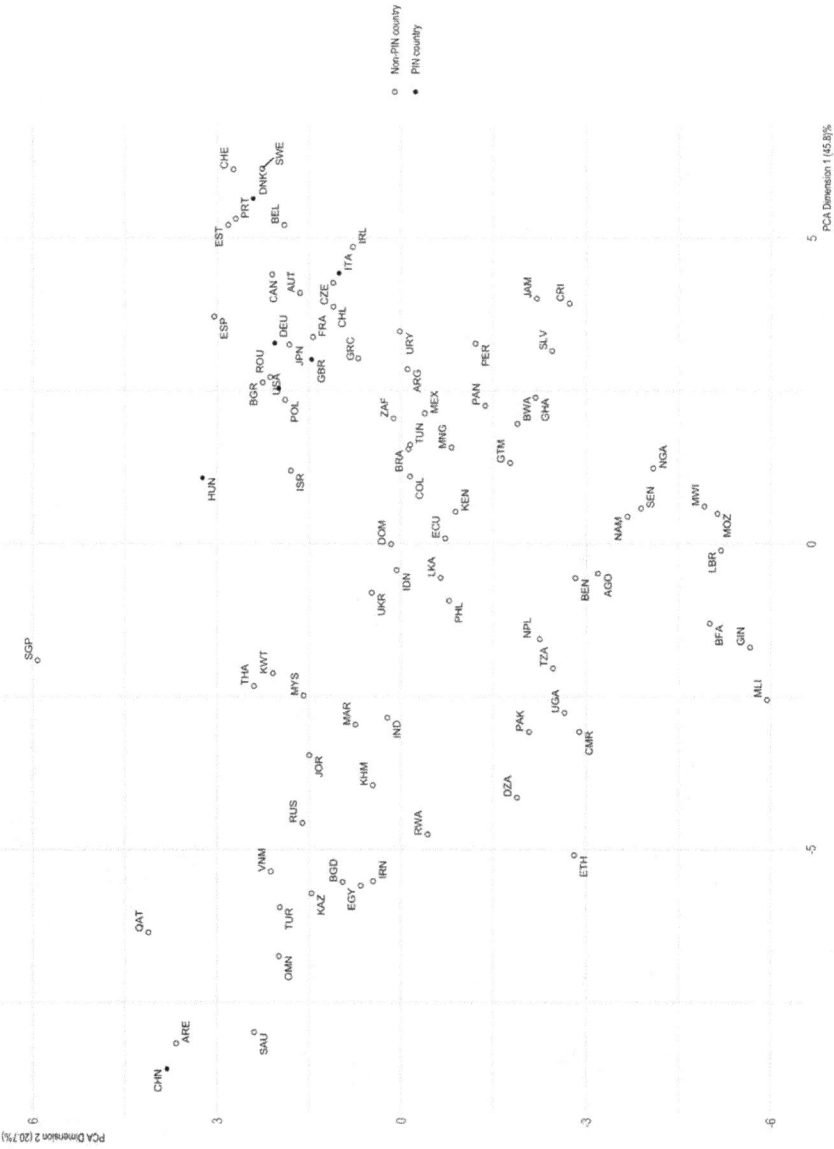

FIGURE 2.1   PCA analysis of 80 world countries on PCA dimensions

Code	Country
AGO	Angola
ARE	United Arab Emirates
ARG	Argentina
AUT	Austria
BEL	Belgium
BEN	Benin
BFA	Burkina Faso
BGD	Bangladesh
BGR	Bulgaria
BRA	Brazil
BWA	Botswana
CAN	Canada
CHE	Switzerland
CHL	Chile
CHN	China
CMR	Cameroon
COL	Colombia
CRI	Costa Rica
CZE	Czechia
DEU	Germany
DNK	Denmark
DOM	Dominican Republic
DZA	Algeria
ECU	Ecuador
EGY	Egypt
ESP	Spain
EST	Estonia
ETH	Ethiopia
FRA	France
GBR	United Kingdom of Great Britain and Northern Ireland
GHA	Ghana
GIN	Guinea
GRC	Greece
GTM	Guatemala
HUN	Hungary
IDN	Indonesia
IND	India
IRL	Ireland
IRN	Iran
ISR	Israel
ITA	Italy
JAM	Jamaica
JOR	Jordan
JPN	Japan
KAZ	Kazakhstan
KEN	Kenya
KHM	Cambodia

KWT	Kuwait
LBR	Liberia
LKA	Sri Lanka
MAR	Morocco
MEX	Mexico
MLI	Mali
MNG	Mongolia
MOZ	Mozambique
MWI	Malawi
MYS	Malaysia
NAM	Namibia
NGA	Nigeria
NPL	Nepal
OMN	Oman
PAK	Pakistan
PAN	Panama
PER	Peru
PHL	Philippines
POL	Poland
PRT	Portugal
QAT	Qatar
ROU	Romania
RUS	Russian Federation
RWA	Rwanda
SAU	Saudi Arabia
SEN	Senegal
SGP	Singapore
SLV	El Salvador
SWE	Sweden
THA	Thailand
TUN	Tunisia
TUR	Turkey
TZA	Tanzania
UGA	Uganda
UKR	Ukraine
URY	Uruguay
USA	United States of America
VNM	Vietnam
ZAF	South Africa

The entire data set was subjected to a PCA (using R [v. 4.0.3] with the package FactoMineR [v. 2.4]) (Husson, Lê, & Pagès, 2017; Jolliffe & Cadima, 2016; Lê, Josse, & Husson, 2008). In addition to being a well-established analytical procedure, facilitating transparency, a specific strength of PCA is its capacity for systematic reduction of dimensionality and, thus, the identification of central analytical categories. A constitutive feature of PCA and our analysis is the clustering of individual cases based on their score on the principal components as constructed during the analysis. This type of cluster analysis also delivers means of assessing the validity of the underlying PCA model, by comparing it against alternative cluster solutions obtained through a different algorithm. The findings of the PCA, detailed in the next section, were compared to an alternative solution obtained through the t-SNE algorithm, as well as to a further solution employing untransformed variables as part of a non-linear PCA. While some numerical differences could be identified, both alternative classifications were in clear agreement with the output of the standard PCA procedure, which is preferred here for its simplicity of interpretation.

The following section, then, stands on the shoulders of existing archives and databases, recognizing that some data have been lost, or they never existed, so that research must work with what data can be found (Jensen, 2012, 2013). For present purposes, we re-make – reconfigure and reinterpret – multiple helpful data sets that a range of international organizations make available and accessible for scholarship. For future comparative studies, an essential task will be to collect and curate more and better data on technological infrastructures and regulatory regimes, in collaboration with public and private agencies, locally and globally, so as to prepare the premises of informed public and policy debate on communication systems as they currently exist.

Modeling communication systems

A model of global infrastructures

To begin with an implication that may be obscured by a multidimensional PCA analysis: Material as well as immaterial resources matter – for the quantities and qualities of communication that are available to people and peoples around the world. The material availability of technologies, and the necessary economic and educational resources for accessing and benefiting from them, intersect with immaterial but equally consequential regulation of how their users may (not) represent their present and imagine future alternatives. Digital divides come with a path dependency on material and institutional divides – follow the divides!

The results of the first step of the PCA analysis are laid out in Figure 2.1, covering all 80 countries. In technical terms, the final model has a good fit with the data, its first two components accounting for a combined 66.5% of the total variance. An inspection of the scree plot of explained variance produced by increasing the number of components clearly indicated that a model of two components has the strongest explanatory power: The addition of a third component only raised the explained variance by 6.7 percentage points. The first, horizontal axis establishes the distinctions between open and closed societies – the haves and the have-nots in terms of de facto opportunities to speak up and speak out, also against the powers that be – whereas the second, vertical axis introduces additional distinctions regarding the quality of the material infrastructures supporting communication (or not).

The visualization in Figure 2.1 juxtaposes countries in Western Europe with a number of Arab and Asian nations on the horizontal axis. At one extreme (to the right), with high, positive scores, are Scandinavian countries such as Denmark and Sweden, as well as Switzerland. At the other extreme (to the left), countries such as China, Saudi Arabia, and the United Arab Emirates have low, negative scores. The scores bear witness to different and distinctive regulatory regimes, with three main aspects as captured by a number of variables.

First, the PCA included variables measuring the ways in which, and the extent to which, the publication of content through online news media (one-to-many communication) as well as interaction on social media platforms (one-to-one and many-to-many communication) is regulated by national authorities. The governments of countries toward the left of the first axis have a wide range of legislative and executive means at their disposal for controlling and constraining communication. The legal provisions that are in place in these countries typically include a right to order both the removal of content from online news media and the filtering of content on other platforms such as social media. The content that is subject to removal tends to be broadly defined so that, in practice, anything deemed unfit for publication or sharing by the powers that be, can be censored. Such control mechanisms further extend to shutting down access to the internet altogether. Governments can switch off communication networks at will, for example, in times of (more or less real) crisis, or they may selectively throttle particular platforms, such as Facebook, rendering them slow or unresponsive, in this way driving users toward sources more amenable to government positions. In comparison, countries toward the right of the first axis will have far fewer provisions in place that allow governments to control communication infrastructures. In these cases, intervention is typically limited to defined and delimited circumstances, commonly subject to legal challenge in a court of law. Here, the wholesale monitoring and banning of content are not an immediate option, and states must regulate citizens' communication within the bounds of the wider criminal justice system. Indeed, a common complaint of public debate in these countries in recent years has been that authorities appear slow or unwilling to introduce regulatory measures, for example, to counteract online harassment in the form of personal threats or the publication of private photographs.

Whereas the first set of variables addressed *potential* state interventions, the second set of variables measured *actual* practices of internet censorship and control. In fact, the data reflect an important difference between regulation in principle and in practice. In a very basic and practical sense, censorship and control take time and effort: Extensive and fine-grained regulation of who says what to whom requires tremendous resources. So, while a good number of governments toward the left side of Figure 2.1 will reserve the legal right to persecute their political opponents and silence their online communications, they may be unable to practice what they preach. Toward the right end of the first axis, again, conditions are quite different. Here, censorship and control are actively prohibited, and the communicative rights of citizens asserted and protected. To a considerable extent, these states promote public debate and governance online, through educational and informational initiatives supporting the digital literacy of citizens, and by utilizing the affordances of digital communication systems for promoting the transparency of public administration and policy making.

The third and final set of variables contributing to the first dimension of the model consists of indicators of the classic freedoms associated with legacy or traditional mass media of the last several centuries. Countries with high, positive scores on this dimension enjoy strong legal protection of news media, and of freedom of expression as such. Media in countries toward the right in Figure 2.1 are typically entirely independent of governments or, in the case of public service radio and television stations, they have de facto editorial freedom. In countries toward the opposite end of the horizontal axis, media have little or no protection of their independence, and a considerable proportion of news media are under direct or de facto control by governments. While hardly surprising, the correlation between (lack of) freedom for traditional media and (lack of) active control with online communication manifests a clear path dependency between the two domains, at least in the countries closest to the extremes of the axis. Old habits die hard, also when it comes to regulatory regimes: The same ends and entrenched interests are likely to reassert themselves and to be served online as offline. As the analysis of the second axis of Figure 2.1 also suggests, however, such path dependencies unfold over time, in lockstep with the gradual implementation of digital infrastructures in a growing number of national settings.

While the first, horizontal axis is the primary dimension of the PCA, accounting for 45.76% of the variance, the second, vertical axis adds important aspects to the analysis (20.69% of the variance). The variables contributing to the second dimension of Figure 2.1 can be collected in two sets.

The first set comprises variables that serve to characterize the scale and scope of basic digital infrastructure. Among the key variables are measures of the coverage of 3G and 4G mobile networks, respectively, as a percentage of the national population. In countries with a high score on this dimension (located toward the top of Figure 2.1), the quality of the mobile broadband networks available to populations tends to be high, as indicated by average download speeds being offered. The quality of service provided is reflected, further, in a variable measuring the complexity of the backbone of national networks: Countries with more so-called internet exchange points (IXPs) per 1,000 inhabitants score higher on the second axis. The number of IXPs is key because these constitute *both* the interconnections among local and regional networks (e.g., telephone companies and internet service providers (ISPs)) *and* the technical points of access for individual countries to the global internet.

The implications for countries as well as citizens are significant. People living in countries toward the top of Figure 2.1 will be in a position not just to access digital communication in the first place, but to take advantage of a wider range of digital services, including bandwidth-heavy services such as streaming audio and video services (provided, of course, that these services are not blocked by national authorities). For countries toward the bottom of the figure, basic access will be limited, often restricted to urban areas, just as the quality of broadband will be comparatively low and the range of services on offer will be modest. In short, the findings bear witness to a relative decoupling not just of individual users and citizens, but of countries and entire world regions from global digital infrastructures. An inspection of Figure 2.1 brings home the fact that many of the countries with an especially low score (below −2) on the vertical dimension are located on the African continent.

The second group of variables contributing to the vertical dimension of the model in Figure 2.1 points to a wider dynamic of private enterprise and public planning intersecting and interacting, which delimits particular windows of opportunity for communication and other social interaction. These variables register the extent to which the diffusion of digital technologies in each country has been stimulated through initiatives undertaken by either private companies or state agencies, or both categories of social agents. In technical terms, the variable measuring market-driven initiatives to promote the popular uptake of digital technologies contributes positively not just to the second, vertical dimension of the PCA, but also to its first, horizontal dimension. The same holds true for the variable measuring backbone connectivity (the number of IXPs relative to population size, as previously mentioned), which depends on diverse forms of state involvement and public planning. The upshot is that some countries and regions have prospered through the development of digital infrastructures, by public as well as private actors: Countries with high scores on both dimensions (i.e., belonging to the top-right quadrant of Figure 2.1, and counting most of the PIN countries) command greater quantities and qualities of digital infrastructure because both private companies and state agencies have continuously promoted the diffusion of communication technologies, if not always as joint ventures or in seamless fashion.

Affluent and privileged by global standards, the countries in this top-right quadrant were among the early adopters of digital networks. Most important, here a fixed-line broadband infrastructure was already in place when the mobile broadband revolution swept (the rest of) the world. It was frequently telephone companies that built a fixed broadband infrastructure, serving as internet service providers, and moving on to implement a mobile broadband infrastructure, as well. But fixed-line broadband has remained in place in these countries, on a par with mobile broadband, and is still in widespread use. As such, fixed broadband feeds into the second dimension of the PCA in decisive respects, differentiating prevalent uses of the internet in various countries: Whereas some countries could be characterized as mobile-first, mobile-mostly, or even mobile-only, in other settings mobiles enter into a division of labor with desktops and laptops, depending on the nature of the interactions and transactions being undertaken in a given context, in public or in private, for professional or personal ends. In sum, rather than serving as a simple indicator of high-tech, low-tech, or no tech resources, the second dimension of Figure 2.1 begins to capture some of the complexity of how national communication systems have been configured and are being reconfigured over time, and how, accordingly, citizens are in a position to do and be certain things (or not) in context, in and by communication.

A model of national infrastructures

Whereas the techniques and visual representations of a PCA might invite polarized thinking in terms of haves and have-nots – countries having or not having technological and economic resources, citizens having or not having the political and cultural rights to translate the resources at hand into rewarding and meaningful lives – Figure 2.1 invites more focused examination of the richly populated spectrum of technological and institutional structures that circumscribe everyday communicative practices in each national setting. In Figure 2.2, we go on to identify some of these details, while simultaneously specifying the location of the PIN countries within the two-dimensional matrix. On the second dimension of Figure 2.2, the seven countries occupy comparable positions; on the first dimension, however, they are located toward the extremes. To begin an analysis of differences and similarities, we further introduce a standard categorization of regime types to characterize the two sets of seven and 80 countries, respectively. Building on categories of social systems that have been consolidated in a long line of previous research, we elaborate on the place of communication systems in the historical trajectories and contemporary configurations of political regimes, with special reference to the seven countries and three regions of the PIN project. In subsequent chapters, we add detail and nuance to the account of how technologies, political economies, and cultural traditions are inscribed in concrete communicative practices in each setting.

Figure 2.2 builds on the Varieties of Democracy project (which also informed several of the variables entering into the wider PCA), specifically the project database for 2019 (https://www.v-dem.net/dsarchive.html, accessed on August 15, 2022). In essence, the project identifies four regime types, namely, two forms of autocracy and two forms of democracy (Lührmann, Tannenberg, & Lindberg, 2018). In *closed autocracies*, there are no multiparty elections for either the chief executive or the legislature; the example in the PIN project is China. In comparison, *electoral autocracies* do grant citizens such rights, but without the sort of freedoms, for example, of expression and association, that make elections free and fair; the PIN example is Hungary. In *electoral democracies* (no PIN example), citizens have the right to participate in free and fair multiparty elections, but they do not enjoy the additional individual and minority rights, rule of law, and legislative and judicial oversight over the executive that are characteristic of *liberal democracies*, represented here by Denmark, Germany, Italy, the United Kingdom, and the United States.

It is particularly striking that even though the closed autocracy (China) and the five liberal democracies and one electoral autocracy are located at opposite ends of the first PCA dimension, all seven countries occupy positions toward the top of the second dimension. As briefly noted with reference to Figure 2.1, like the cultivation of participatory forms of public communication, censorship and control depend on resources. With comparable resources and infrastructures at their disposal, states may pursue radically different policies of communication

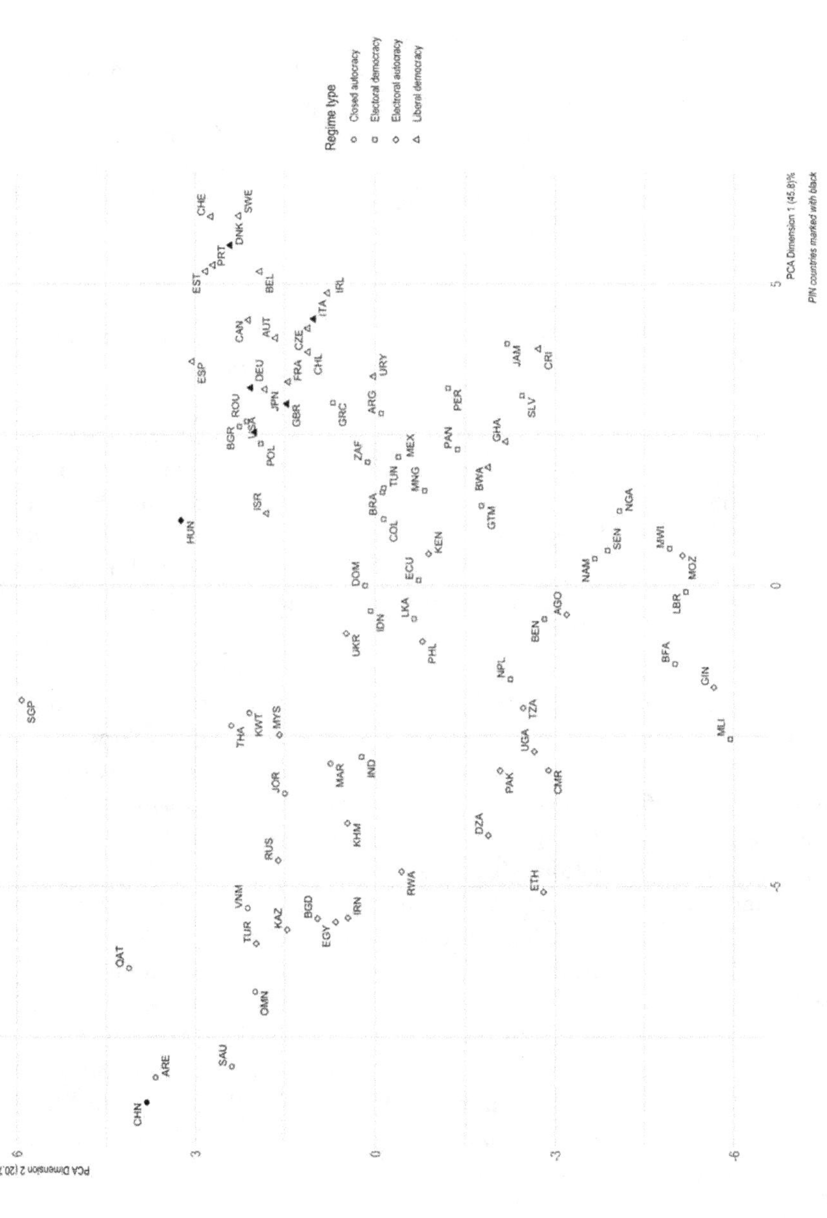

FIGURE 2.2   PCA analysis of 80 world countries on PCA dimensions with regime type

– of communicating like a state. China is located at the negative extreme of the first dimension not only because it is a closed autocracy in the traditional political sense, but because the Chinese state engages in extensive automated and manual control of online communication by media and citizens. In order to obtain the PCA score in question, a state must emphatically practice the policy that it preaches, enacting communicative prerogatives and prosecuting transgressors. In a networked public sphere pervaded by myriads of messages, some of which will originate outside its jurisdiction, a closed autocracy depends on both substantial infrastructures of surveillance and human operators with high-level and specialized technological capabilities. Indeed, dedicated technologies of surveillance and filtering are active export items, from China to the rest of the world, not least other autocratic regimes (Polyakova & Meserole, 2019).

Moving toward the right along the first dimension of Figure 2.2, one first encounters Hungary, which illustrates the distinction between closed and electoral autocracies. Where closed autocracies seek a total control of sorts through comprehensive and fine-grained filtering and monitoring, electoral autocracies rather dedicate their resources toward specific concerns such as public disorder, criminal activity, or the prevention of terrorism. While such categories are, evidently, slippery in legal as well as practical terms, they help to explain why, for example, Hungary engages in targeted surveillance of particular kinds of organizations and groups of professionals such as NGOs and investigative journalists (Mills, 2019; Nagy, 2017). At the same time, such regimes also benefit tremendously from the bulk collection of metadata that is enabled by digital technologies (Kaminski, 2017). A related case in point is Poland, which, like Hungary, has been sliding from liberal-democratic toward an authoritarian or autocratic regime type. In Poland, legislation is in place that provides access to various digital archives for the investigation of an expansive range of potential wrongdoing, including even "the breach of rules of sports competition" (Rojszczak, 2021: 21).

In overview, Figure 2.2 brings home the further point that all closed autocracies among the 80 countries in the present sample command relatively strong digital infrastructures (as indicated by their positive coordinates on the second dimension): Digital surveillance has become constitutive of twenty-first-century autocratic statecraft. Not all surveillance, however, is of the manifest, blatant, autocratic kind. For one thing, it is by now common knowledge that the users of infrastructural digital platforms are subject to continuous surveillance by commercial interests (Zuboff, 2019). We return, in Chapter 6, to the underlying ecology of tracking and monetizing data and metadata, and, in Chapter 7, to some of the implications for the future national and international regulation of digital communication systems. For another thing, it is equally well known, through the 2013 whistleblowing of Edward Snowden on its National Security Agency, that the government of the United States has access to substantial portions of global digital information and communication flows, implemented through the tapping of broadband backbone infrastructures, the server farms of platforms, and cloud service providers.

Less familiar in either research or public debate is the communicative state of Denmark, a country that otherwise occupies a privileged position toward the far top right of Figure 2.1 and among the liberal democracies of Figure 2.2. The Danish government has continued to uphold a legal requirement for Danish telephone companies to retain detailed logs of call records and location data for all mobile phone subscribers, motivated by their potential uses in investigating serious crime. This is in spite of the fact that the practice is almost certainly illegal under EU law, as an invasion of privacy disproportionate to the likely benefit. Nevertheless, shifting governments from across the national left–right political spectrum have maintained the requirement while also, paradoxically, recognizing its conflict with EU law. Both the Danish lilliput and its big American brother highlight the profound implications of digitalization for the availability and exchange of private as well as public information, and thus for the formation of identities and communities, and for human existence and social coexistence. Because of their flexible, programmable nature, digital communication systems lend themselves to diverse and proliferating business processes feeding on information, which in turn renders the resulting records of significant interest to state agencies (Lyon, 2010). In the American case, the information of interest to NSA – what people say and do online – presumably corresponds well with the business proposition of the central corporations of the surveillance economy, which therefore are first in line for state surveillance, as well (Zuboff, 2019). At issue, locally and globally, is the classic balancing of private interest in both senses of that term – commercial gain and personal privacy – and public interest. It is this balancing that is still being articulated and contested in national and international contexts at the time of writing.

Summary of findings

This chapter has offered a basic and preliminary mapping of communication systems around the world, as a contribution to further comparative research, with special reference to the diffusion and regulation of digital infrastructures. Summarized in Figures 2.1 and 2.2, the analysis of available data sources, on the one hand, documents pervasive and, to a degree, predictable variations across different world regions and political economies, reflecting entrenched disparities of material and immaterial resources – wealth and knowledge – alongside distinctive political and cultural traditions. On the other hand, the dimensions of the two models identify a complex dynamic of technological and institutional forces and factors that remain subject to negotiation and modification. Most striking, perhaps, are the ambiguous affordances of digital technologies: The upper, comparatively resourceful regions of the models are home to state regimes that apply their resources, on balance, for purposes of either censorship and control or deliberation and participation.

At the same time, it is noteworthy that the most distinctive practices in both respects lie at the extremes of the first dimension of the PCA models, in closed autocracies and liberal democracies. Between these extremes, a wide and mixed middle ground includes many states with relatively scarce digital infrastructures and other states, for example, in the former Eastern European bloc, where rights and responsibilities of information and communication at present are being negotiated both in public debate and through institutional action. Further aspects of internet governance fall outside the scope of this chapter, as noted in the introduction. As we complete this volume, however, struggles over the regulation of communication systems may be entering a new phase, within Europe, but also among world regions, as the European Union is set to introduce new regulatory frameworks with implications for the rest of the world. Following on the General Data Protection Regulation (GDPR) of 2018, which sought to limit commercially as well as politically motivated tracking of users, the Digital Markets Act (DMA) and the Digital Services Act (DSA) address broader questions regarding the relationship between states and markets. The DMA is designed to counteract monopolistic tendencies among the largest (Western) data aggregators such as Alphabet, Amazon, and Meta, promoting cross-platform communication and transactions for users. The DSA, in turn, engages further and even more difficult issues of how to balance free speech and free enterprise, and how to regulate hate speech while protecting the legitimate expression of opinion as a defining constituent of political democracy. As rule-bound frameworks, and in combination with potentially corporation-breaking fines, the two legal acts will play into the ongoing global reconfiguration of the regulatory regimes circumscribing human communication (for an overview, see Flew, 2021).

In analyzing and discussing the analytical models at the core of this chapter, we noted a variety of path dependencies in the contemporary configuration of communication systems, from the great disparities of material and immaterial resources between the Global North and the Global South, to the carry-over of regulatory principles and procedures from traditional mass media to digital media and communication systems. Writ large, these path dependencies make up the histories and cultures that people and peoples both shape and are shaped by, as they communicate, and which they will refer to in order to make sense of the rest of the world. Having mapped the technological and institutional outlines of communication systems of the world, in the following chapters we dive deeper into such historical and cultural trajectories, and into their consequences for how people communicate today, here and there.

In conclusion, we also offer the findings in this chapter as a small contribution to the study of communication systems as systems in their own right, intersecting with other local and global systems of social interaction. In Chapter 6, we return to a distinctive feature of digital communication systems – the fine-grained registration of users' actions as they communicate into the system (Jensen & Helles, 2017), to commercial and state interests listening in. This latest variant of communication technology recalls the insight of early communication theory that humans "cannot *not* communicate" (Watzlawick, Beavin, & Jackson, 1967: 49): We constantly express ourselves and interpret others. And, when communication is carried by technologies, we necessarily regulate the institutions and practices circumscribing technologies and inscribing communication. If only by default, as non-intervention, states cannot *not* regulate communication systems, which presents classic issues of negative and positive freedom (Berlin, 1969/1958): Freedom *from* interference by public agencies, and freedom *to* pursue communicative and other ends in life, enabled by public regulation. In the concluding Chapter 7, we reconsider these contested normative issues in the light of findings presented in subsequent chapters.

3

THE INTERNET AND OTHER MEDIA OF COMMUNICATION

Jacob Ørmen, Sascha Hölig, Signe Sophus Lai,
Jesper Pagh, Fiona Huijie Zeng Skovhøj, Uwe Hasebrink,
Julia Behre, Rasmus Helles, and Klaus Bruhn Jensen

Media, meta-media, and communication repertoires

It is a common insight from the long history of human communication that new media rarely replace old media (Simonson, Peck, Craig, & Jackson, 2013). Video did not kill the radio star, despite song lyrics to the contrary (The Buggles, 1979). Instead, old and new media typically establish a division of communicative labor in which different media acquire distinctive and complementary social uses. For example, breaking news has been shifted from special editions of newspapers, via radio and television, to the internet and mobile phones, while newspapers, radio, and television as institutions (and in their online versions) have retained much of their role (so far) as analysts and interpreters of local and global events. At the same time, new media rework or remediate (Bolter & Grusin, 1999) the contents and forms of old media, and vice versa. Early websites adapted the graphic designs of various print media to the online domain, just as television has adopted the multiple windows of personal computers for its newscasts and documentaries. And, for interpersonal or one-to-one communication at a distance, the media of choice have been, in turn, handwritten letters, landline telephone calls, text messages, and digital messaging services. This is in spite of the fact that handwritten messages have kept some of their attraction and fascination as media of physical contact and witnesses of authentic relations among true selves with unique identities (Peters, 2001).

Taken together, the technologies and institutions of a given historical time and cultural place constitute an environment in which people will turn to different media for different ends of communication and other interaction. People communicate to say things, but also to do things, and to become and remain particular kinds of persons and social beings. Communicative practices are ways and means of doing, being, and becoming.

DOI: 10.4324/9781003057055-3

The internet presents itself as a prime candidate for the sort of super-medium that might be thought to substitute some, even all, previous media. In fact, as we go on to show in this chapter, the current age represents no exception to the historical rule that different media, old and new, complement each other in the lives of individuals, social segments, nations, and world regions. As such, the chapter provides an overview and first mapping of contemporary communication systems, including the presence and configuration of various media within these systems, and their place and function in diverse communicative practices.

In this opening section, we refer to three sensitizing concepts (Blumer, 1954) that serve to structure the presentation of the empirical findings. We depart from the idea of *communicative prototypes* introduced in Chapter 1: Basic forms of interaction in signs and symbols that have traveled across technologies, societies, and cultures down through history – one-to-one, one-to-many, and many-to-many communication. We go on to recognize the distinctive nature of the internet as a *meta-medium*, which we confer with media as traditionally understood, and with face-to-face interaction, to cover the range of media forms that currently carry the communicative prototypes. In a third step, we introduce the idea of *repertoires* – of media and of communication – to refer to the concrete communicative practices that people engage in: Everyday actions and events in which communicative prototypes are coupled to specific media. Importantly, people will turn to more medium than one and will perform a wide variety of communicative practices amounting to media and communication repertoires, which can be expected to vary across sociodemographic segments and cultural contexts.

We begin by revisiting Table 1.1, which identified three prototypes of human communication in historical perspective, and we specify synchronous and asynchronous variants, which produce six prototypes in all, laid out in Table 3.1. In each cell, we include illustrative examples of the media and applications that are current and characteristic carriers of the prototype in question. On the vertical axis, one-to-one communication, which remains an evolutionary and historical reference point, has been extended from face-to-face interactions, via personal letters and landline telephony, to emails and online messaging. One-to-many or mass communication, next, introduced the possibility of sharing information on a grand scale to support economic enterprise, political deliberation, and cultural expression. And, in recent decades, many-to-many communication has added

TABLE 3.1 Communicative prototypes

	Asynchronous	*Synchronous*
One-to-one	Letter, email, text message	Voice telephony, instant messaging
One-to-many	Book, newspaper, audio and video recording, 'Web 1.0'/webpage, download	Broadcast radio and television
Many-to-many	'Web 2.0'/wiki, blog, social network site	Online chatroom Online multiplayer games

further options of networked and multi-step interaction, whose potentials and implications are still being discovered through technological, commercial, and other social experimentation.

On the horizontal axis, Table 3.1 distinguishes between synchronous and asynchronous variants of each of the three types on the vertical axis. With writing systems and subsequent technologies have come a wide range of media and genres for recording, reflecting upon, and acting on extant information and earlier interactions, both in interpersonal relations and in the context of society-wide mass communication. In the case of many-to-many communication, the formal distinction between synchronous and asynchronous interaction proves difficult to uphold, as illustrated by rapid-fire texting and messaging – an issue to which we return later in this chapter.

Media, as traditionally understood, have commonly been the vehicles of single communicative prototypes. Newspapers and broadcast television have carried asynchronous and synchronous mass communication, respectively, even if they have included elements of letters to the editor and moments of phone-in programming. In comparison, the internet belongs to a different category of *meta-media*, which collect and configure several other media on one platform of hardware and software. The idea was first articulated in the early days of personal computing and instantiated in prototypes of notebook and laptop computers (Kay & Goldberg, 1999/1977). With the addition of networking capacities, and still grounded in the general capacity of the digital computer to simulate the full range of human expression, the internet has reproduced all previous media forms, while adding several new ones, from blogging and multiplayer gaming to social network sites. It is not only that computers and the internet "can be *all other media*" (p. 112); they can also be *several media at once*, integrating diverse connections between content elements and individual media: Intertextuality and intermediality (Jensen, 2008a, 2008b). Accordingly, the internet holds all six communicative prototypes as potentials for users to take advantage of. The question is whether people have begun, or may begin, to do things with the internet that they used to do with other media separately.

The third and final sensitizing concept (Blumer, 1954) – *repertoires* – captures how, concretely, individuals select and combine various media in characteristic sets or patterns as they engage in various communicative practices in the context of their everyday lives. For the last two decades, in response to a more complex media environment, research has examined media repertoires as "meaningfully structured composition[s] of media" (Hasebrink & Domeyer, 2012: 760). They are meaningful because users associate particular communicative functionalities and psychological gratifications with particular media. Beyond the immediate encounter of medium and user, media repertoires lend structure to people's everyday lives, and, over time, such repertoires serve to pattern their participation in societies and cultures at large, feeding into long-term processes of socialization and social structuration. Empirical studies have confirmed that media repertoires vary with the sociodemographic backgrounds of users, notably age, gender, educational level, and ethnicity (Edgerly, 2015; Hasebrink & Popp, 2006; Kim, 2016; Sin & Vakkari, 2017; van Rees & van Eijck, 2003). Moreover, media repertoires correlate with political attitudes and with the 'capitals' or (unequally distributed) resources that different sociodemographic groups command as part of their involvement in other social and cultural practices (and which Chapter 5 addresses in detail) (Lindell, 2017; Oblak Črnič & Luthar, 2017). Media repertoire research has begun, further, to document the extent to which, and the ways in which, 'new' online media complement or challenge 'old' legacy media as constituents of contemporary media repertoires (Behre et al., 2020; Bucholtz, 2015; Hasebrink & Popp, 2006; Nimrod, 2019; Sin & Vakkari, 2017). To capture this development, we introduce a category of *communication repertoires* that are associated specifically with digital media.

We first consider 'passive' mass communication as a communicative prototype that now unfolds both online and offline. Indeed, as we detail in the next section, mass communication comes out as a key component of media repertoires across both sociodemographic segments and the seven countries and three regions of the present study. In the subsequent sections, we examine how people engage more 'actively' in one-to-one and many-to-many communication. Because digital media, in principle, afford contact with anyone else, anytime, and anywhere, one-to-one and many-to-many communications reach multiple 'audiences' of radically different sizes. In the last part of the chapter, we return to the question of how people combine not just particular media, but a range of communicative practices in configurations that bear witness to distinctive ways of being a person, a society, and a culture, including communication by expats and other migrants as they relate to their significant others (Mead, 1934). In this regard, the present chapter anticipates a more detailed analysis, in Chapter 4, of different ways of being and remaining social, in and by communication.

Mass communication – online and offline

The internet has been widely associated with active and interactive uses by the general public; it equally lends itself to classic mass communication. As laid out in Table 3.1, mass communication includes both synchronous and asynchronous variants: Watching broadcast television and listening to radio as well as streaming audiovisual content and reading online news(papers). Covering different variants of mass communication, the Peoples' Internet (PIN) surveys asked how many days in a typical week respondents would watch television or listen to radio in traditional fashion, read a newspaper, or use the internet in order to follow news and current affairs. We defined regular users of a medium as those who engaged in the specific activity at least several times a week. And, because earlier studies have consistently identified age or generational differences as central to variations in both internet and other media use (Blank & Groselj, 2014; Dutton & Reisdorf, 2019; Van Deursen & Helsper, 2017), we gave special attention to the age factor. Concretely, we 'went to extremes' by singling out the age segments between 18 and 34 and between 55 and 74 years, respectively, and then compared these groups, both with each other and with the total adult population of each country. The following tables and discussions, then, begin to compare and contrast different media uses and communicative practices across the human lifespan and in three world regions.

Figure 3.1 brings home a first important insight: Mass communication remains a central component of media repertoires in all seven countries and across age groups, if to varying degrees. Anywhere between 94% (Italy) and 71% (China) of the adult population use traditional broadcast *television* several times a week. Whereas these numbers are lower for the younger age groups, in all countries it is still a majority in the 18–34 age range who habitually turn to television in the classic sense. Indeed, in Italy, this applies to more than 90% of young respondents. When it comes to regular *radio* listening, the numbers are comparable, ranging from 70% of the adult population in Italy to 61% in Hungary, again with slightly fewer listeners in the 18–34 age range. [For radio, China represents a clear exception, with only 7% of the adult online population listening to the radio several times a week. National statistics indicate that only 38% of Chinese households have a radio set and that as many as 20% of those using radio only listen rarely (National Radio and Television Administration, 2021).] *Newspapers*, finally, reach a relatively low proportion of respondents across the seven countries, from 7% in China to 34% in Italy, again with the young as the least likely to read newspapers regularly. The internet, in other words, has not replaced classic mass media, at least so far and in the aggregate, even if their twentieth-century incarnations – broadcast radio and television – appear more robust than (one of) the print variants carried over from the eighteenth and nineteenth centuries: Newspapers.

The internet appears in Figure 3.1 as a central carrier of mass communication, as well, at least when it comes to delivering news and current affairs to the general public. This finding reemphasizes the premise of the present volume, namely, the importance of studying and comparing communication systems, above and beyond media systems as typically understood (Hallin & Mancini, 2004): Even if *mass media*, to a degree, may be receding, *mass communication* could be considered a social and cultural resource that, once invented and adopted, people will want, whatever other media and communicative practices they also want to engage in. In the seven countries and three world regions of the PIN study, between 69% (China) and 89% (Hungary) of respondents use the internet for news and current affairs, with comparatively minor variations across the age groups, roughly similar to those for television, radio, and print newspapers. In fact, Figure 3.1 further indicates that, in most of the countries examined here (except for China and the United Kingdom), the older group is more likely than both the young and the population average to go online for news. While this might be, in part, an artifact of the online samples employed here, the finding, along with high levels of online mass communication (OMC) in general (seven to nine out of ten media users across all seven countries engage in OMC), does

TV

China   Germany   Denmark   Hungary   Italy   UK   US

Radio

China   Germany   Denmark   Hungary   Italy   UK   US

Newspaper (NP)

China   Germany   Denmark   Hungary   Italy   UK   US

Online Mass Communication (OMC)

China   Germany   Denmark   Hungary   Italy   UK   US

■18+ ▨18-34 ☐55-74

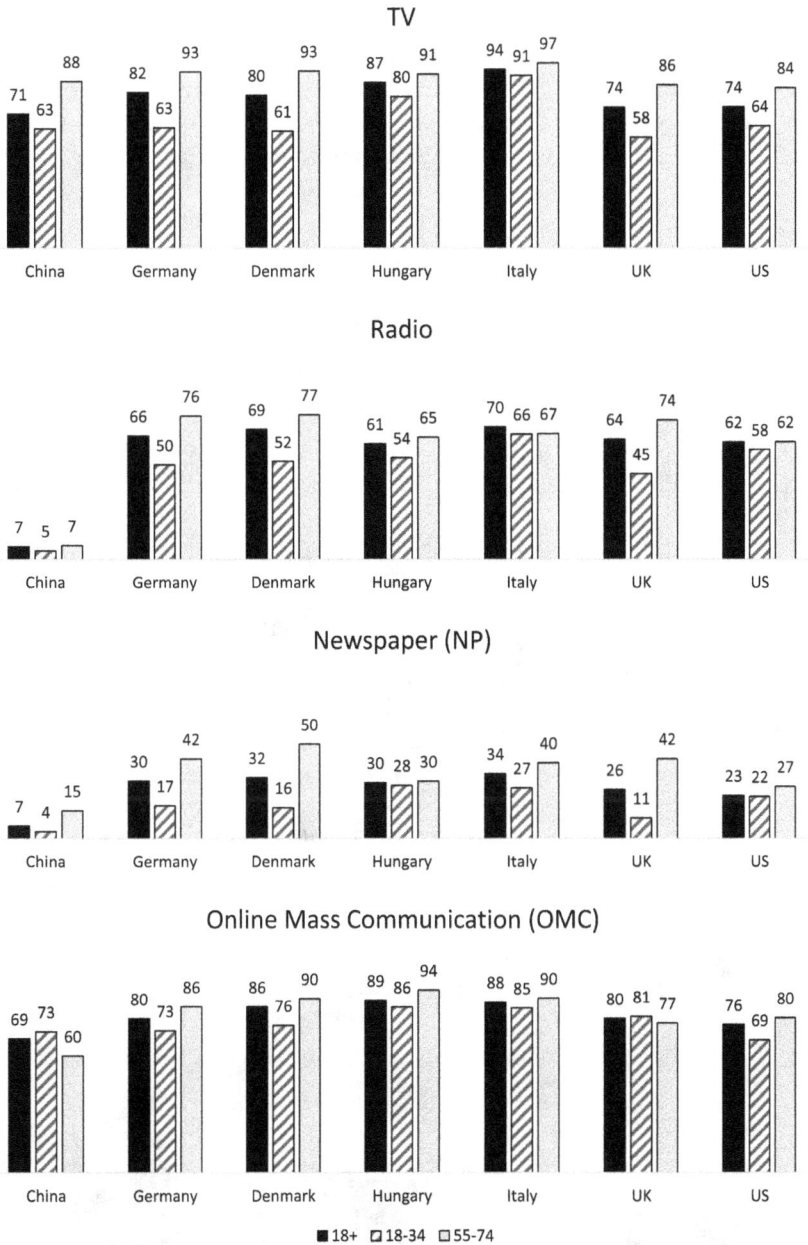

FIGURE 3.1 Mass communication at least several times a week, by age (in percentages)

suggest media and communication environments in which the internet is emerging as an equal, even preferred, platform of *mass communication*.

Figure 3.2 adds detail concerning the relevance of connecting to a wider world through some form of mass communication; the figure lays out combined measures of newspaper reading and online news use. The takeaway is that the great majority of the general public in all seven countries attend to news at least weekly. While there are significant variations in whether people turn to either newspapers, the internet, or both of these platforms to follow the news, most people by far seek to stay updated on what is happening in the wider world (even if China represents somewhat of an outlier in this regard, since 27% here get

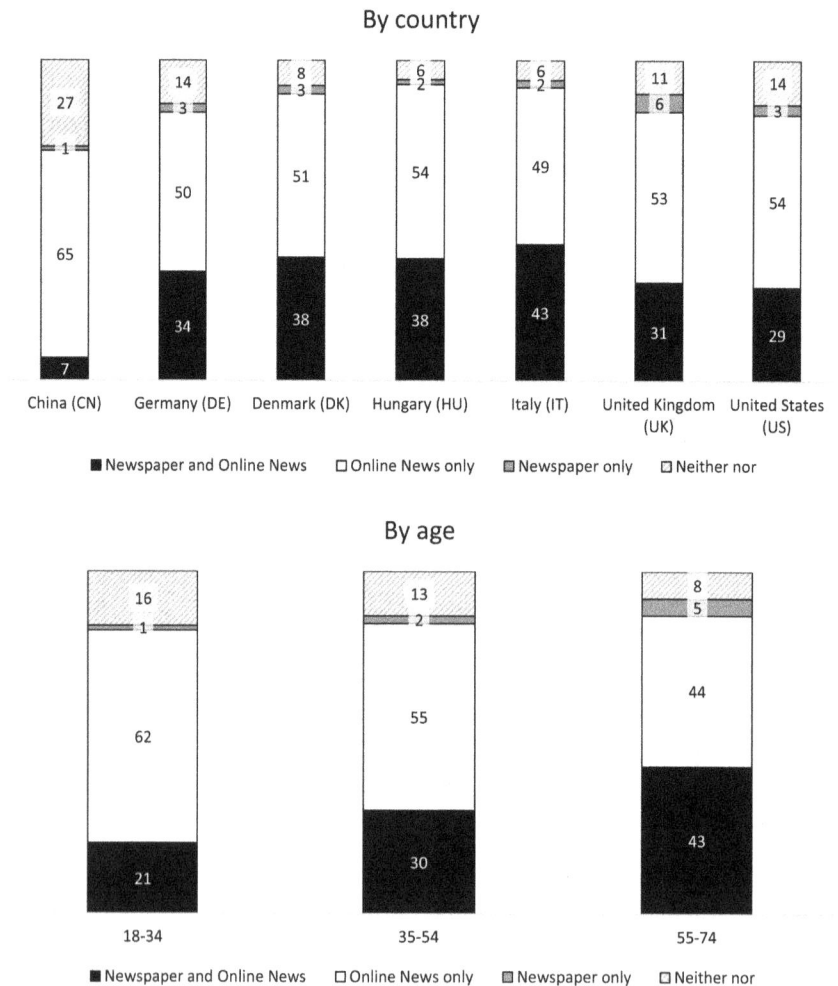

FIGURE 3.2 Weekly news use – print newspapers and online news combined (in percentages)

news less often than weekly). Looking across the age groups, the general pattern of staying in touch with the world still holds: The young, as one would expect, primarily go online for news, but for the sample as a whole, around 85% get news updates at least weekly. And, the proportions who use both newspapers and the internet weekly to be updated are substantial: Depending on age, between a fifth and a little less than half of the respondents across countries and regions get news on paper as well as on screens.

The resilience of mass communication invites further analysis and interpretation. Mass communication affords the experience of the same information (or entertainment) by large groups of individuals, including the experience that *other* people are having the *same* or similar experiences, perhaps at the same time or, at least, within a relevant time frame. Whether time-shifted or not, mass communication serves social integration, if only, in some instances, for collectives to agree to disagree on particular agendas of problems and potential solutions, as represented through (mass) communication in both factual (McCombs & Shaw, 1972) and fictional genres (Newcomb & Hirsch, 1983). The tradition of uses-and-gratifications research has consistently identified social integration as a central experienced value of media and communication (Blumler & Katz, 1974; Rosengren, Wenner, & Palmgreen, 1985), and the literature on media repertoires has specified how different combinations of media contribute to the ongoing socialization of audiences and the maintenance of social identities. Contemporary communication scholarship, thus, reconfirms Aristotle's insight that humans are social beings (*zoon politicon*), who will communicate – must communicate – to be updated on events in the world so as to become and remain social, even if conceptions of what it means to be 'social' and to 'communicate' have varied considerably across historical time and cultural place.

To differentiate variants of mass communication, Figure 3.3 lays out the repertoires of media use for each country, again distributed by age. The most common repertoire combines regular use of television, radio, and internet, ranging from 29% (Germany) to 36% (Italy) of the adult online population. Second place, in most countries, goes to the combination of television, radio, newspapers, and internet. On both counts, China represents the exception, because radio use, as noted, is relatively more limited here. It is remarkable, however, that the media repertoire combining regular television viewing and regular internet use for mass communication accounts for as much as 45% of the total adult online population in China. Across the seven countries and three world regions, then, and bridging the online–offline divide, mass communication remains a key component of the general public's media use.

Figure 3.3 suggests two additional points. First, respondents with a single-medium repertoire are very few indeed. The highest shares of television-only (16%) and internet-only (14%) users are found in China. In all other countries, these shares are in the single digits, even if single-medium repertoires are marginally more widespread in the 18–34 age range than in the 55–74 group. Second, in all countries except China, the most common repertoire – television,

18+

18-34

55-74

Legend:
- ■ TV-Radio-OMC
- □ TV-OMC
- ▨ TV-Radio-NP-OMC
- ▢ OMC
- □ TV
- ◨ Radio-OMC
- □ TV-NP-OMC
- ▨ none
- ▥ TV-Radio
- ■ TV-Radio-NP
- ▦ Radio
- □ Radio-NP-OMC
- □ NP-OMC
- □ TV-NP
- ▤ Radio-NP
- ◧ NP

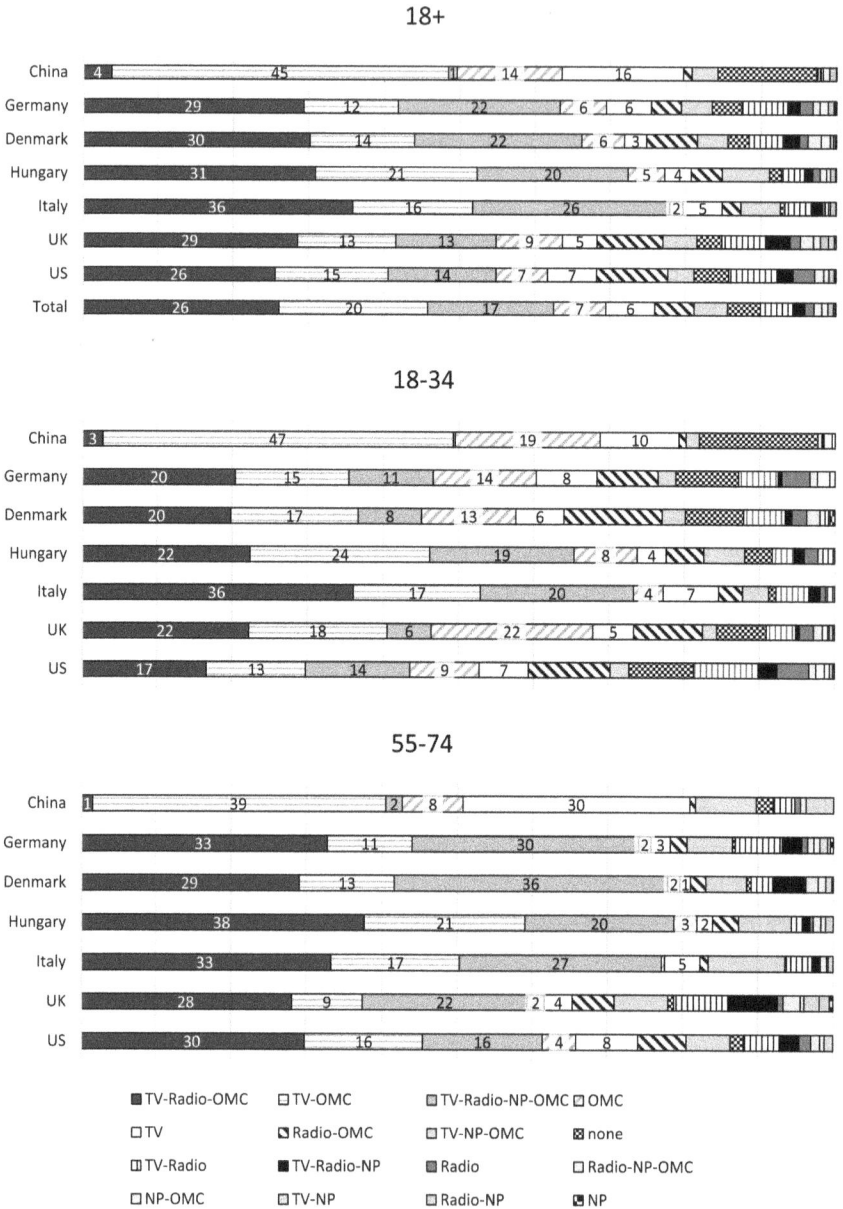

FIGURE 3.3 Mass communication repertoires of media used at least several times a week, by age (in percentages)

radio, and internet – is shared by young and old respondents alike. And, when it comes to the television-and-internet repertoire, young and old respondents are strikingly similar across all seven countries, including China.

The internet, thus, complements broadcasting (and print media), offering one more medium of one-to-many or mass communication for publics to choose from. At the same time, the internet hosts and integrates both one-to-one and many-to-many forms of communication, which we consider next.

Speaking to the few, the many, and the masses

The internet enables, in principle, anyone to communicate to and with anyone else, anytime, and anywhere in the world – one-to-one, many-to-many, and even one-to-many (if one can find a mass audience) (Table 3.1). As such, the internet gives rise to *communication repertoires* in which people combine several communicative practices, and which complement the media repertoires identified so far. We start by noting the prevalence and distribution of four different communicative practices: Individualized communication (*one*), closed-group communication (*some*), communication to all of one's personal contacts (*all*), and communication to, potentially, anybody on the internet (*mass*). The four practices constitute points on a continuum extending from one-to-one to many-to-many interactions. But, in each case, the person in question is an active party to the communication going on – a sender affording information and, perhaps, involvement to and with others. In practice and with current communication technologies, the question is *both* how often *and* in which combinations people use social media and messaging apps to relate to other people.

Figure 3.4 first notes the frequency with which people engage in each of the four *communicative practices*, as distributed across countries and age groups. For individualized communication, first, China stands out: 80% of the adult online population interacts one-to-one with friends, family members, or colleagues several times a week, whether by sending texts, photos, or videos. In this respect, the other countries make up three formations, from Italy (66%) and Hungary (65%) at approximately two-thirds of respondents, via the United Kingdom (52%), the United States (47%), and Germany (45%) at about half, to Danes (36%) representing the lowest level of individualized communication, at a little more than a third of the population. Second, communication with delimited groups of friends, family members, or colleagues is somewhat less common than individualized communication, ranging from 64% of the online population in China to 23% in Denmark. The third type – interaction with all of one's personal contacts – represents a further decline, again with the highest numbers in China (57%) and the lowest in Denmark (20%). The last, and least common, practice is that of addressing anybody on the internet, for example, by commenting on news sites or joining online debates. And yet, it is engaged in by close to half of the respondents in China (43%), Italy (43%), and Hungary (42%), and by more than a third in the United States (35%). Across all four communicative practices and

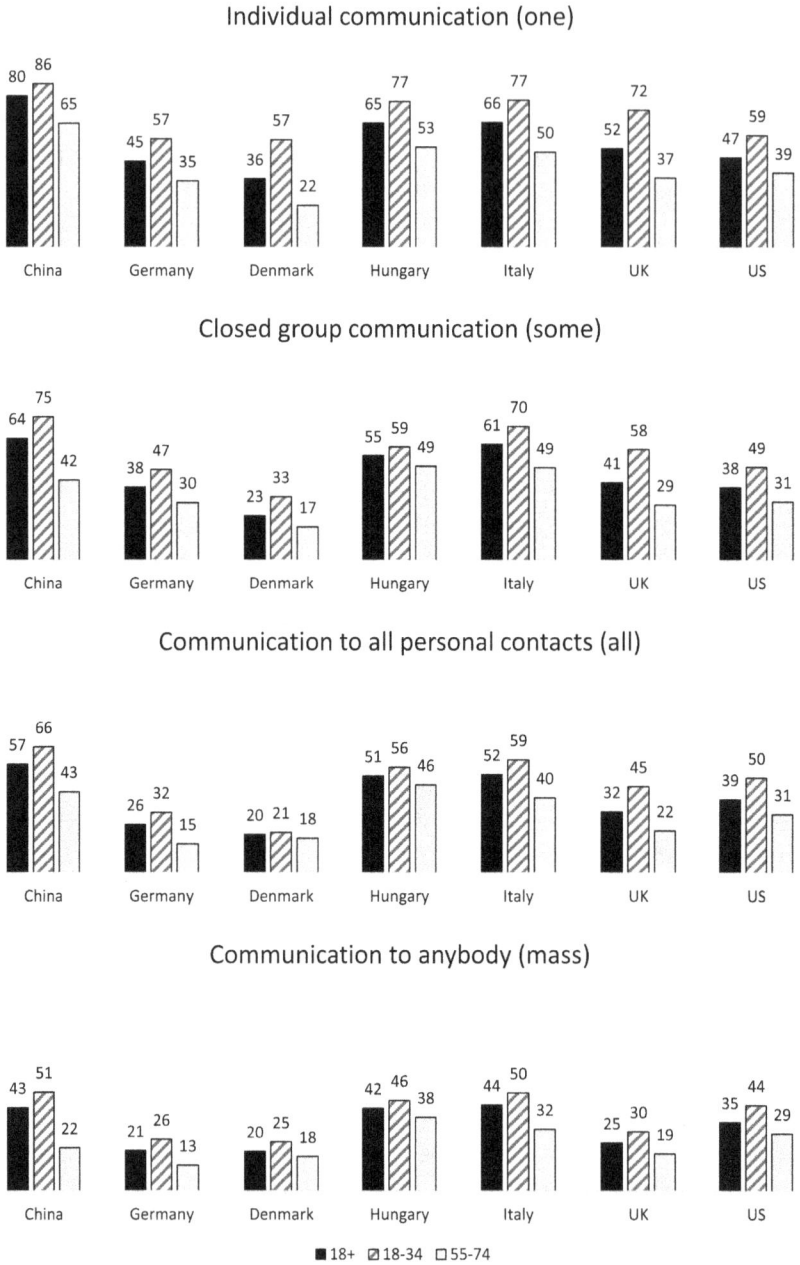

FIGURE 3.4 Online communicative practices at least several times a week, by age (in percentages)

seven countries, age makes a (small) difference, so that people in the 18–34 age range are slightly more likely to engage the few, the many, as well as the masses in communication.

Figure 3.5 summarizes the *communication repertoires* that combine the four different communicative practices to varying degrees. The most striking finding is that a clear majority of adult internet users either *do* or do *not* join online communication: Between 66% (the United States) and 44% (China) of the respondents engage in all four communicative practices or none at all. This pattern holds across younger and older respondents, despite some variations, so that the older group is more likely to engage in *none*, the younger group in *all* of these practices, especially in China, Hungary, and Italy. In spite of the affordances of the internet for diverse combinations and configurations of one-to-one and many-to-many communication, then, all-or-nothing repertoires come out as the most common in all three regions of the world, at least so far. It is also noteworthy that, across regions as well as age groups, the 'nothing' repertoire characterizes a considerable proportion of the population in most of the seven countries, from 53% (Denmark) to 14% (China). We return in Chapter 4 to some distinctive national and regional differences in how the internet is used for interpersonal communication throughout the diverse engagements of everyday life.

The next question is how *communication* repertoires and *media* repertoires go together to make up full diets of media and communication. The following section describes the diets of different national populations and sociodemographic groups, relating them to the six communicative *prototypes* noted at the outset of this chapter and to the understanding, outlined in Chapter 1, of *cultures* as configurations of communicative practices. In and through communication, cultures produce, maintain, repair, and transform themselves (Carey, 1989b/1975), sometimes in surprisingly similar ways.

Converging cultures of communication

Table 3.2 displays a variety of communicative practices covering one-to-many and many-to-many prototypes. It notes in the middle column the corresponding survey questions that addressed different kinds of media use. To the right, the table includes a brief characterization of each communicative practice as a prototype.

In overview, the surveys asked how often people would engage in the following media uses and communicative practices: Linear television, recorded television, streaming television (including videos and feature films), linear radio, podcasts, streaming music, printed newspapers, printed magazines, printed books, audiobooks, e-books, games, internet for news and information, internet for practical purposes, internet for personal interests and hobbies, and social network services (SNS – including messaging applications). We split the responses into two categories: Daily use and less than daily use. And to gauge the relative importance of national contexts and individual characteristics, the analyses considered

18+

China   14 | 30 | 15 | 10 | 11
Germany   47 | 13 | 7 | 8 | 11
Denmark   53 | 8 | 3 | 12 | 6
Hungary   28 | 33 | 8 | 8 | 7
Italy   27 | 34 | 9 | 6 | 9
UK   40 | 16 | 9 | 10 | 11
US   44 | 22 | 6 | 6 | 4

18-34

China   8 | 39 | 19 | 7 | 9
Germany   34 | 15 | 10 | 10 | 13
Denmark   36 | 10 | 3 | 19 | 12
Hungary   19 | 37 | 8 | 11 | 9
Italy   18 | 40 | 12 | 6 | 10
UK   22 | 21 | 14 | 9 | 18
US   32 | 31 | 6 | 5 | 5

55-74

China   27 | 12 | 16 | 17 | 8
Germany   58 | 7 | 4 | 8 | 10
Denmark   66 | 7 | 3 | 6
Hungary   35 | 28 | 7 | 6 | 5
Italy   39 | 22 | 8 | 5 | 10
UK   54 | 11 | 6 | 9 | 6
US   51 | 16 | 6 | 6 | 3

■ none	□ one-some-all-mass	▨ one-some-all	□ one
□ one-some	▨ one-all	■ one-some-mass	▨ one-all-mass
▥ mass	■ one-mass	▦ some	□ some-all-mass
□ all	□ some-all	■ all-mass	□ some-mass

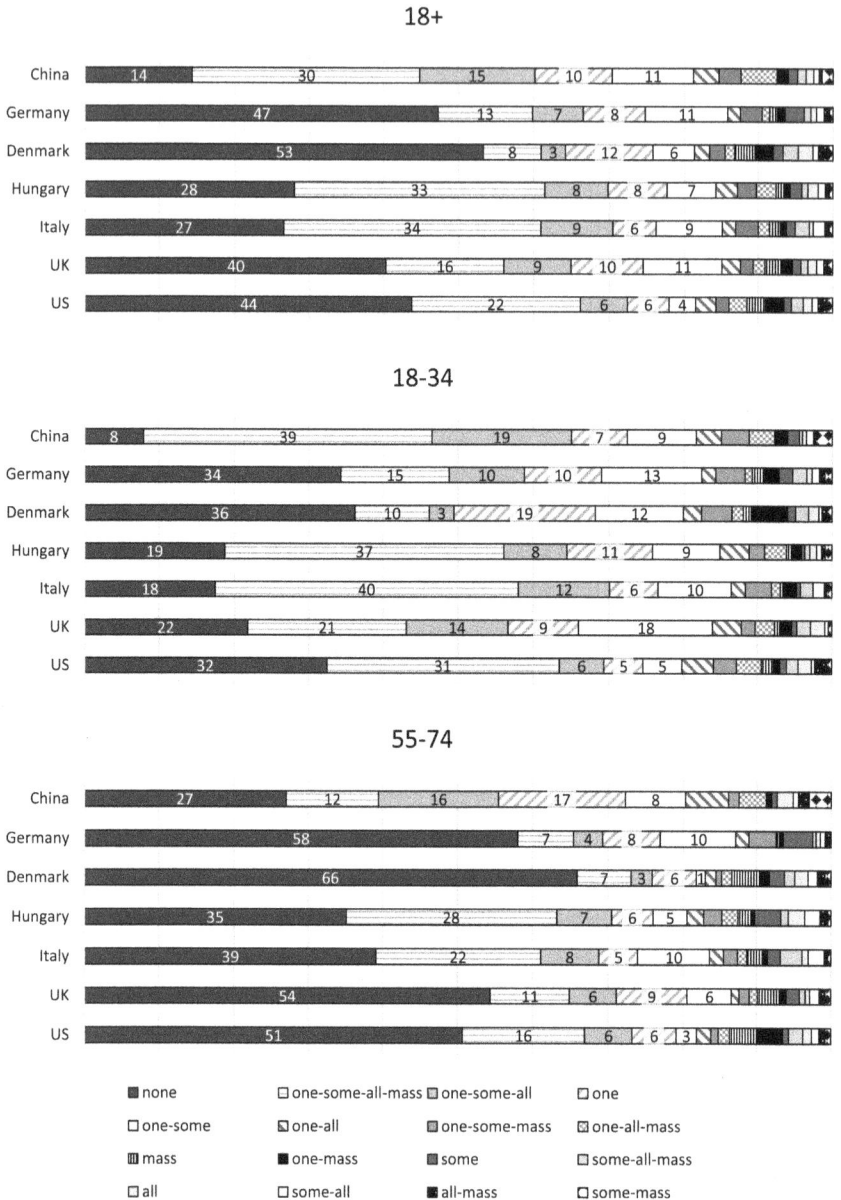

FIGURE 3.5 Repertoires of online communicative practices at least several times a week, by age (in percentages)

TABLE 3.2 Communicative practices

Communicative practices	Survey questions	Prototypical characteristics
Broadcast	Watching linear TV, or listening to linear radio	Synchronous, one-to-many
Print	Reading print newspapers, or reading print magazines, or reading physical books	Asynchronous, one-to-many
Streaming	Watching recorded content, or using video streaming services, or using podcast services, or using music streaming services, or using audiobooks or e-books	Primarily asynchronous, one-to-many
Browsing	Using the internet for news and info, or using the internet for practical matters, or using the internet for personal interests	Asynchronous, one-to-many
SNS	Using social network services or messaging apps	Primarily asynchronous, one-to-one, few-to-few, or many-to-many
Gaming	Playing video games	Primarily asynchronous, one-to-many

both country of residence and standard sociodemographic factors: Gender, age, education, occupation, and income, all of which have proved their explanatory value in previous studies (Blank & Groselj, 2014; Dutton & Reisdorf, 2019; Van Deursen & Helsper, 2017). Gender was treated as a binary category, and age was divided into three groups (18–34, 35–54, and 55–74 years of age, in line with the analyses of media and communication repertoires earlier in this chapter). Because different countries typically have different educational systems, we relied on the International Standard Classification of Education (ISCED) (developed by the United Nations, http://uis.unesco.org/en/topic/international-standard-classification-education-isced, accessed August 15, 2022), which comprises three levels: Primary, secondary, and tertiary education. The definitions of occupations, similarly, tend to vary across countries, so we employed five standardized categories: Office job, service job, physical labor, student, and unemployed (including retirees). Lastly, in order to reflect the very different levels of GDP and costs of living in the seven countries, we asked respondents to compare their personal income to the median income of the country in question, summarized as below average, about average, or above average.

To begin mapping some general patterns of contemporary media and communication diets, we relied on so-called latent class analysis (LCA) (see the Methodological Appendix in Chapter 8 for details on this and other analytical procedures). In essence, LCA serves to identify classes of respondents whose (responses regarding a range of) media uses and communicative practices are similar and, at the same time, distinct from those of the members of other classes. Importantly, LCA also facilitates the analysis of such classes in terms of age, gender, nationality, and other sociodemographic characteristics. In the following pages, we introduce additional statistical techniques to explore some of the wider patterns of communication emerging from the surveys.

As a first step, an LCA of the entire sample produced the five classes visualized in Figure 3.6 (the names of the classes are explained in the next paragraph). This opening analysis bracketed other variations across the seven historically and culturally distinctive nations in order to arrive at a baseline of different media and communication diets, which we subsequently compared across countries and sociodemographic backgrounds.

In Figure 3.6, the various communicative practices that are listed in Table 3.2 appear on the left-hand side, and their prevalence in the different classes is suggested by the bars, with percentages at the bottom of the figure. Each bar indicates the likelihood (probability score) that members of the class in question engage in that particular communicative practice on a daily basis. It includes a line noting the so-called confidence interval (CI), which represents the statistical range within which the true value of the measure can be expected to fall (with a 95% confidence level). For example, the bar for SNS in the class named 'Socializers' registers an 83.8% likelihood of using SNS daily (with a CI ranging from 80.9% to 86.7%). In other words, people who are 'Socializers' are highly likely (more than 8 in 10) to use social network services on a daily basis.

The largest class, *Socializers* (approximately 28% of the sample), primarily use the internet to browse information and for social network services; they are not likely to stream content, read print publications, or play games. *Adapters* (c. 23%) tend to both use broadcast media and browse the internet on a daily basis. But they are unlikely to play games, stream content, or use SNS. As the name suggests, *Allrounders* (c. 21%) have a diverse media and communication diet. They browse the internet, watch or listen to broadcasts, and rely on SNS as part of their daily routines; they also quite likely engage in streaming, gaming, as well as reading print media. In contrast, *Rarelies* (c. 16%) will use media relatively little. If engaging in any media use on a daily basis, they will prefer broadcast media, SNS, or browsing the internet. Lastly, *Streamers* (c. 12%) have the highest score of all the classes identified when it comes to streaming content; they also tend to browse the internet and use SNS on a daily basis.

The first-step LCA, thus, covered traditional one-to-many (print, broadcast), digital one-to-many (streaming, browsing), and networked communication (social network services). In the second step, we included interpersonal communication in the analysis, as well – one-to-one or few-to-few interactions – to produce another baseline for comparative purposes. By initially keeping these two baselines separate, we were able to compare and contrast not just countries and sociodemographic segments, but also familiar prototypes of human communication: Interpersonal, mass, and networked.

Figure 3.7 lays out so-called boxplots indicating the extent to which the five classes of media users also engage in various kinds of interpersonal communication. The survey singled out five communicative practices as variants of

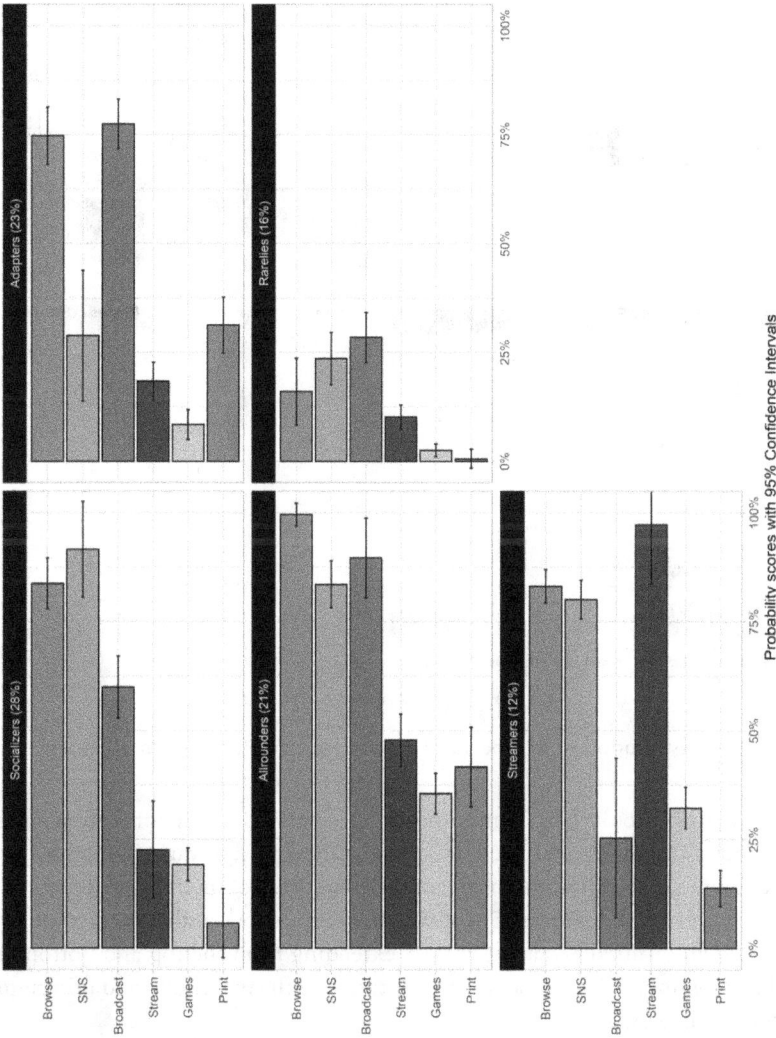

FIGURE 3.6 Five–class solution using LCA in Latent Gold 5.1, weighted $n = 10{,}450$

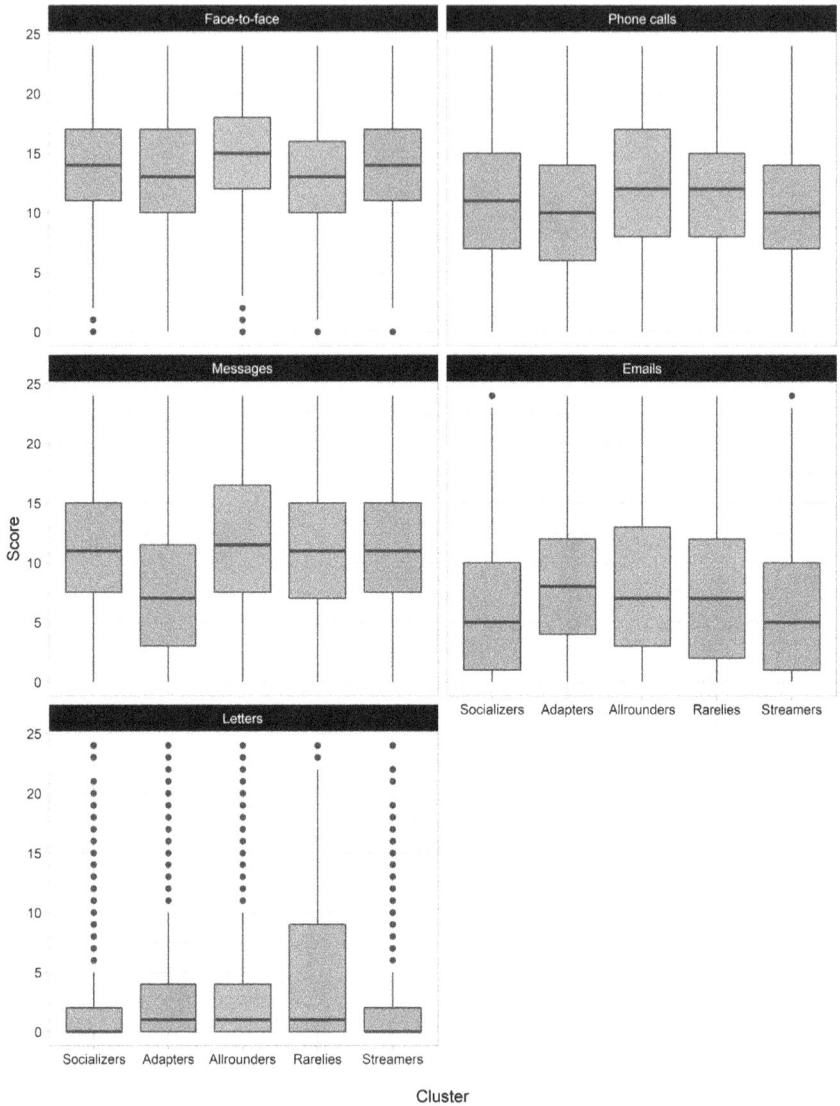

FIGURE 3.7 Distribution of interpersonal communicative practices across classes

the one-to-one prototype: Communication face-to-face, by phone, messaging, email, and traditional letter. The boxes suggest the spread or variation in how the different types of media users engage in different types of interpersonal communication. Each box represents 75% of the class in question, with a horizontal line at the median or middle value; the lines extending from the top and bottom of each box (commonly known as whiskers) stretch to the maximum and minimum points of each class.

The boxplots suggest several points. Allrounders make phone calls more frequently than the other classes (apart from Rarelies). For messaging, it is noteworthy that Adapters are less likely than anyone else to text other people, be it by phone or through instant messaging. As might be expected, it is comparatively rare by now for all five classes of respondents to send either letters or (more surprisingly) emails. Socializers and Streamers are even less likely to use email than the other three classes. For traditional letters, it is somewhat puzzling that Rarelies tend to score higher than all the other classes of media users, followed by Adapters and Allrounders (with no statistically significant difference between them) and Socializers and Streamers (again no difference). Perhaps Rarelies constitute a traditionalist segment with limited use of (or access to) modern communication technologies, or they are made up of multiple categories not captured by the present summative analysis.

Across all five classes of media users, however, and across all five communicative practices, the boxplots bring home another striking finding: Interpersonal communication appears to be a different category of interaction altogether, different from networked as well as mass communication. Even a cursory comparison of Figure 3.7 with Figure 3.6 suggests that the variations between the classes are much smaller when it comes to the respondents' interpersonal interactions. Only Adapters stand out with a slightly less intensive pattern of interpersonal communication than the other four classes. Most notably, Rarelies, who are decidedly light users of mass and networked communication, are quite similar to the other classes when it comes to interpersonal communication. This also goes for digital formats such as instant messaging and email. Rarelies might, in fact, be renamed 'interpersonalists': They primarily turn to communication technologies, in addition to face-to-face interactions, to connect with their social networks, rather than to seek news or entertainment as traditionally understood.

As an intermediate conclusion, then, we note that, on top of the fact that *mass communication* remains a key practice in all of these three world regions, also *interpersonal communication* represents a common denominator for the sample as a whole and across the five different classes of media users. The next question is how these prototypical patterns vary by respondents' backgrounds: How similar or different are these national populations and their constituent sociodemographic segments when it comes to the combination of interpersonal, mass, and networked communication?

To address this question, we relied on so-called multinomial logistic regression analysis, which assesses the extent to which several different factors may explain an outcome, for example, belonging to one of the five classes of media uses and communicative practices. In addition to relating these classes to the respondents' country of residence, we explored five sociodemographic factors: Gender, age, education, income, and occupation. Table 3.3 summarizes the findings.

In review, Socializers tend to be relatively young and to work in service jobs or physical labor, and they are most commonly found in China and Italy.

TABLE 3.3 Multinomial regression on cluster membership with covariates

	Socializ.	Adapters	Allround	Rarelies	Streamers	Wald statistic[+]
Cluster size	0.25	0.24	0.24	0.15	0.12	230.2107★★
Sociodemographic						
Gender						90.3502★★
Female	0.52	0.35	**0.59**	0.45	0.55	
Male	0.48	**0.65**	0.41	0.55	0.45	
Age						291.4495★★
18-34	**0.44**	0.03	0.07	**0.46**	0.77	
35-54	**0.48**	0.33	0.41	**0.46**	0.22	
55-74	0.08	**0.64**	0.51	0.09	0.02	
Mean	*1.65*	*2.61*	*2.44*	*1.63*	*1.25*	
Education						2.9744
Primary	0.27	0.20	0.16	0.28	0.16	
Secondary	0.48	0.52	0.52	0.46	0.51	
Tertiary	0.25	0.28	0.31	0.26	0.33	
Mean	*1.98*	*2.08*	*2.15*	*1.98*	*2.17*	
Income						28.066★★
Below median	0.28	0.33	0.29	0.22	0.38	
Around median	**0.49**	0.38	**0.40**	**0.49**	**0.43**	
Above median	0.23	0.29	0.31	0.29	0.19	
Mean	*1.94*	*1.96*	*2.02*	*2.06*	*1.81*	
Occupation						89.0295★★
Office job	0.17	0.17	0.22	0.21	0.21	
Service job	**0.37**	0.17	0.18	**0.29**	0.22	
Physical work	0.23	0.15	0.10	0.21	0.14	
Student	0.07	0.01	0.01	0.07	**0.25**	
Unemployed	0.15	**0.49**	**0.48**	0.22	0.17	
Country						6529.115★★
China (CN)	**0.27**	0.02	0.00	**0.30**	**0.19**	
Germany (DE)	0.15	**0.19**	0.10	0.14	0.07	
Denmark (DK)	0.12	0.14	**0.21**	0.10	**0.20**	
Hungary (HU)	0.13	0.14	**0.20**	0.12	0.11	
Italy (IT)	0.19	0.14	**0.19**	0.10	0.07	
United Kingdom (UK)	0.09	**0.18**	0.16	0.09	0.21	
United States (US)	0.06	**0.18**	0.13	0.16	0.15	

Multinomial regression carried out as a step-three covariate analysis in Latent Gold 5.1 with proportional classification and maximum likelihood (ML) adjustment (Vermunt and Magidson, 2016). The scores indicate the distribution within each covariate for each cluster; they sum to 1 vertically within each covariate. The scores with the largest distance to the rest are shown in bold.

[+]The Wald statistic indicates the likelihood of getting the observed result if the covariate does not predict values on the outcome (Hypothesis 0). It is a standard measure of how much variables contribute to the overall fit of the model. The statistic for the overall clusters is the intercept.

★★Wald test significant at $p < .01$.

Adapters are predominantly male (c. 65%), above 55 years of age (c. 64%), and outside the workforce (primarily retired), and they are most common in Germany, the United Kingdom, and the United States. Allrounders are similar to Adapters in their sociodemographic profile (albeit with a majority of women), but Allrounders are most common in a different set of countries: Denmark,

Hungary, and Italy, in addition to the United Kingdom. Rarelies come out as a mixed category with few distinct features, but they are likely to be young, and they are overrepresented in China. Finally, Streamers are distinctively young (77% below 35 years of age), and they are most commonly found in China, Denmark, and the United Kingdom.

It is, however, age and country of residence which provide by far the best explanations for differences between the five classes, as suggested by the numbers in bold in Table 3.3. As a final step in this portion of the analyses, therefore, we probed the relationship between age and country of residence across the classes identified in the latent class analysis.

Figure 3.8 visualizes the interaction or relationship between country and age group for each of the five classes of respondents. The most important finding is the remarkable similarity of the youngest age group across the seven countries. People below the age of 35 are about equally likely to be either Socializers,

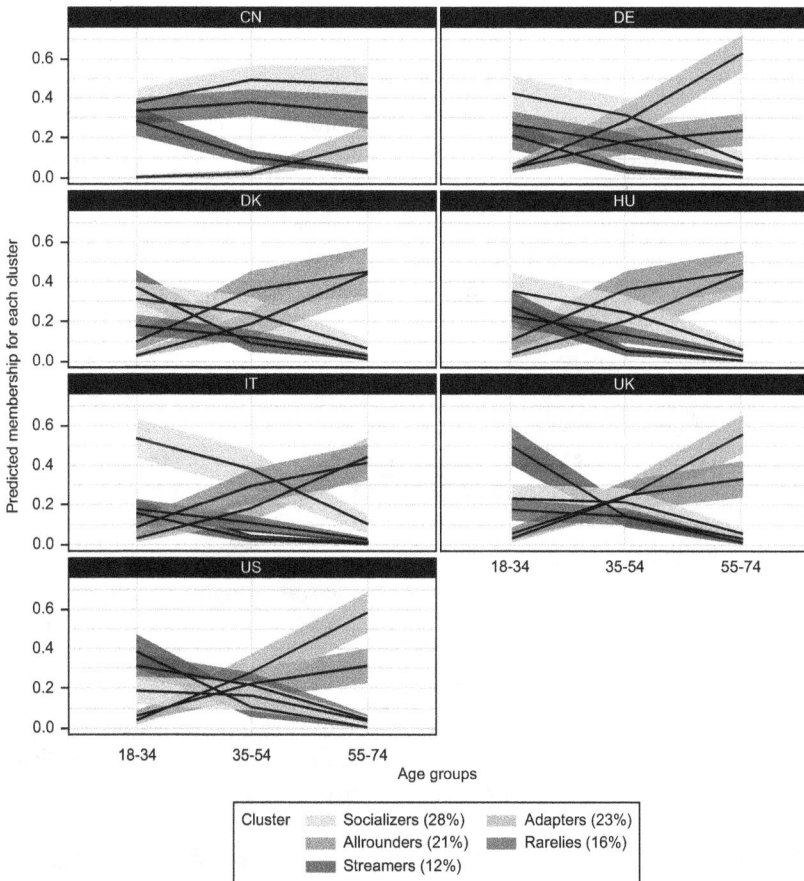

FIGURE 3.8 Predicted class memberships across age groups

Streamers, or Rarelies. In the United Kingdom, the young are distinctively Streamers, while in Italy they tend to be Socializers. It is not surprising, of course, that the youngest respondents rely more heavily on social network sites and/or streaming services than their older compatriots. Also, earlier research has found that a considerable share of young people live a life largely 'without media,' even in high-income countries such as Sweden (Westlund & Bjur, 2014). Nevertheless, the media and communication diets of the young are evidently similar in the aggregate. The implication is that, in terms of media uses and communicative practices, the youngest generation in the three different and distinctive regions of the world is unified in its diversity.

Looking beyond the youngest age group, one finds greater variation. China, in particular, exhibits striking similarities from the youngest to the oldest groups – a pattern that could be described as one of continuation. Socializers and Rarelies predominate in China across all age groups (for the youngest group, Streamers enter the mix). (The absence of Allrounders for China in Figure 3.8 is explained by the limited use here of radio, which is a defining constituent of being an Allrounder.) Different from China, people in the six other countries are less likely, as they grow older, to belong to the three 'young' classes: Streamers, Socializers, and Rarelies. Conversely, Allrounders and Adapters become more numerous with age, and they make up the majority of the oldest age group. The starkest contrast between the young and the old is found in Denmark, the United Kingdom, and the United States, where the oldest respondents are more likely to belong to Adapters than to any of the other classes. To appreciate the scale of these differences, consider the oldest age groups in China and Germany, respectively: Older Germans are about six times more likely to belong to Adapters than to Socializers or Rarelies, whereas their Chinese counterparts are about twice as likely to be Socializers than to be Adapters.

In summary, while the youngest generation may be converging around comparable media and communication diets, the older age groups bear witness to multiple patterns of retention, displacement, and complementarity as media systems around the world are being reconfigured in a protracted process of transition from analog to digital media and communication environments. In Germany, the United Kingdom, and the United States, the oldest age groups *retain* traditional media as their preferred channels, if combined with news and information online. For the same group in China, the internet – in particular, social network sites – has either largely *displaced* legacy media *or* respondents may only have started using media as such as they came online. On a retention–displacement continuum, Denmark, Hungary, and Italy occupy a middle ground of *complementarity*. In these three countries, people above the age of 55 are as likely to be Allrounders (integrating new and old media) as they are to be Adapters (supplementing legacy media with digital services, primarily for web browsing). We return, in the final chapter of the book, to the outlooks for communication systems as their digital components are being consolidated in China, Europe, and the United States.

Communicating now or later

As part of the initial mapping of media uses and communicative practices, in this section we explore the distinction between synchronous and asynchronous interaction, and its intersection with one-to-one, one-to-many, and many-to-many practices of communication (Table 3.1). In one sense, the always-on affordance of digital technologies might favor more synchronous modes of interaction. In another sense, the capacities of these same technologies for storing information and time-shifting access, anytime and anywhere, might invite more asynchronous, user-driven, and user-centered interactions. Potentially at least, digital systems could reconfigure human communication in each of these respects, as both information transmission and social ritual (Carey, 1989b/1975).

Since the 1990s breakthrough of the internet as a public medium, both research and public debate have regularly returned to the question of whether digital media and communicative practices would displace or, at least, marginalize classic forms of one-to-one communication, notably face-to-face conversations, but also phone calls (Dimmick et al., 2000). With smartphones and personal computers enabling perpetual contact (Katz & Aakhus, 2002) with other people and continuous access to diverse offerings of news and entertainments, would people still want to speak to one another as part of the flow of everyday life and of their participation in communities, large and small?

Table 3.4 provides part of an answer, laying out the relationship between synchronous and asynchronous forms of *interpersonal* communication. The numbers indicate that people who talk a great deal with other people (either face-to-face or on the phone) also tend to be frequent users of messaging, emails, and letters to stay in touch with others (correlations in Table 3.4 between .304 and .709

TABLE 3.4 Correlations of interpersonal communicative practices

Correlations

		f2f_scale	phone_scale	mess_scale	email_scale	letters_scale
f2f_scale	Pearson correlation	1	.624**	.618**	.474**	.304**
	Sig. (two-tailed)		.000	.000	.000	.000
	N		7,784	7,641	7,675	7,455
phone_scale	Pearson correlation		1	.709**	.504**	.418**
	Sig. (two-tailed)			.000	.000	.000
	N			7,698	7,728	7,516
mess_scale	Pearson correlation			1	.528**	.422**
	Sig. (two-tailed)				.000	.000
	N				7,628	7,435
email_scale	Pearson correlation				1	.641**
	Sig. (two-tailed)					.000
	N					7,561
letters_scale	Pearson correlation					1
	Sig. (two-tailed)					
	N					

**Correlation is significant at the 0.01 level (two-tailed).

suggest as much). And, with minor differences, this pattern applies across all seven countries and three world regions. Of course, displacement may occur over time, perhaps for particular kinds of interactions or in specific sociode-mographic groups. But the implication, once again, is that digital media and communicative practices are approached by their users as additions or comple-ments, rather than as alternatives to or replacements of long-established forms of interaction. People who frequently communicate with each other will carry on the conversation across the range of available media, and in synchronous as well as asynchronous modes.

Earlier in this chapter, we noted the continued centrality of one-to-many or *mass* communication across countries and world regions. Table 3.5 elaborates on the relationship between different kinds of mass communication. Broadcast (linear television and radio) represents the synchronous prototype, and the asynchronous equivalent comprises three variants: Print (newspapers and maga-zines), Streaming (video, music, and audiobooks), and Internet for informa-tion (Int_info in Table 3.5, a category which covers use of websites and other text-based information). The numbers suggest that use of one variant is largely unrelated to use of other variants (as indicated by modest positive correlations) – which means that the general pattern is one of combination or complementarity. For one thing, whether or not people stream or otherwise access content online has little bearing on their use of print media, and vice versa. For another thing, while streaming is, to a degree, replacing traditional broadcasting, the effect appears relatively small (as indicated by a modest negative correlation of −0.121). Such displacement has been documented over the past decade (Nimrod, 2019; (Tefertiller, 2018), but the present findings from three world regions suggest that any epochal transition from broadcasting to streaming is taking place at a slower pace than has been widely assumed in research as well as public debate.

TABLE 3.5 Correlations of mass and networked communicative practices

		Broadcast	Print	Streaming	SNS	Int_info
Broadcast	Pearson correlation	1	.176**	−.121**	.000	.165**
	Sig. (two-tailed)		.000	.000	.985	.000
	N		10,704	10,744	10,566	10,648
Print	Pearson correlation		1	.026**	−.065**	.169**
	Sig. (two-tailed)			.008	.000	.000
	N			10,718	10,548	10,631
Streaming	Pearson correlation			1	.166**	.160**
	Sig. (two-tailed)				.000	.000
	N				10,570	10,653
SNS	Pearson correlation				1	.229**
	Sig. (two-tailed)					.000
	N					10,537
Int_info	Pearson correlation					1
	Sig. (two-tailed)					
	N					

**Correlation is significant at the 0.01 level (2-tailed).

Many-to-many communication – the final prototype – is represented here by social network sites (the second-to-last column and row in Table 3.5), and it completes and confirms the pattern of complementarity, rather than any momentous shift toward asynchronous interactions. It is true that heavy use of social network sites (SNS) and heavy use of informational websites, both of which belong in the asynchronous category, go together (even if the correlation is modest). But, in fact, the correlations regarding SNS are small and mixed. For the synchronous broadcast mode, the correlation is zero; for (asynchronous) print it is negative (but almost indistinguishable at -0.065); and for (asynchronous) streaming, the correlation is positive (at a moderate 0.166).

It is, admittedly, difficult to assess whether and how SNS use is synchronous or asynchronous through a survey, which depends on self-reports by ordinary media users – the distinction may not be an intuitive aspect of everyday communicative practices (see further the Methodological Appendix in Chapter 8). Chapter 4 returns to diverse aspects of the embedding of different communicative practices in everyday life. To conclude the initial mapping in this chapter of media uses and communicative practices, we turn in the following section from the administration of time in and through communication, to communication as a mode of moving, and relating to others, across space.

Communicating here and there

As elaborated in Chapter 1 and in the Methodological Appendix in Chapter 8, the Peoples' Internet project combined quantitative and qualitative forms of evidence to characterize contemporary communication systems. Ethnographic fieldwork was conducted in each of the three world regions: In mainland China, Denmark, and the United States. An iterative interview–diary–interview methodology (Lai, Pagh, & Zeng, 2019) – comprising an establishing interview, followed by participants keeping a diary, which then provided both reference points and prompts for a second interview – offered insights into participants' communicative practices in the context of their everyday lives. Whereas most of the present chapter has drawn on findings from the quantitative surveys, this section adds insights from the qualitative fieldworks in order to explore the constitutive role of communication in experiencing oneself as part of a wider world, and in situating oneself within that world. To do so, we depart from informants with migrant backgrounds, including both transnational migrants and domestic migrants. The internet, in principle, affords contact with the whole world. In practice, our informants orient themselves in complex geographic as well as cultural territories, integrating, to varying degrees, into new locations and relations, while maintaining ties that still bind at a distance. Information and communication technologies offer migrants (and other users) a distinctive set of navigational resources that might empower them to be, at once, local and global.

As a mediating and sensitizing concept, we add here Benedict Anderson's (1991) notion of *imagined communities*. Originally developed to account for the development of modern nation-states and nationalism, the concept has been widely influential in communication and cultural studies to refer to a sense of belonging to collectives beyond families and locales. The communities in question are imagined, but not imaginary: Even in the smallest of nations, it is impossible for all of its citizens to have direct contact and, in this way, to relate to and come to know one another. And yet, few Chinese, Danes, or Americans are in doubt that they belong to communities known as China, Denmark, and the United States, respectively, likely participating in additional local and global communities and subcultures, as well. By virtually migrating in and by communication, they may remain members of all of these imagined communities while, in the process, cultivating multiple identities.

The fieldworks bear out informants' reliance on distinctive media and communication repertoires to maintain a presence both 'here' and 'there.' While it is hardly surprising that the internet comes out, across the three national settings, as a particularly important resource – a meta-medium with multiple communicative uses – it intersects in the course of everyday life with other media and with face-to-face interactions, too. Messaging apps, for instance, represent means both of reaching out to contacts hundreds or thousands of miles away, and of arranging to meet up with contacts, old or new, for coffee at a local café. Complementing the patterns of communicative prototypes and practices identified through the surveys, the fieldworks add contextual depth regarding "media repertoires [...] as integral part[s] of lifestyles, and they have to be interpreted with regard to their practical meaning" (Hasebrink & Popp, 2006: 373). Some of our informants communicate, not least, to manage their lives – produce, maintain, repair, and transform themselves – as migrants located in China, Denmark, and the United States. We briefly illustrate their experiences of media and their communicative practices, and of the widely differing conditions enabling and constraining them, with reference to a family that had migrated from Mexico to the United States, a Bosnian family living in Denmark, and a domestic migrant family in China.

Figure 3.9 displays the members of a Mexican immigrant family living in the United States: Mariah (female, 39 years old), her husband Javier (male, 40), and

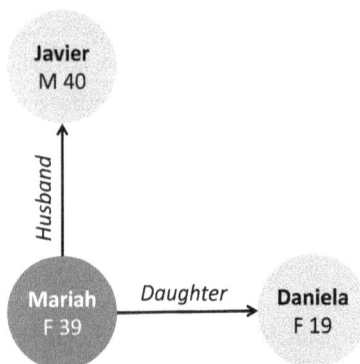

FIGURE 3.9 Mexican family living in the United States

their daughter Daniela (female, 19). (The sampling of qualitative informants, the notations of the figures, and other methodological details are described in the Methodological Appendix in Chapter 8.) Mariah and Javier are both first-generation immigrants, with most of their families still living in Mexico. Because of their immigrant status, the three of them would not be able to return to the United States if they were to travel to Mexico for a visit. In this condition of long-term, even permanent, physical separation from the rest of their families, Daniela responds to the question of which medium of communication she could not live without:

> Probably the app, WhatsApp, because my grandma, that's the only way I get to talk to her. So, ah, every now and then we send each other messages or a voice message. I mean, me and my grandma are really close, so for me, I would be really heartbroken if I wasn't able to talk to my grandma. So that would be one of the things that I couldn't live without.

Whereas, in our US sample, it is only immigrant informants who refer to WhatsApp, which is singled out as their preferred application, the other US informants will use Facebook Messenger, Snapchat, or Instagram to communicate with families and friends.

Among the advantages of WhatsApp, Mariah and Javier noted that this app allows them to create voice messages. This is particularly convenient if they need to relay substantial or complex information. At other times, if they want to keep things short, they will resort to text messaging. Mariah described how, through the voice messaging function of WhatsApp, she can make the most of the brief breaks in between her everyday chores and, thus, conveniently stay in contact with her mother, who still lives in Mexico:

> Because I can leave a message, like a voice. A voice record. If my life is on rest, I can push just one button and say "good morning mom, have a great weekend!" And if she was sick last night I can ask "how are you feeling today?" Ah, sometimes she has little accidents and I ask "how are you feeling today, what did the doctor say?" And it's easy for me to record, because texts are very slow, super slow, and I don't have too much time. And I feel, WhatsApp, I need everybody on WhatsApp [laughing]. If I need to say something to my husband, if he needs a lot of information – I need to be short in texts, you know?

It is noteworthy, however, that the Mexican family relates quite selectively to their country of origin. The interviews and the media diaries (which all informants completed, and which, as mentioned, served as a point of departure for a second round of interviewing) suggested that, in fact, they are not all that interested in being updated about events in their native country or relating to some wider national community. It is, instead, a small set of family relations that drives their

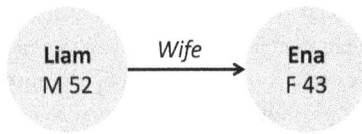

FIGURE 3.10   Bosnian family living in Denmark

communications to stay socially connected. The internet does come across as a relevant source of traditional news and information, but only for events relating to their current local community and to the rest of the United States.

The members of the Bosnian family living in Denmark (Figure 3.10) tell a rather different story about getting news from and about a wider world. Liam (male, 52) and his wife Ena (female, 43) are refugees, who came to Denmark in 1995, following the wars in the Balkans after the breakup of the former Yugoslavia. Liam is currently a factory worker; Ena works as a part-time pedagogue in an after-school program. In addition to following local news about Denmark, Liam will use news apps dedicated to what is going on in Bosnia-Herzegovina and Croatia. And, beyond news, they relate to their region of origin through other genres, as well, such as a TV series about a Turkish sultan that Ena is currently watching.

Indeed, Liam and Ena became early adopters of the internet because of their life circumstances, acquiring a stationary home computer and an internet connection back in the late 1990s when the internet was still an emerging technology. At the time, they had just moved from an asylum center into regular housing, and they were on a tight budget. Nevertheless, they found that they needed the internet connection to stay in touch with family and friends around the world, taking advantage of the unique opportunities for interpersonal communication afforded by the internet.

Compared to the Mexican family, who chose to migrate to the United States, the Bosnian family are refugees. During the war, Ena and Liam had fled to Denmark, and did not know what had happened to many of their social relations. By the time of this study, their friends and family had been scattered all over the globe, with people living in Germany, Sweden, and the United States, in addition to Bosnia and Croatia. Ena noted that, besides maintaining regular contact with various relations, the internet had allowed her to reconnect with old friends and family. Being able to relocate people that she dreaded might not have survived the war, through social media, has been a great relief to her:

> We're all over the world, family, friends, and all that, and it's nice when you hear from someone writing [on social media], I mean we haven't heard from each other for 20 years or more, since the war, it's like, it's something else, it's not like [you young guys], thank God, you haven't had to experience something like that, but to us it means so much to hear from someone we went to school with.

FIGURE 3.11 Domestic migrant housekeeper living in China

To sum up, for Ena, the internet has enabled all of three forms of connectivity: Identifying other people's whereabouts, reestablishing social ties with them, and staying in touch across great physical distances. We return in Chapter 4 to the range and types of social contacts, and sociality as such, that communication enables and carries.

Unlike our American and Danish fieldwork participants, Qing (female, 30) is a domestic migrant worker within mainland China (Figure 3.11). At the time of the fieldwork, she was occupied as a housekeeper in Beijing. Her family, however, still resides in her hometown, a small village in Hebei province in the northern part of China. This, importantly, includes her son, Shuai (male, 7), who lives with and is being cared for by Qing's father, Long (male, 53). Qing considers herself a temporary migrant worker in Beijing, and her plan in life is to return to her hometown after earning enough funds in the big city to start a small family business. This self-conception and imagined future explain her approach to internet use: To Qing, it turns out, the internet is basically a tool for work, not a medium for relating to people back home, nor for integrating into Beijing as her local community.

Qing only finished primary school, but though her literacy is relatively limited, she has acquired a high level of specific digital skills, and she utilizes multiple mobile applications to undertake a wide variety of daily tasks at work. For example, Qing relies on the app of a housekeeping company to manage the orders and accounts of different customers; she navigates Beijing via Baidu Maps (a mobile map service) to arrive at customers' houses; and she coordinates work with her boss and colleagues via group chats on WeChat, a key social medium in China.

Before coming to Beijing at the age of 24, Qing had never used the Internet. Her hometown had not been connected to the internet, and many of its residents, including Long and Shuai, have remained non-internet users. As a result, Qing still relies on phone calls to communicate with her family back home. And, when Qing returned to help her family harvest cotton in the fall of 2017, during all this time she did not use the internet at all. Qing basically described living two different lives, one in Beijing, and the other in her hometown:

> In Beijing, my hands were always holding the smartphone. I need it for my work and for surviving in Beijing. But when I came home, it did not matter to me that my phone was power-off for two days [...]. But in Beijing, I cannot live without my smartphone. If I go out of my room and cannot

find a place in Beijing, I use Baidu Maps. When I buy something, I use WeChat Pay. At home, I cannot use WeChat Pay. We still use cash everywhere. And I am with my family all the time, doing farming activities or staying in the house. Even if I am not with them sometimes, I will come back to the house after a short while.

The three migrant families in the United States, Denmark, and China illustrate distinctive ways of navigating physical and virtual spaces along a local–global continuum, with the internet as a recent and welcome pivot of communication, but with other media, from phones to television series, as additional resources for reaching out to others and representing the past as well as the present. On the one hand, locally oriented communicative practices embed migrants in new communities, from the Mexican family following general news about the United States (but not about their native Mexico), to Qing taking care of local business in Beijing through instrumental uses of the internet (but without treating it as a general information resource). On the other hand, more globally oriented communicative practices, enhanced by the internet, allow the Mexican and Bosnian families to maintain personal relations at a distance, and to stay updated on social developments in their region of origin (Mexico) – or not (Bosnia). For Qing, in contrast, her Beijing present represents a reality separate from the village life to which she hopes to return, connected in the interim by traditional phone calls and visits in person. In her case, time and, more specifically, an imagined future trumps space: Whereas the Mexican and Bosnian families accept, or resign themselves to, a state of suspension between two geographic and cultural poles, both of which are communicated with and about, the Chinese temporary migrant worker communicates in what amounts to different shifts, anticipating a time when the two poles of her life will be reunited.

Summary of findings

This chapter has provided a first mapping of contemporary communication systems and associated media and communication repertoires, across three world regions, seven countries, and their respective sociodemographic segments, against the background of an ongoing worldwide process of digitalization. The one-line takeaway is that the internet as a meta-medium, far from displacing other media, coexists with both broadcast and print media, and with face-to-face interaction, in slowly shifting configurations. Among the communicative prototypes, one-to-one interpersonal communication stands out as a human universal with significant similarities despite other social and cultural differences; one-to-many mass communication has retained its attractions as a source of factual information and fictional entertainments; and many-to-many networked communication has been added as a resource for variable degrees of contact to and interaction with other individuals and institutions. Synchronous and asynchronous communication, similarly, come out as complementary modes of managing personal and social time. And, across space, communicative practices in a range of media afford flexible ways and means of relating to, and acting in, both physical and virtual settings, as brought home by migrants in different life circumstances. While migrants face specific challenges of navigating local and global contexts of social interaction, their communicative practices will be broadly familiar or, at least, recognizable to other inhabitants of contemporary media environments.

As a preliminary conclusion, we find that what we designated, in Chapter 1, as *communication cultures* – distinctive combinations and configurations of one-to-one, one-to-many, and many-to-many communicative practices – are converging in different parts of the world. Most notably, the youngest age groups share more characteristics with each other *across* national borders than with the oldest age groups *within* those same borders: In the latent class analyses, the young are virtually indistinguishable across the seven countries and three world regions. This is in spite of the equally important finding that the young have *not* abandoned mass communication (or interpersonal communication, for that matter). It is up to further research, including longitudinal studies, to specify whether and how the young will go on to reproduce and maintain the common culture of communication they appear to have produced for themselves (a generational phenomenon), or whether they may abandon or transform that culture as they grow older (a life-course phenomenon). We return to potential future trajectories of communication systems in the concluding Chapter 7.

Anticipating more detailed analysis and discussion of theoretical and normative implications in later chapters, we carry forward three main insights. First, the findings in this chapter highlight mass communication as a key element of contemporary communication systems, across political economies, regulatory regimes, levels of digitalization, and distinctive cultural traditions. Indeed, the internet roundly delivers the familiar experience of television as audiovisual flows of fact and fiction (Williams, 1974), which presumably continue to hold essential qualities for the public(s) at large. In Europe and the United States, also radio retains an important place in media and communication repertoires; in China, radio comes out as more marginal, at least at the present aggregated level of analysis. A first lesson of studying contemporary communication systems, then, is that, at least so far, the internet has killed neither broadcasting nor mass communication as such. Mass *media* as traditionally understood may be fading as businesses and institutions, but mass *communication* remains an appreciated mode of interaction, a valuable asset, and a social resource with global attractions.

Second, interpersonal communication presents itself as another common denominator. If different repertoires of *mass* and *networked* communication divide people into classes of Socializers, Adapters, Allrounders, Rarelies, and Streamers, *interpersonal* communication reunites them, representing a much more evenly distributed set of communicative practices. Human communication is a generic mode of becoming and remaining a part of and a participant in shared realities, as enhanced by different historical technologies and configured through local social institutions.

The internet, undeniably, has afforded greatly enhanced opportunities for people to communicate to and with each other: The few, the many, and the masses. Third, however, the present findings suggest that, at least so far, people will either 'do everything' or 'do nothing' online – with other individuals, closed groups, all personal contacts, and anybody on the internet. The following chapter explores the multiple meanings of 'many' in many-to-many communicative practices. In this respect, the aggregated findings in the present chapter have pointed to important differences among the seven countries and across the three regions. At one end of the spectrum, in China, Hungary, and Italy, internet users tend to 'do everything' online; at the other extreme, in Germany and Denmark, they 'do nothing'; while respondents in the United States and the United Kingdom occupy a middle ground.

As part of these intermediate conclusions, we note two explanations likely contributing to these patterns of many-to-many communication. On the one hand, China, Hungary, and Italy all represent high, if variable levels of so-called political parallelism (Hallin & Mancini, 2004): Countries where media outlets are affiliated with and, to a degree, promote the positions of established political parties or interests. Networked online communication provides means of circumventing, compensating for, or coping with the powers that be. On the other hand, internet penetration remains comparatively low in China, Hungary, and Italy (see Chapter 2 and the Methodological Appendix in Chapter 8), so that the present internet-using samples could be considered early adopters embracing new technological potentials. In the chapters ahead, we return to these and other potential explanations for differences as well as similarities in the trajectories of contemporary communication systems.

4

BEING SOCIAL

Baohua Zhou, Nicoletta Vittadini,
Piermarco Aroldi, Francesca Pasquali, Jesper Pagh,
Fiona Huijie Zeng Skovhøj, Signe Sophus Lai,
Chris Chao Su, Jun Liu, and Klaus Bruhn Jensen

Qualities and quantities of sociality

Human beings become and remain social, across time and space, in and by communication (Carey, 1989b/1975). Communication accomplishes the socialization and acculturation of individuals in the mostly ordinary, if occasionally extraordinary, processes of their everyday interactions. By the same token, communication establishes and maintains the valued relations, ties, and networks that make up identities, communities, and societies. Increasingly throughout history, social networks have been extended from the local to the national and transnational levels of social organization by technologically mediated communication. And yet, face-to-face interaction remains essential to all social life throughout a great variety of cultural practices. Communication systems include humans as the oldest media of them all (Jensen, 2022). Humans are both necessary and sufficient conditions of communication in signs and symbols, even if this unique human capability has been extended in significant and consequential ways by a long line of technologies, from writing to computing.

Referring to digital environments, and extending the classic division of social ties into the strong and the weak (Granovetter, 1973), previous research has referred to *media multiplexity* (Haythornthwaite, 2005) or *multimodal connectedness* (Schroeder, 2010) to capture the varieties and combinations of different media and modalities of experience through which people engage each other, both face-to-face and in technologically mediated forms. In this chapter, we introduce the idea of *affordances* (Gibson, 1979) from ecological psychology to specify the scaling of human communication and social networks in current communication systems. The concept of affordances draws attention to the *relational* nature of interactions between humans and their natural environments, but also between one human being and another, and between humans and technologies,

DOI: 10.4324/9781003057055-4

as well: Humans and technologies afford or enable different and distinctive kinds of interaction that depend on acquired competences as well as momentary circumstances. Affordances emerge in relational fashion, and are cultivated over time, on biographical as well as historical time scales.

We first identify some general patterns – differences as well as similarities – in how people in the three world regions of this study become social, in and through a range of media and modalities. Across China, Europe, and the United States, respondents rely on *both* face-to-face *and* technologically mediated modes of communication to relate to their more or less significant others. While we detail variations across age, gender, and material and intellectual resources, the findings suggest that, given access to comparable media and modalities, people in different parts of the world may communicate in increasingly similar ways, at least when it comes to maintaining social relations writ large. Complementing the survey data tapping these patterns, the second section draws on the ethnographic fieldwork data from each region to explore the contexts in which, and the criteria by which, people elect (not) to engage in communication with others, and to make themselves available for communication (or not) in the first place. Whereas the internet, in principle, allows for being always-on (Baron, 2008), its socially and culturally situated users will negotiate the finer terms of whether and how to be available to various social networks, small and large.

The third section of the chapter explores the extended range of ways in which it has become possible to be social through 'social media.' Departing from the notion of *scalable sociality* (Miller et al., 2016), we examine the different kinds and degrees of being social that social media afford, and which turn out to vary not just with world region, age, and gender, but also with different spheres of human and social activity. The findings suggest that scalable sociality entails familiar formats of private and public communication, but also a variety of hybrid formats in which people may articulate, at once, individual and social identities (Papacharissi, 2010). In this regard, the present chapter adds detail and depth regarding two of the main conclusions that emerged in Chapter 3: People unequivocally still wish to engage in mass communication, if not necessarily via mass media as traditionally understood, and they further seek to maintain both their individuality and their sociality in characteristic repertoires of interpersonal and networked communication. This is in spite of the fact that political economies and regulatory frameworks may incline people to do different things with social media in the context of different national communication systems – either 'everything' or 'nothing' – so as to become and remain social in distinctive ways.

In the final section, we briefly consider the question of how communicative practices relate to people's affiliation with social and cultural organizations – which constitute consolidated, institutionalized indicators of specific ways of being social. Notwithstanding Robert D. Putnam's (2000) worry, expressed and widely circulated around the time of the public breakthrough of the internet

– that people (Americans) were increasingly bowling alone and otherwise with-drawing from classic social engagements – 20 years on, our respondents report being social both online and offline, on three continents: Being a member of offline organizations does not represent any contrast to being an online commu-nicator. The somewhat grander question – how organizational, communicative, and other involvement in the affairs of community and society relates to indi-viduals' capabilities and capitals, their positions in society, and their opportuni-ties in life – brings back fundamental issues of privilege and power throughout and beyond the individual's lifespan; Chapter 5 next turns to these difficult and important normative questions.

The communicative affordances of humans and technologies

Chapter 1 outlined the material, institutional, and discursive conditions that inter-sect in communication systems, circumscribing the communicative practices that are possible (and impossible) in a given historical time and cultural place. Chapter 2 reviewed the diffusion of communication technologies in the seven countries and three world regions of the present study, and characterized the political economies that variously enable, discourage, or prevent particular forms and contents of com-munication. And Chapter 3 mapped the media and communication repertoires of different sociodemographic and national segments, as societies undertake a long-term transition from analog to digital environments of social interaction. Implicit in these accounts has been the premise that, throughout historical time, humans have increasingly come to rely on a range of complex technologies to commu-nicate, for instrumental as well as reflective ends. At the same time, face-to-face interaction remains constitutive of all human and social life. Current social media have returned research to the question of how communication – face-to-face and mediated by technologies – shapes and is, simultaneously, shaped by social relations and networks.

The concept of affordances helps to bridge what has remained a persistent divide between studies of interpersonal and mass communication, respectively (Rogers, 1999), including but not delimited to communicative practices that are either embodied or technologically mediated. Originating from the field of psychology, the concept was coined by James J. Gibson (1979) to capture the rela-tionship between a biological organism and its environment, highlighting the fact that various elements and structures of the natural environment afford dif-ferent things to different organisms. Unlike human beings, insects can walk on water. Unlike other living organisms, humans systematically rework the natural goods they find, and they redesign the artifacts, tools, and technologies they inherit across generations, including reprogramming the forms and contents of older media. Gibson (1977: 67) started out, literally, from the surface of things, describing an affordance as "a specific combination of the properties of its sub-stance and its surfaces taken with reference to an animal." Research on human–computer interaction took Gibson's cue and transferred it to another category of surfaces: Computer screens and the designs that would facilitate user-friendly navigation and stepwise procedures of performing tasks (Norman, 1990). Studies of mobile media and communication, similarly, have often focused on the ways in which mediating interfaces reconfigure access to information across space and time (Hutchby, 2001; Ling, Goggin, Fortunati, Lim, & Li, 2020).

Gibson (1979), however, had highlighted one basic affordance of the environments in which humans find themselves, namely, other animals, including human beings. One of the most important affordances of the natural environment for humans is exactly other humans:

> The richest and most elaborate affordances of the environment are provided by other animals and, for us, other people [...] Behavior affords behavior, and the whole subject of psychology and of the social sciences can be thought of as an elaboration of this basic fact.
>
> *(p. 135)*

A distinctive affordance of other people is that they speak, and that they speak to me or to us. To a considerable degree, it is through speech and face-to-face nonverbal communication that we find out what other people are both able and willing to afford us in numerous other respects. In our ecological niche, other humans are as unavoidable as they are indispensable, in part as media of communication.

In Chapter 1, we briefly noted some long lines of media and communication history with reference to the three degrees or categories of media that have supported human communication, in different combinations in different eras. Humans are media in their own right, necessary and sufficient conditions of communication (Jensen, 2022). Here, we underline the continued and central importance of embodied communication, alongside technologically mediated interaction, for being and remaining human and social. In order to specify, measure, and understand the qualities and quantities of communication between individuals in the contemporary world, we consider both frequency and diversity: How often do people make contact with various kinds of social relations, and how diverse are the media and modalities through which they stay in touch?

The Peoples' Internet (PIN) surveys, accordingly, addressed the respondents' communicative contact with:

- a partner (e.g., spouse, girlfriend, boyfriend, a person they have a romantic relationship with)
- immediate family (e.g., parents, siblings, children)
- other family members or relatives
- close friends
- acquaintances
- colleagues

For each type of contact, respondents were asked to indicate the modalities they would rely on:

- conversations face-to-face
- telephone or voice calls
- messages to one person
- messages to several people at once
- emails
- letters

And, for each contact and modality, respondents reported the frequency of their interactions during an ordinary week on a five-point Likert-type scale (1 = never, 2 = less than weekly, 3 = once or a few times a week, 4 = several times a week, 5 = daily). The responses begin to delineate the affordances of different media and communicative practices for being social, their complementarity and configurations, for different sociodemographic groups and in different national and cultural settings.

Twelve degrees of contact

It was the work of the sociologist, Stanley Milgram, that brought to wider public attention the idea of six degrees of separation: The notion that all humans are, on average, six social connections away from each other (Travers & Milgram, 1969). While debated on theoretical as well as methodological grounds, the idea was carried into the age of the internet where, in theory, anybody might relate directly to anybody else, but where studies found Milgram's principle to still apply, for example, in networks of instant messaging (Leskovec & Horvitz, 2007). For most people most of the time, however, they themselves occupy the precise center of a world with a more manageable periphery. Alongside potentially global networks of both one-to-many and many-to-many communication, people will maintain contact with much smaller and much more local sets of nodes. What, then, are the different degrees not of separation, but of contact? How often, and how, through which forms of interaction, do people relate to their significant others (Mead, 1934), in face-to-face communication and by the media that be?

As in the initial mapping of media uses and communicative practices in Chapter 3, we employed a latent class analysis (LCA) (Hagenaars and Halman, 2019; Magidson and Vermunt, 2004) to first identify distinctive patterns of interpersonal interaction for the sample as a whole; we next related these patterns to respondents' sociodemographic and national backgrounds. Departing from the findings in Chapter 3, which depicted interpersonal communication as a universal and, potentially, unifying, if far from homogenizing human practice, the present chapter covers some of the complexities of how communication makes us human in socially and culturally distinctive ways. Tables 4.1 and 4.2 first lay out 12 repertoires or patterns of communication (classes of respondents) in terms of

TABLE 4.1 Six degrees of diversity in interpersonal communication

	Partner	Immediate	Relatives	Friends	Acquaintances	Colleagues	Description (this class scores …)
Every-things	High	High	High	High	High	High	High on diversity for all six types of relationships
Middle-roaders	Median	Median	Median	Median	Median	Median	Median on diversity for all six types of relationships
Family circlers_1	Median	Median	Low	Median	Median	Low	Median on diversity except for relatives and colleagues
Family circlers_2	High	High	Median	Median	Median	Median	High on diversity for close relationships, median for other relationships
Networkers	High	Median	Median	High	High	High	High on diversity except for immediate family and relatives
Low keys	Low	Low	Low	Low	Low	Low	Low on diversity for all six types of relationships

TABLE 4.2 Six degrees of frequency in interpersonal communication

	Partner	Immediate	Relatives	Friends	Acquaintances	Colleagues	Description (this class scores …)
Intensives	High	High	High	High	High	High	High on frequency for all six types of relationships
Family–extended	High	High	Median	Median	Median	Median	High on frequency for close relationships, median for other relationships
Middlers	Median	Median	Median	Median	Median	Median	Median on frequency for all six types of relationships
Family–plus	Median	Median	Low	Median	Median	Median	Median on frequency except for relatives
Family–only	Median	Median	Low	Low	Low	Low	Median on frequency for close relationships, low for other relationships
Extensives	Low	Low	Low	Low	Low	Low	Low on frequency for all six types of relationships

the ways in which (diversity) and the extent to which (frequency) they establish and maintain social relations through different media and modalities.

Table 4.1 bears witness to repertoires extending from all-or-nothing profiles to respondents who rely on different media for different folks. *Everythings*, *Middle-roaders*, and *Low keys* use the same range of media and modalities, but to varying degrees, to interact with their various social relations. The other three groups, in comparison, can be seen to articulate distinctive social relations through their selection and combination of different media and modalities. While *Networkers* give priority to extended networks in which friends, acquaintances, and colleagues, along with partners, are included as key nodes, both *Family circlers_1* and *Family circlers_2* communicate more diversely closer to home, centering on their partners and immediate relations, while reaching out, with variable degrees of diversity, to a circle or periphery of more distant relatives, friends, and colleagues.

Table 4.2, similarly, brings out two broad varieties of interpersonal communication in terms of its frequency. *Intensives*, *Extensives*, and *Middlers* will have equally frequent (or infrequent) contact with all of their social relations. In comparison, the other three groups, not surprisingly, all give priority to their close relationships, and include wider social spheres into their communications to different degrees. Whereas the *Family-only* group tends to restrict their interactions to close relationships, the *Family-plus* segment includes collegial as well as friendship relations to similar degrees. The *Family-extended* group might be taken as a contemporary variant of families extending across space, generation, or both, facilitated by (digital) communication technologies: Though anchored in high-frequency communication with close ties, this last group engages in significant interaction with all of their other social relations, as well. In Facebook terminology, they engage an extended range of 'friends' with certain family resemblances in and through their ongoing communications.

It should be noted, of course, that the two sets of six communicative degrees constitute analytical constructs and ideal types – they capture general, if characteristic, ways in which people may manage the mundane communicative business of relating to other people. The types, however, represent robust characterizations of communicative styles, both in themselves and in combination: Overall *diversity* and overall *frequency* of interpersonal communication are strongly correlated, ranging from .60 ($p < .001$) in the United Kingdom to .82 ($p < .001$) in Italy. Quantity and quality, it turns out, go together: If you communicate a great deal, you are also likely to be a diverse communicator in relating to other people. The further question, addressed in the next two sections, is how these 12 types and degrees of contact apply to media users with different sociodemographic backgrounds and in different national and cultural contexts.

Social contacts

Table 4.3 first lays out the *diversity* of interpersonal communication for various social segments. Among the *Everythings*, it is noteworthy that one finds not

TABLE 4.3 Sociodemographic characteristics of interpersonal communication classes, by diversity

Covariates/clusters	Every-things	Middle-roaders	Family circlers_1	Family circlers_2	Networkers	Low keys	Total
Gender							
Female (%)	44	50	51	60	50	31	53
Male (%)	56	50	49	40	50	69	47
Age	2.93	2.62	3.13	2.96	3.15	3.52	3.04
Education	3.80	3.18	3.31	3.75	3.78	3.06	3.56
Income	2.13	2.01	1.86	2.00	2.08	1.67	1.96
Occupation							
Office job (%)	38	21	20	34	40	15	30
Service job (%)	36	54	33	37	32	34	38
Physical work (%)	21	23	36	21	21	43	25
Student (%)	5	3	10	7	7	8	6

Note: Age is measured in five categories ("1" = 18–29 years old, "2" = 30–39 years old, "3" = 40–49 years old, "4" = 50–59 years old, "5" = 60–74 years old, "6" = 75 years and above); education is measured in six categories ("1" = primary education, "2" = lower secondary education, "3" = upper secondary education, "4" = post-secondary non-tertiary education, "5" = tertiary education, "6" = master's level or above); income is measured in three levels as low level (=1), medium level (=2), and high level (=3) by comparing the individual's income with the average income in the country in question.

only more young (and more male) respondents, but also more with a longer education and a higher income. In contrast, the *Low keys* include more older respondents and more respondents with lower incomes (and again more males, as well). The implication is that the two extremes of the diversity spectrum align with relatively resource-rich and resource-poor backgrounds, in terms of people's material opportunities, informational and communicative competences, or both. More resources enable more diverse communications. In this spectrum, the *Middle-roaders*, indeed, occupy a middle position, comprising respondents mostly working in the service industry as well as being the youngest cluster overall. For the remaining types, gender enters into the social equation in important ways. Interestingly, *Family circlers_1* has a predominance of older male respondents (who also have the least amount of education and the least income, and who are more frequently employed in manual labor); *Family circlers_2*, in contrast, are more likely to be female and younger (while also having more education, but less income than the sample average). It is plausible that, in family circles, it falls especially upon female household members to maintain the ties that bind, by any media necessary, including more distant relatives. *Networkers*, finally, come out as similar to this last group of *Family circlers_2* in terms of (relatively high) educational and (relatively low) income levels, but with an older profile and a 50–50 gender distribution, representing a more outgoing style of interpersonal communication centered in the (single) individual. This profile, further, aligns with the respondents' marital status: 41% of singles belong to the *Networkers* cluster, which holds the largest percentage of singles across clusters.

Table 4.4 next considers the *frequency* of interpersonal communication for various sociodemographic backgrounds. Here again, a spectrum extending from the resource-rich to the resource-poor is manifest. At one end, *Intensives*, but also *Middlers* and, notably, the *Family-extended* class all represent a combination of relatively high educational and income levels. Along similar lines, respondents in these classes are commonly occupied in office or service jobs. There are also slightly more male respondents across these three segments (while *Intensives* are distinctively younger than all other classes). At the opposite end of the frequency spectrum, *Extensives* tend to be older, with relatively low education and income, occupied in physical jobs, and with a much higher share of male respondents. The two intermediate groups – *Family-only* and *Family-plus* – in addition to having a comparable distribution of occupations as well as similar income and educational levels, again point to the centrality of gender: Both 'family' groups include more female respondents, bearing out the understanding of communication as, in part, a continuous practice of sociability and care for others (Gilligan, 1982). Respondents in the *Family-only* class, in addition, tend to be older than those in the *Family-plus* class, suggesting communication in a more delimited social circle as part of a more sedentary lifestyle.

In terms of both its quantity (frequency) and its quality (diversity), then, and unsurprisingly, interpersonal communication is conditioned by entrenched social structures, which communication, in turn, maintains and may modify over time. Indeed, the two sets of findings map onto each other in what amounts to a homologous structure, generated by three mechanisms intersecting in and,

TABLE 4.4 Sociodemographic characteristics of interpersonal communication classes, by frequency

Covariates/classes	Intensives	Family-extended	Middlers	Family-plus	Family-only	Extensives	Total
Gender							
Female (%)	49	47	47	52	54	36	53
Male (%)	51	53	53	48	46	64	47
Age	2.49	2.79	2.77	3.03	3.19	3.48	3.04
Education	3.55	3.75	3.59	3.58	3.56	3.02	3.56
Income	2.13	2.12	2.06	2.00	2.02	1.70	1.96
Occupation							
Office job (%)	38	37	33	28	30	11	30
Service job (%)	35	38	39	34	39	26	38
Physical work (%)	19	20	23	30	27	51	25
Student (%)	7	5	6	7	4	12	6

Note: Age is measured in five categories ("1" = 18–29 years old, "2" = 30–39 years old, "3" = 40–49 years old, "4" = 50–59 years old, "5" = 60–74 years old, "6" = 75 years and above); education is measured in six categories ("1" = primary education, "2" = lower secondary education, "3" = upper secondary education, "4" = post-secondary non-tertiary education, "5" = tertiary education, "6" = master's level or above); income is measured in three levels as low level (=1), medium level (=2), and high level (=3) by comparing the individual's income with the average income in the country in question.

arguably, pervading social life: An unequal distribution of (material and immaterial) resources, a gendered allocation of communicative roles, and a biological-cum-biographical mechanism by which, early in life, people communicate to make a way and a place for themselves in society and the world, by any media necessary. Around the turn of the millennium, as the internet was becoming a staple of social life, it was common to overstate the status of its youthful early adopters as a distinctively sophisticated generation of digital natives (Prensky, 2001). On reflection and with hindsight, it was entirely to be expected that younger age groups would communicate, frequently and diversely, to become who they would like to be, turning to the media of their times. Like gender, age is articulated in communication; like other experienced realities of gender and age, communication is circumscribed by socially structured and historically less than equal opportunities.

Cultural configurations

Chapter 1 outlined an understanding of *cultures of communication* as configurations of communicative practices which, over the long historical haul, have been enabled by the available material technologies, institutionalized through variable political economies, and expressed in cultural and discursive forms and contents, from alphabets to narrative genres and conventions of (not) addressing or presenting oneself to (some) other people. For interpersonal communication in contemporary communication systems, an important question is whether and how online as well as offline interactions correspond to what are commonly recognized as national or regional cultures: Whole ways of life (Williams, 1975/1958) that are experienced as meaningful across decades and centuries, and which have been invoked, repeatedly and sometimes notoriously, to justify collective action both within and beyond national borders. While the nation-state should not be approached, for comparative purposes, as an innocent default category (Esser and Vliegenthart, 2017; Livingstone, 2003), it remains a social fact of centuries whose manifestation in contemporary communicative practices is an empirical issue. How does interpersonal communication, its diversity and frequency, enter into wider cultures of communication, with long histories and associations with particular locations in the world, and to what degree do such cultures differ, coincide, converge, or overlap?

Table 4.5 presents the distribution of the seven national samples across the interpersonal communication classes, first by *diversity*. In this respect, two outliers are evident. In China, first, almost three-fourths (74%) belong to the *Middle-roaders* category (who are moderately diverse in staying in touch with all of their social contacts), and if one adds the more prolific group of *Every-things*, close to nine out of ten (88%) Chinese respondents present themselves as, if not always-on, then always-available for social interaction. Second, close to two-thirds of respondents in Hungary (63%) and somewhat less than half in Italy (42%) go into the highest category of *Every-things*. (As explained in the Methodological

TABLE 4.5 National characteristics of interpersonal communication classes, by diversity

	China (%)	Germany (%)	Denmark (%)	Hungary (%)	Italy (%)	UK (%)	US (%)
Every-things	14	29	19	63	42	16	34
Middle-roaders	74	6	6	5	13	12	6
Family circlers_1	3	23	30	9	16	23	19
Family circlers_2	4	21	23	10	13	25	23
Networkers	3	12	17	10	14	19	10
Low keys	2	9	5	2	2	4	8
Total	100	100	100	100	100	100	100

TABLE 4.6 National characteristics of interpersonal communication classes, by frequency

	China (%)	Germany (%)	Denmark (%)	Hungary (%)	Italy (%)	UK (%)	US (%)
Intensives	2	4	1	12	14	3	7
Family-extended	4	8	2	22	15	6	14
Middlers	42	19	15	34	45	17	26
Family-plus	13	32	42	13	13	44	20
Family-only	23	22	21	16	9	24	24
Extensives	16	14	18	4	4	6	9
Total	100	100	100	100	100	100	100

Appendix in Chapter 8, especially the Hungarian sample likely is somewhat skewed toward tech-savvy or elite respondents.) The remaining four countries – Denmark, Germany, the United Kingdom, and the United States – in comparison, exhibit both relatively more even distributions across the classes and comparable profiles overall, even if the United States and Germany constitute one subgroup with a substantial proportion of *Every-things* (34% and 29%), the United Kingdom and Denmark another subgroup with rather similar profiles.

Table 4.6, addressing *frequency*, supports and specifies such an understanding of differently configured interpersonal communication cultures. In the case of China, Hungary, and Italy, the more active *Intensives* and *Middlers* account for close to – or in the case of Italy (59%) more than – half of all respondents. The United Kingdom and Denmark, again, come out with similar, less active profiles overall (although Denmark holds considerably more of the least active, *Extensive* respondents, 14%), whereas the United States and Germany each make up a separate subgroup, at least when it comes to the frequency of interpersonal interactions.

By way of an intermediate conclusion, the surveys begin to specify the extent to which, and the ways in which, national contexts, along with sociodemographic factors, may explain distinctive configurations of the universal human practice of interpersonal communication, online and offline. We return, later in this chapter, to additional and similarly variable ways of being social specifically on 'social' media. First, however, we complement the quantitative findings with ethnographic fieldwork data in order to unpack some of the fine-grained aspects of the lived realities behind the numbers – the practices and processes in which people come to communicate (or not), more or less frequently, and to rely on particular media to relate to particular others in particular contexts. People do things with media, and with each other, according to criteria that highlight the different affordances of different media as situated means to social ends.

Can we talk?

As noted in earlier chapters and specified in the Methodological Appendix in Chapter 8, the Peoples' Internet project included ethnographic fieldwork in mainland China, Denmark, and the United States, centering on fieldwork participants' diverse practices and flows of communication in the context of their everyday lives. A central component of such practices and flows, not surprisingly, was the continuous maintenance of social relations but, importantly, through different kinds and degrees of contact. Communicative contact may serve as either ground or figure – a backdrop to other essential endeavors, but also, from time to time, a focused activity of reaffirming both strong and weak ties (Granovetter, 1973). Whereas the fieldwork covered digital platforms as well as other media in each of the three world regions, the strategy was to follow *people* (Marcus, 1995) across different contexts of communication, including face-to-face interactions, complementing self-reports from the interviews with diary records and follow-up interviews about the latter. In addition to the opportunity to triangulate factual details, this combination of several sources of evidence further facilitated reflection by fieldwork participants, as they reported on their communications across the full range of contacts and media available to them.

Mark Granovetter's (1973) founding classic of social-ties theory had suggested that people will look to a delimited set of strong ties for emotional support, while gaining (more or less) useful information from a broader range of weak ties. In the early days of the internet, Caroline Haythornthwaite (2005) specified, on the one hand, that strong ties support both emotionally intense and information-heavy exchanges, whereas weak ties primarily deliver instrumental information. On the other hand, she clarified a qualitative distinction with important analytical implications, namely, that strong ties will be cultivated through multiple channels of contact, and weak ties through fewer channels. Recent work has confirmed the centrality of strong ties in providing diverse forms of social support on social media (Krämer, Sauer, & Ellison, 2021). As further suggested by our survey findings, both the diversity and the frequency of communicative contacts entail different ways of being social and, presumably, different ways of understanding and experiencing sociality. Across the three regions, the participants in the fieldworks consistently emphasized a three-way distinction between the affordances of different media and modalities: Text-based communication (text messages, emails), voice-based communication (voice messages, phone calls [and for a minority, at the time of these field-works, occasional video messages]), and face-to-face communication. But how do people enact such complex distinctions between channels as they go on (not) to communicate?

To address this question, we conducted a comparative thematic analysis of fieldwork data from China, Denmark, and the United States, identifying five criteria (see further Pagh, Zeng Skovhøj, & Lai, 2021):

- *Efficiency*: How efficiently can the communication convey potentially complex information?
- *Sensibility*: To what degree can the communication accommodate emotionally charged topics?
- *Ephemerality*: Might the communication be accessed by outsiders, with social consequences for the sender, the receiver, or both?
- *Insistency*: How urgent is the communication, as perceived by the sender and/or on behalf of the receiver?
- *Availability*: To what extent, with what frequency, should people accept the role of being a receiver in communication?

The rest of this section explores the place of these criteria – as explicit and sometimes implicit premises – in communications with strong as well as weak ties and across regions. Whereas the contexts and contents of concrete interactions in China, Denmark, and the United States evidently vary, all five criteria can be seen to guide communicative practices in all three settings, most of them with similar evaluations of when and how (not) to communicate.

Efficiency. In one sense, communication is all about getting one's message across to other people. For both strong and weak ties, and across regions, our fieldwork participants give priority to face-to-face communication, specifically to share instrumental and, at times, intricate information. The moment-to-moment control of a conversational flow, they agree, makes for clarity and, hence, a better understanding of the points either being expressed by one person or emerging from the interaction. Chun, a 19-year-old student in Beijing, noted how complex matters that require detailed exchanges, do not lend themselves to text-based communication:

> For example, if you discuss a topic for the debate competition, you should do it face to face. Or when it is a group assignment. So, if things get complicated, I will choose to handle them through face-to-face communication. […] Typing in text messages is way more troublesome, as you cannot convey your ideas clearly through only one or two sentences.

As a second choice, voice-based communication preserves aspects of the face-to-face modality, despite an intervening medium. Textual media and modalities, in comparison, come out as people's last choice for offering information and making oneself understood.

Sensitivity. The same ranking applies to the second criterion of sensitivity: Human communication carries not only instrumental information, but emotional exchanges, as well. Fieldwork participants bring up the sensitivity – of exchanges and of the people having them – particularly in relation to strong ties (even if emotion may also figure in weaker ties, as well; see Small, 2017). In sensitive matters, they prioritize face-to-face interaction because, with the embodied person as the medium, a wider range of social cues is on offer. Jane, a 63-year-old retired lawyer who volunteers at a foundation in the United States, explained that she had recently fallen out with a colleague, who had emailed her something that upset her, and she wanted to have a conversation with her. Although it would have been quicker, an email or even a phone call, in Jane's view, would not have worked in engaging the situation:

> About that particular incident, when I got the first email […] I wrote immediately a couple of emails but I waited a while before I sent them, and I reread them and I – I'm aware of how easy it is to misconstrue things in email, and I think that emotional kind of outbursts are not well suited to email. Sometimes I will write the emails just to do it and then I will delete it. Just like, "OK, now how am I really gonna deal with this?" […] And, as it turned out, fortunately I think, we didn't end up talking on the phone, and I ended up seeing her that night.

Jane added that, in fact, the conflict had been initiated when her colleague had sent her an email instead of breaking some bad news to her in person. The choice of the right and wrong communication channel, thus, may either create or resolve interpersonal tension.

Ephemerality. People are well aware that, in textual and, more specifically, digital media, communication leaves a trace for future reference. In China, Denmark, as well as the United States, fieldwork participants were concerned that, particularly if emotional exchanges were to be leaked in their social networks, this might affect especially their strong, trusted ties with particular significant others. More generally, there was a clear preference for face-to-face communication even when emotional and otherwise intense exchanges are kept between the parties: Ephemerality, even deniability, may serve a common interest of mending things and making up without revisiting what was once said and done. In the Danish setting, Hanne, a 21-year-old real-estate intern, suggested that personal disagreements should not be handled by texting or instant messaging, because digital media can leave behind proof of harsh and potentially hurtful statements expressed in the heat of the moment:

> It also depends on what it is you're writing about and stuff like that, but actually, in a way it can also be nice to have talked [face-to-face] and that you don't have the proof of what each other wrote, right?

Interestingly, however, in none of the three regions did participants refer to either governmental or commercial online surveillance as a reason for observing the criterion of ephemerality.

Insistency. If ephemerality addresses conditions under which it may be preferable *not* to communicate, the criterion of insistency applies to communication as a matter of urgency. How pushy or polite should senders be, in timing their communications, but also in choosing their medium? Such questions arise for both informational and emotional exchanges, among strong as well as weak ties. The urgency may follow from an imbalance between the communicating parties, when one is dependent on the other, for instance, in order to tackle a particular problem, and may be at risk of being ignored or even denied assistance when reaching out. The participants pointed to several considerations in scaling insistency: How quickly they would want the receiver(s) to respond; what degree of attention they wish them to devote to the exchange; and which degrees of freedom to leave for receivers to either engage or overlook the invitation to communicate. Sophia, a 19-year-old student in the United States, found that she would initiate communication through text messaging to allow other people to respond in their own time. Along similar lines, Fatma, a 25-year-old Danish schoolteacher, described phone calls as more insistent than text messages, requesting both immediate contact and sustained attention:

> I just think sometimes it is a bit more manageable and easier in writing [...] I can take care of it when I have time and feel like it, whereas with phone calls, then I have to take care of it at that moment.

Once again, and in all three national settings, participants ranked face-to-face contact as the most insistent modality, an offer of communication that may be difficult to refuse.

Taken together, four out of the five criteria – efficiency, sensitivity, ephemerality, and insistency – bear witness to interpersonal communication as a universal human practice, carried and differentiated by local, situated uses of embodied, textual, and auditory media and modalities, but according to strikingly similar considerations of how to be social.

Availability. The final criterion, while also shared across national and cultural contexts, will be administered in two distinctive ways. On the one hand, fieldwork participants in the United States and Denmark evaluated the three categories of media and modalities – text, voice, bodies in context – according to whether they would minimize their availability to other people, that is, to *avoid* communication; this strategy was said to apply especially to weak ties. On the other hand, our Chinese participants approached the same media and modalities as means of maximizing their availability to their entire social network. In Denmark and the United States, participants described how they would both limit and delimit their text-based as well as voice-based communications in time and space, for instance, by placing their smartphone in the bedroom all day, leaving their laptop at work, or dedicating particular hours to social media use. In mainland China, in contrast, participants elaborated how they would have not just one, but several channels of contact open, using multiple media in parallel. A characteristic concern here was that, unless the social medium of WeChat is kept running on one's smartphone, even while one is engaged in someone or something else, whether media use or other work or leisure activities, one might be out of touch with a person needing and reaching out for help. Yuan, a 27-year-old human-resources (HR) employee in Shanghai, relates how she always has WeChat open on her mobile phone while watching television:

> I have to constantly check if something comes up from work, and if my boss contacts me. You know, it is very intense at my work. Or to check if my friends or family need anything from me. I will always try to reply to them immediately if I can.

We return, in the concluding section of the present chapter, to the implications of both the qualitative and the quantitative findings on interpersonal communication for the understanding of sociality and individuality in the three world regions. In Chapter 3, we noted how technological infrastructures and political economies help to explain media and communication repertoires at large in each of these regions. Before turning to specific ways of being social on social media, we reiterate the point, addressed in Chapter 1, that also one-to-one and few-to-few patterns of communication are explained by cultural traditions as well, some of which are shared across civilizations. It was the eighteenth-century philosopher, Johann Gottfried von Herder, who contributed the idea that culture simultaneously unites and differentiates members of the human species (*Ideas for the Philosophy of History of Humanity*, 1784–1791) (Forster, 2008): All human beings have and hold culture, but the cultures that we articulate and participate in set us apart over time. The present survey and ethnographic data converge on the related insight that humans cannot *not* communicate (Watzlawick, Beavin, & Jackson, 1967); that we will negotiate comparable ways of being human and social as meaningful and appropriate through the historically and cross-culturally available range of media and modalities; and that some of these ways of life (Williams, 1975/1958) will vary across historical time and cultural place.

The concrete difference between China, on the one hand, and the United States and Denmark, on the other, in administering one's availability for communication, aligns with several theoretical conceptions of cultural difference. Beyond the commonly cited individualism–collectivism axis (Inglehart, 1990), studies of the formation and management of social networks in China – from the classic work by Fei Xiaotong (1939) to more recent contributions (e.g., Herrmann-Pillath, 2017) – have noted that persons of Chinese heritage tend to emphasize their relations with the same individuals across contexts and domains of relevance, which helps to explain the priority given by our fieldwork participants to keeping all of one's channels open all of the time. In comparison, this line of research has argued, in

Western settings people will orient themselves towards different individuals and communities at different times for different ends and, hence, may be more likely to switch channels on and off. More generally, *guanxi* – the dynamic of personalized, reciprocal relationships that is specific and essential to Chinese society and culture (Yang, 1994) – suggests the importance of being always-available: Communication is a necessary condition of offering instrumental and emotional support to one's full social network, as needed, whenever possible. In contemporary Danish and American contexts, different variants of social safety nets may fill this function, through welfare states, religious communities, or private charities.

The conjuncture of mobile devices and social media has made always-being-social, as practiced in China, a real option in much of the world; in China, mobile phones had become the predominant point of access to the internet at the time of this fieldwork (CNNIC, 2019). The following section elaborates on what it means to be social on social media across the seven countries and three regions.

Scalable sociality

Listening, searching, and sharing

Communication on social media can be understood, most basically, as acts of sending or receiving information about either private or public matters, in more or less focused fashion, as ways of relating to other individuals, but also to small and large groups, and to anybody online. Over the last two decades, research has identified several kinds of online communicative practices, from *background listening* by following people online for updates (Crawford, 2009); via more dedicated information seeking, divided into *social searching* for information on family, friends, and friends-of-friends, and *social browsing* for the activities of politicians, celebrities, and institutions (Lampe et al., 2006); to *information sharing* along a private–public continuum (Quinn, 2016b). Importantly, although social browsing might be thought of as less than committed participation in the affairs of community and society as conventionally understood, it can, in fact, be seen to establish and maintain consequential forms of *public connection* (Couldry, Livingstone, & Markham, 2007) beyond private or personal life. At the same time, internet users may still be negotiating appropriate ways of presenting themselves, but also their relations with other people, to multiple audiences of varying sizes, as they practice a form of *public intimacy* (Kaplan, 2021). All of these communicative practices articulate what Daniel Miller and his collaborators have referred to as *scalable sociality* (Miller et al., 2016). In communication, online as offline, people engage a range of more or less significant others in a process which, over time, generates social structures and meaningful communities around particular endeavors.

Most, but certainly not all, internet users are also social media users. To begin, we noted the distribution of the entire sample, across countries, regions, and sociodemographic groups, into users (daily or weekly) and non-users (rarely or never). 85.2% were social media users (three out of four on a daily basis), whereas

14.8% were non-users. Users would spend slightly below two hours daily on social media (mean = 1.75).

We next considered the sample's interest in following different sources of information as a form of background listening. Table 4.7 lists the ranking of such sources, indicating a marked preference for following relatives and friends (the latter slightly above family relations, in fact). In comparison, less than one in three relate to wider social spheres of either state, market, or civil society in this manner. News media attract a little more than one in four, surpassing entertainment media; commercial brands trump both political parties and NGOs. Religious or spiritual leaders come out as the least important sources of information and insight on social media. Sociality, at least on social media and for the online populations of these seven countries and three world regions, thus comes out as distinctively secular; in Chapter 5, we return to the preferred sources of guidance on moral dilemmas (which, again, are secular).

A factor analysis of the list in Table 4.7 served to identify three broad forms of sociality. In Table 4.8, the three resulting categories can be seen to cover familiar domains of individual and social existence: personal relations; entertainment and lifestyle interests; and political, economic, and other public affairs. These findings, further, align with the respondents' practices of social searching (personal) and social browsing (public), respectively. Table 4.9 reaffirms a primary orientation towards family and friends, with well over half (56.7%) getting a least daily updates from their personal circles. When it comes to the other two domains, classic public issues of politics and economy garner the least attention, even if the level of interest here is roughly comparable to that for entertainment, sports, and culture.

TABLE 4.7 Background listening on social media (multiple responses possible)

What kinds of people are you connected to or do you follow on social network sites?	%
Friends	81.9
Family members and relatives	79.1
Acquaintances or friends-of-friends	56.8
Colleagues or former colleagues	51.1
News media	28.0
Celebrities	17.2
Musicians	17.0
Lifestyle or retail brands	16.5
Politicians or political parties	14.3
Entertainment media	14.1
Non-profit organizations, grassroots movements	12.5
Sports stars	10.4
Religious or spiritual leaders	3.8
Other	1.7
Don't know/prefer not to respond	3.4

TABLE 4.8 Three components of social media connections

What kinds of people are you connected to or do you follow on social network sites?

	Components		
	1	*2*	*3*
Celebrities	**.759**	.051	.075
Musicians	**.749**	.071	.093
Entertainment media	**.630**	.053	.215
Sports stars	**.622**	.010	.095
Lifestyle or retail brands	**.601**	.110	.131
Family members and relatives	.027	**.726**	−.049
Friends	.026	**.704**	.009
Colleagues or former colleagues	.087	**.682**	.129
Acquaintances or friends-of-friends	.106	**.631**	.049
Non-profit organizations or grassroots movements	.196	.103	**.704**
Politicians or political parties	.286	.042	**.648**
Religious or spiritual leaders	−.015	−.049	**.648**
News media	.439	.133	**.469**

Note: The table derives from a principal component factor analysis with varimax rotation. An eigenvalue of greater than 1 (Kaiser criterion) was used to determine the number of components, which was confirmed by a scree test (Cattell, 1966). Numbers in bold highlight the elements of each of the three components.

TABLE 4.9 Private searching and public browsing of social media (%)

Do you ever get updates about ...	*Many times a day*	*Once or a few times a day*	*Weekly (one or more times a week)*	*Rarely*	*Never*	*Don't know/ prefer not to respond*	*Total*
... your friends, family, or acquaintances?	24.5	32.2	27.6	9.4	3.7	2.6	100.0
... entertainment, sports, or culture?	11.2	21.3	25.6	21.5	17.0	3.5	100.0
... political or economic affairs?	10.5	18.8	20.6	24.9	21.8	3.5	100.0

In terms of sending or sharing information, finally, the pattern repeats itself. Table 4.10 shows how people will share information more frequently with closer social contacts; more than one in three (35.6%) will send texts, photos, or videos at least daily to individuals, and more than one in four (26.2%) will do the same to groups. Sharing information with one's entire social network or the public at large is less common. In fact, there is an inverse relationship between the size of the audience and the frequency of communication. In sum, social media are not approached as means of mass communication if one considers the full sample across China, Europe, and the United States. The question is whether some users, in some settings, are more likely to be social at scale.

TABLE 4.10 Speaking up on social media (%)

How frequently do you ...	Many times a day	Once or a few times a day	Weekly (one or more times a week)	Rarely	Never	Don't know/ prefer not to respond	Total
... send text messages, photos, or videos to other people individually?	14.6	21.0	30.8	24.5	7.1	1.9	100.0
... share text messages, photos, or videos to groups of friends, family, or colleagues?	8.8	17.4	28.1	31.3	12.3	2.0	100.0
... share text messages, photos, or videos so that all your connections can see them?	7.1	14.9	25.1	33.3	17.6	2.0	100.0
... post comments that can be seen by anybody on the internet?	6.0	12.5	20.6	32.4	26.5	2.1	100.0

TABLE 4.11 Background listening across countries and cultures (%) (multiple answers possible)

What kinds of people are you connected to or do you follow on social network sites?	CN	DE	DK	HU	IT	UK	US	Total
Family members and relatives	95.6	65.6	79.5	83.5	71.8	80.7	71.4	79.1
Friends	88.2	76.2	83.9	82.2	78.2	84.4	78.1	81.9
Acquaintances or friends-of-friends	77.8	51.7	44.6	66.5	56.2	46.0	47.9	56.8
Colleagues or former colleagues	57.8	37.6	58.8	67.5	41.3	55.1	34.9	51.1
Celebrities	3.6	15.4	25.2	16.8	19.1	22.5	21.4	17.2
Sports stars	2.1	9.8	11.8	11.4	12.6	15.2	11.8	10.4
Musicians	3.6	14.2	22.0	21.8	18.0	22.1	20.5	17.0
Politicians or political parties	1.2	9.0	19.6	11.0	13.5	23.1	27.7	14.3
Religious or spiritual leaders	0.4	2.6	3.4	4.5	3.2	5.3	9.1	3.9
News media	6.2	21.2	36.7	38.7	29.9	35.6	33.3	28.0
Entertainment media	2.8	11.4	10.8	24.4	12.0	23.2	17.0	14.1
Lifestyle or retail brands	6.5	11.9	23.3	16.8	21.0	17.9	21.1	16.5
Non-profit organizations or grassroots movements	0.6	8.8	17.5	13.7	8.6	21.6	20.7	12.5
Other	0.3	1.4	3.6	1.4	1.2	2.5	2.4	1.8
Don't know/prefer not to respond	1.2	8.8	3.6	1.9	3.2	3.1	3.3	3.4

Cultural configurations

Social media use, as noted in this and preceding chapters, is widespread across the three regions and seven countries. However, people in different cultural settings will communicate with different kinds of social relations to different degrees. Table 4.11 first lays out the variations in background listening. Beyond the primacy of family and friends across the board, three patterns stand out. First, respondents in China are much more likely to connect to the full range of their offline contacts, from family and friends to colleagues. In contrast, the same respondents are highly unlikely to follow practically all other potential contacts; the figure for news media (6.2%) even falls below that for commercial brands (6.5%). Second, also within the European region and the Western set of countries overall, there is considerable variation. German respondents, in particular, display comparatively low figures both for family, friends, and colleagues, and for news media as well as political parties and NGOs. Third, additional variations emerge, for example, between the United States and the United Kingdom, which have commonly been understood as having the same category of *media* system (Hallin & Mancini, 2004). Their *communication* systems, in comparison, differ in important respects, for instance, when it comes to relating to relatives, colleagues, and religious leaders.

Tables 4.12 and 4.13 move on from background listening to actively searching or browsing information and speaking up. While Table 4.12 reconfirms that, across regions and countries, the strength or closeness of a relation entails frequency of communication (even if the number of Chinese respondents who report getting updates on their close contacts "many times a day" is comparatively low),

TABLE 4.12 Searching and browsing across countries and cultures (%)

Do you ever get updates about ...	CN	DE	DK	HU	IT	UK	US	Total
... your friends, family, or acquaintances?								
Many times a day	19.7	20.6	22.9	31.8	27.0	23.8	26.7	24.5
Once or a few times a day	33.2	29.5	29.1	30.4	33.6	35.9	33.6	32.2
Weekly	36.1	30.6	24.9	27.5	22	25.8	24	27.6
Rarely	8.7	11.4	11.2	7.2	10.3	8.1	9.1	9.4
Never	1.9	4.3	5.2	1.5	6.1	3.3	4.2	3.7
Don't know	0.4	3.7	6.8	1.6	1.0	3.1	2.4	2.6
Total	100.0	100.0	100.0	100.0	100.0	100.0	100.0	100.0
... entertainment, sports, or culture?								
Many times a day	5.6	8.8	12.1	16.1	14.3	11.8	10.5	11.2
Once or a few times a day	21.2	15.1	19.0	24.4	24.0	21.7	23.3	21.3
Weekly	34.3	20.1	21.3	31.6	25.5	20.6	22.4	25.6
Rarely	25.6	24.1	19.4	19.3	20.0	22.0	18.7	21.5
Never	12.2	28.1	18.5	6.4	15.2	19.1	22.4	17.0
Don't know	1.1	3.8	9.7	2.3	0.9	4.9	2.6	3.5
Total	100.0	100.0	100.0	100.0	100.0	100.0	100.0	100.0
... political or economic affairs?								
Many times a day	2.9	9	8.5	16.4	10.3	11.4	17.6	10.5
Once or a few times a day	11.1	16.1	15.2	23.5	21.4	22.5	23.6	18.8
Weekly	24.8	17.6	19.9	22.5	22.1	17.8	17.5	20.6
Rarely	36.1	24.1	21.6	25.1	24.4	20.4	19.3	24.9
Never	23.8	29	25.4	10.0	21.0	23.8	19.5	21.8
Don't know	1.4	4.1	9.5	2.6	0.8	4.1	2.4	3.5
Total	100.0	100.0	100.0	100.0	100.0	100.0	100.0	100.0

TABLE 4.13 Speaking up across countries and cultures (%)

How frequently do you …	CN	DE	DK	HU	IT	UK	US	Total
… send text messages, photos, or videos to other people individually?								
Many times a day	13.1	10.9	7.7	20.2	22.3	13.6	14.0	14.6
Once or a few times a day	23.9	21.0	11.3	22.4	26.8	19.7	20.6	21.0
Weekly	43.8	25.5	24.2	32.2	24.0	32.7	30.1	30.8
Rarely	17.1	26.8	39.7	21.0	20.8	24.3	24.4	24.5
Never	2.0	12.1	13.6	2.8	4.9	7.5	9.2	7.1
Don't know/prefer not to respond	0.1	3.8	3.6	1.4	1.2	2.2	1.5	1.9
Total	100.0	100.0	100.0	100.0	100.0	100.0	100.0	100.0
… share text messages, photos, or videos to groups of friends, family, or colleagues?								
Many times a day	4.5	6.8	2.8	14.3	17.0	7.0	9.7	8.8
Once or a few times a day	18.8	15.2	7.2	21.0	26.3	15.0	17.2	17.4
Weekly	41.7	26.4	18.0	27.5	24.5	29.6	25.5	28.1
Rarely	27.8	28.6	48.6	28.9	23.2	33.2	30.3	31.3
Never	6.8	19.0	19.8	6.7	7.8	13.0	15.8	12.3
Don't know/prefer not to respond	0.4	3.9	3.6	1.6	1.2	2.3	1.4	2.0
Total	100.0	100.0	100.0	100.0	100.0	100.0	100.0	100.0
… share text messages, photos, or videos so that all your connections can see them?								
Many times a day	5.1	4.8	1.7	13.6	12.1	4.2	7.7	7.1
Once or a few times a day	19.3	10.3	5.9	18.1	20.6	11.0	17.5	14.9
Weekly	33.6	17.2	16.7	26.8	24.9	25.7	28.1	25.1
Rarely	31.5	27.3	48.1	31.6	26.9	36.9	31.2	33.3
Never	10.0	35.7	24.3	8.4	14.1	19.9	14.0	17.6
Don't know/prefer not to respond	0.4	4.7	3.3	1.4	1.5	2.2	1.5	2.0
Total	100.0	100.0	100.0	100.0	100.0	100.0	100.0	100.0
… post comments that can be seen by anybody on the internet?								
Many times a day	2.8	4.8	2.5	10.4	10.1	4.3	7.9	6.0
Once or a few times a day	13.7	7.0	5.3	16.2	18.6	9.8	15.6	12.4
Weekly	26.9	14.5	16.5	21.9	20.4	17.3	25.0	20.6
Rarely	27.9	29.4	38.4	32.7	30.2	38.1	31.0	32.4
Never	28.1	40.4	33.8	17.1	19.4	28.1	18.9	26.5
Don't know/prefer not to respond	0.7	4.0	3.6	1.6	1.3	2.4	1.6	2.1
Total	100.0	100.0	100.0	100.0	100.0	100.0	100.0	100.0

there are noteworthy differences when it comes to following news and entertainments. At the high end of interest in entertainment, sports, and culture, one finds around 40% of respondents in Italy and Hungary getting updates at least once a day (again recognizing the likely skewed nature of the Hungarian sample); at the other end, more than half (52.2%) in Germany receive such updates rarely or never. For political and economic affairs, whereas China, again, occupies the lowest point with almost 60% getting updates on social media rarely or never (59.9%), Germany comes rather close at 53.1%, and the remaining countries (excluding Hungary) occupy a spectrum between 35% and 47% of people not being informed about political and economic affairs, at least in this manner – even though, in the United States, the United Kingdom, and Italy, roughly a third of respondents get such information daily.

Table 4.13, lastly, reiterates the finding that audience size and communication frequency are inversely related, across national and cultural backgrounds. People will reach out much more frequently to significant individuals and small groups than to their full social networks or the general public. Behind this global picture, a second pattern emerges from what are admittedly complex configurations of communicative practices. The Italian and Hungarian respondents, again, are the most active communicators, as senders as well, for audiences of all sizes. Danes and Germans, at the other end of the spectrum, are the most passive (or modest) communicators across audience types: If the German respondents accounted for the most limited background listening, they also are quite unlikely to share information with the general internet public (rarely or never for 69.8% of the German sample), only trumped by the Danes at more than seven in ten (72.2%). Interestingly, the middle ground for practices of speaking up, including to anybody online, is occupied jointly by China and the United States, along with the United Kingdom. Before assessing these mixed cross-cultural patterns of interpersonal and networked communication in the conclusion of this chapter, we address variations across sociodemographic backgrounds, which add further nuances to the meaning of being social on social media.

Social contacts

The final step of the analysis of communication on social media considered whether and how different social segments send and receive information, respectively. Table 4.14, first, presents the results of a binary logistic regression analysis, indicating the extent to which social media users with specific sociodemographic background characteristics receive updates about various social domains and contacts. The most pertinent features are gender, age, and education, in addition to country. Women tend to orient especially toward personal domains, men toward public domains, most clearly so for political and economic affairs. The youngest age group is the most likely to use social media for any purpose, if most manifestly for entertainment, sports, and culture. And a higher educational level entails greater use of social media, notably for political and economic affairs. In contrast, respondents with a low educational level are about 50% less likely to rely on social media for either political and economic information or entertainment; the same (absence of) communicative practices coincide with low income. For the different countries, the results reaffirm that our Chinese respondents orient quite emphatically toward their personal contacts and as prominently *not* toward political and economic affairs. In a comparison between Europe and the United States, the two regions come out with close to identical communicative practices

TABLE 4.14 Receivers on social media

| | Friends, family, acquaintances[1] | | Entertainment, sports, culture[2] | | Political and economic affairs[3] | |
| | N: 8,874 (82.1%) | | N: 8,789 (81.4%) | | N: 8,794 (81.4%) | |
	OR	95% CI	OR	95% CI	OR	95% CI
Gender (**Male**)	0.724**	0.630–0.832	1.375**	1.248–1.515	1.528**	1.389–1.680
Age (**55–74**)	1.000**		1.000**		1.000**	
Age (**18–34**)	1.337**	1.100–1.625	2.268**	1.976–2.603	1.195**	1.045–1.367
Age (**35–54**)	0.970	0.809–1.162	1.347**	1.181–1.535	0.952	0.835–1.085
Education (**High**)	1.000*		1.000**		1.000**	
Education (**Low**)	0.761*	0.615–0.942	0.522**	0.450–0.606	0.512**	0.443–0.592
Education (**Medium**)	0.791**	0.666–0.940	0.796**	0.707–0.897	0.635**	0.566–0.712
Having a partner (**Yes**)	1.137	0.976–1.324	0.949	0.849–1.060	1.112*	0.999–1.239
Children living at home (**Yes**)	1.275**	1.078–1.508	1.025	0.915–1.148	0.994	0.890–1.109
Income (**High**)	1.000		1.000*		1.000	
Income (**Low**)	0.895	0.735–1.090	0.830**	0.721–0.955	0.855*	0.746–0.981
Income (**Medium**)	0.980	0.822–1.170	0.967	0.855–1.093	0.919	0.817–1.035
In employment (**Yes**)	1.268**	1.077–1.493	1.197**	1.065–1.346	1.061	0.946–1.191
Country (**USA**)	1.000**		1.000**		1.000**	
Country (**China**)	1.519*	1.096–2.107	1.626**	1.307–2.024	0.687**	0.557–0.847
Country (**Europe**)	0.986	0.793–1.226	1.214*	1.041–1.416	0.851*	0.731–0.991
Urbanization (**City**)	1.000		1.000**		1.000**	
Urbanization (**Village**)	0.787	0.597–1.037	0.661**	0.549–0.796	0.667**	0.557–0.800
Urbanization (**Town**)	0.873	0.752–1.013	0.948	0.853–1.053	0.945	0.853–1.046
Belonging to an organization (**Yes**)	1.090	0.944–1.259	1.355**	1.223–1.502	1.455**	1.317–1.606

Note: The table derives from a binary logistic regression analysis (maximum likelihood estimation, MLE), dividing respondents into users and non-users of social media and noting the distribution of sociodemographic characteristics for each of three social domains (personal contacts, entertainments, political and economic affairs). **bold**: reference category. Cox and Snell's R^2: [1]0.116; [2]0.161; [3]0.261.
Legend: *p < 0.05; **p < 0.01; OR, odds ratio; CI, confidence interval.

when it comes to personal contacts, with Europeans slightly more active in seeking entertainments, and slightly less so for political and economic affairs.

It is noteworthy, moreover, that people living outside cities and towns are significantly less likely to receive information about the two public-oriented domains and, further, that respondents participating in some form of organized social life are more likely to also relate to these domains through social media. We return – briefly in the next section and in Chapter 5 – to the relationship between communicative and other social engagement.

Table 4.15, which addresses the uses of social media for sending information, both reiterates and specifies the social patterning of communicative practices. As senders as well as receivers of information, women and men tend to orient toward personal and public domains, respectively. The youngest age group clearly shares information on social media, but relatively less so when it comes to wider social networks and publics. And resources – education and income – again condition whether or not people speak up, even if this pattern is not statistically significant for wider social networks and publics. Urbanization and organizational involvement, similarly, foster or promote communicative expression. An interesting, if unsurprising, pattern is that respondents with children living at home are particularly active sharers, likely in large measure of representations of their children, even more so to wider social networks and, indeed, for the whole world online to see. China, once again, is home to the most avid communicators for all audiences. On this last point, it is remarkable that our Chinese respondents are as likely as their American counterparts to share comments for anybody on the internet to receive, whereas the European respondents are much less likely to do so, compared to both China and the United States.

On a more global note, it is striking that the greatest differences across various sociodemographic characteristics pertain to the sharing of information on social media with other people individually: The larger the audience, the less socially differentiated the communicative practice of sending information. The implication appears to be that, at least on current social media, and in these three world regions, people will devote special attention, energy, or care to their already strong ties, with information overflowing, more or less incidentally, to others who are online, as well.

Organizations, communities, worlds

To conclude the examination of communication and sociality, the surveys addressed both formal membership in various kinds of organizations and the informal, imagined sense of belonging to particular communities (Anderson, 1991). While organizations and communities can be said to exist in and by individuals' communicative practices, they are, simultaneously, collectively recognized and regulated social structures, from local arts, activity, and interest groups, via nation-states and diasporas, to the communitarian understanding of all of humanity as one community (Kleingeld & Brown, 2013).

TABLE 4.15 Senders on social media

	Sending text messages, photos, or videos to other people individually[1]		Sharing text messages, photos, or videos to groups of friends, family, or colleagues[2]		Sharing text messages, photos, or videos so that all your connections can see them[3]		Posting comments that can be seen by anybody on the internet[4]	
	N: 8,937 (82.7%)		N: 8,928 (82.6%)		N: 8,923 (82.6%)		N: 8,917 (82.5%)	
	OR	95% CI	OR	95% CI	OR	95% CI	OR	95% CI
Gender (**Male**)	0.746**	0.673–0.826	0.973	0.886–1.07	1.032	0.940–1.134	1.240**	1.127–1.363
Age (**55–74**)	1.000**		1.000**		1.000**		1.000**	
Age (**18–34**)	3.019**	2.608–3.496	1.931**	1.691–2.206	1.616**	1.417–1.844	1.499**	1.309–1.716
Age (**35–54**)	1.365**	1.196–1.559	1.155*	1.016–1.313	1.162*	1.021–1.322	1.203**	1.052–1.375
Education (**High**)	1.000**		1.000**		1.000		1.000	
Education (**Low**)	0.773**	0.660–0.905	0.761**	0.658–0.881	0.890	0.770–1.029	0.884	0.763–1.025
Education (**Medium**)	0.860*	0.759–0.973	0.934	0.834–1.047	1.026	0.917–1.147	0.989	0.883–1.108
Having a partner (**Yes**)	0.986	0.878–1.107	0.965	0.867–1.075	0.938	0.843–1.043	0.836**	0.75–0.932
Children living at home (**Yes**)	1.278**	1.131–1.444	1.212**	1.086–1.353	1.351**	1.212–1.504	1.394**	1.250–1.555
Income (**High**)	1.000**		1.000**		1.000**		1.000**	
Income (**Low**)	0.820**	0.710–0.948	0.734**	0.640–0.840	0.875	0.764–1.001	0.901	0.784–1.036
Income (**Medium**)	1.173*	1.032–1.334	1.064	0.945–1.197	1.173**	1.044–1.317	1.193**	1.060–1.342
In employment (**Yes**)	1.168*	1.034–1.319	1.133	1.011–1.27	1.123*	1.002–1.259	1.067	0.949–1.199
Country (**USA**)	1.000**		1.000**		1.000**		1.000**	
Country (**China**)	3.053**	2.367–3.938	2.394**	1.925–2.978	1.797**	1.452–2.223	1.067	0.866–1.314
Country (**Europe**)	1.060	0.903–1.245	1.192*	1.026–1.384	0.785**	0.676–0.910	0.673**	0.58–0.782
Urbanization (**City**)	1.000**		1.000**		1.000**		1.000**	
Urbanization (**Village**)	0.443**	0.358–0.547	0.576**	0.478–0.694	0.546**	0.454–0.657	0.594**	0.494–0.714
Urbanization (**Town**)	0.891*	0.798–0.995	0.981	0.886–1.086	0.940	0.850–1.039	0.905	0.817–1.003
Belonging to an organization (**Yes**)	1.137*	1.022–1.265	1.262**	1.143–1.394	1.402**	1.271–1.547	1.666**	1.508–1.84

Note: The table derives from a binary logistic regression analysis (maximum likelihood estimation, MLE), dividing respondents into users and non-users of social media and noting the distribution of sociodemographic characteristics for people sending to each of the four audiences (individuals, groups, all contacts, anybody online). Legend: *p < 0.05; **p < 0.01. Legend: OR: odds ratio, CI: confidence interval, **bold**: reference category. Cox and Snell's R^2: [1]0.189; [2]0.155; [3]0.250; [4]0.248.

Formal membership of organizations is, on the whole, limited among our respondents, below 10% on average across the three world regions. The surveys referred to political, religious, cultural, and sports organizations as well as civil society and community groups. Whereas, in China, membership is below 5% for all types of organizations, the numbers are higher in other countries and for specific domains. More than 20% of US respondents are members of a religious organization; Denmark exhibits 10–20% ranges for sports, cultural, and civil society organizations; in the United Kingdom and the United States, 10–15% are members of political organizations.

The surveys also explored the relationship between online and offline engagement, broadly speaking: Are people, in fact, increasingly bowling alone, now also online (Putnam, 2000)? Tables 4.16 and 4.17 report the extent to which

TABLE 4.16 Organizational membership and receiving on social media (%)

	About friends, family, acquaintances		
	China	*Europe*	*US*
Member	86.5	87.9	92.8
Non-member	89.5	84.8	83.7
	About entertainment, sports, culture		
	China	*Europe*	*US*
Member	77.9	67.9	60.0
Non-member	65.1	55.9	49.8
	About political and economic matters		
	China	*Europe*	*US*
Member	53.9	63.9	71.3
Non-member	44.5	47.7	53.5

TABLE 4.17 Organizational membership and sending on social media (%)

	To individuals		
	China	*Europe*	*US*
Member	83.9	67.0	70.9
Non-member	83.9	63.2	59.2
	To groups		
	China	*Europe*	*US*
Member	81.9	57.9	58.6
Non-member	67.1	51.0	44.7
	To all contacts		
	China	*Europe*	*US*
Member	63.9	49.8	58.4
Non-member	61.1	41.2	47.0
	To anybody		
	China	*Europe*	*US*
Member	53.2	44.7	53.3
Non-member	45.1	33.1	42.3

members and non-members of organizations, respectively, either receive information about various social domains, or send information to particular audiences, on social media. The implication seems clear, despite the relatively small proportions of members in these samples: Offline organizational involvement goes together with more, not less, online activity of either sending or receiving information.

To gauge sociality as an imagined construct – something that people will think and communicate a good deal about – the concluding background questions of the survey, posed in each country and region, included reference to locations or communities that respondents might feel (most) connected to: local, regional, or global; ethnic or religious; past or present. Respondents ranked each of these on a ten-point scale, and Table 4.18 lays out the findings. Not surprisingly, the country and local community where people currently live come out as their primary experienced affiliations. Interestingly, however, the world as a whole is ranked well above regional or ethnic communities. Spiritual or religious communities, again, hold the lowest rank overall.

There are variations in imagined sociality, as well: In China, respondents tend not to conceive of themselves as belonging to any world community. In small and ethnically homogeneous Denmark, respondents rank country highest of all, ethnic belonging lowest of all communities. In the United States and in Italy, spiritual or religious community is ranked higher than in the other five countries. The general picture of a world revolving around countries and local communities, however, holds up across the three regions, as represented and interacted about in the combined legacy and social media of contemporary communication systems.

TABLE 4.18 Imagined socialities

	N	*Minimum*	*Maximum*	*Mean*	*Std. Deviation*
The country one lives in	10,172	0	10	6.72	3.020
The local community one lives in	10,137	0	10	5.89	3.049
The world as a whole	9,877	0	10	4.58	3.234
A local community other than the one one currently lives in (e.g., place of birth)	9,926	0	10	3.76	3.359
A regional community (e.g., Europe, Asia, America, Africa)	9,886	0	10	3.42	3.366
An ethnic or national community (e.g., White, Black, Hispanic, Asian)	9,915	0	10	3.38	3.508
A country other than the one one currently lives in	9,922	0	10	2.84	3.256
A spiritual or religious community (e.g., Christianity, Islam, Judaism)	10,051	0	10	2.82	3.443
Valid *N* (listwise)	9,172				

Summary of findings

Whereas Chapter 3 noted the special status of interpersonal communication as a universal human practice, the present chapter has explored the varieties of interpersonal and networked communication that maintain and modify social networks. Across world regions and sociodemographic segments, respondents give special priority, as both senders and receivers, to one-to-one and few-to-few interactions with their significant others for instrumental information and emotional and other social support. Supplementing the quantitative surveys, the qualitative fieldwork data offer reminders that face-to-face interaction is a unique, greatly appreciated modality, still carrying decisive details of fact as well as affect. At the same time, online and offline interactions come out as complementary modes of engaging both persons and institutions, sometimes as small acts of engagement (Picone et al., 2019) with public relevance and experienced consequence. Just as video did not kill the radio star, people are still bowling, not alone, but mostly sharing lanes close to home with a relatively few others, while more occasionally visiting alleys at a distance.

Beyond its standing as an everyday staple, interpersonal communication, like mass communication, is socially stratified. Most generally, more resources – as associated with education and income, but also with urbanization and privileged gender positions – enable more diverse communications, including an orientation toward the public contexts of personal lives. Women more likely end up taking (or being given) primary responsibility for the frequent, mundane everyday communications with the ties that bind, and which make much of the world go round. The young, not surprisingly, will communicate especially frequently and diversely, on social media and beyond, arguably less thanks to technological sophistication than because of a conjuncture of biography and history: So-called digital natives (Prensky, 2001) were born into a transitional moment in the history of human communication which, like earlier cohorts and generations, they are making the most of, as they live their lives and make their own histories.

Regarding the national and regional configurations of interpersonal communication, our Chinese respondents paint a picture of a culture of communication that is always-available to (what a Western sociological paradigm would characterize as) both strong and weak ties (Granovetter, 1973). The same respondents, in comparison, will pay little attention to public news and entertainments as conventionally understood, at least on social media. Respondents from the United States and the five European countries partly differ from, partly resemble this Chinese baseline. In Italy and Hungary, respondents are similarly active senders as well as receivers in relating to their personal contacts, if not with the same intensity as their Chinese counterparts. German respondents, in their turn, are almost as *unlikely* as Chinese respondents to attend to either classic news or entertainments on social media. Remarkably, however, the American and Chinese respondents are about equally *likely* to share comments with anybody online, whereas Europeans will restrict their commentary to smaller social circles.

We return, in Chapter 7, to theoretical explanations and normative implications of these patterns of interpersonal and networked communication, and their interrelations with mass communicative practices. We conclude the present chapter by noting, across the three world regions, what amounts to a dual sense of belonging or sociality – through relatively localized one-to-one and few-to-few interactions, and through affiliation with the larger nation-states that remain the economic, political, and infrastructural reference points of the modern world system (Wallerstein, 1974), as represented in and interacted about through both legacy and social media. The communicative agency of individuals is circumscribed, at once, by globally competing national political economies and by the (relatively more) local production and distribution of scarce resources – capitals. The following chapter turns to the place of these economic, cultural, social, and, increasingly, digital capitals in conditioning what people (can) do with media.

5

HOW TO DO THINGS WITH MEDIA

Adrian Leguina, Jacob Ørmen, Fiona Huijie Zeng Skovhøj,
Signe Sophus Lai, Jesper Pagh, John Downey,
Rasmus Helles, and Klaus Bruhn Jensen

Communication as representation and action

Media are typically understood, in research and in common parlance, as forms of *representation* – ways and means of rendering diverse aspects of reality in either factual or fictional formats. Chapter 3 mapped the multiple media of representation that people rely on to relate to and understand their natural and cultural environments. Chapter 4 developed a complementary perspective on media as means of social interaction – *resources* for people to engage both individuals and institutions, so as to become and remain a part of social networks and a member of meaningful communities. In this chapter, we shift attention toward the broader and deeper social structures that are the products, in part, of innumerable distributed acts of communication: Representations and interactions that produce, maintain, repair, and transform reality over time and, increasingly, across space (Carey, 1989a). In the process, communication participates in the accumulation of capitals – material and immaterial resources – and in their (unequal) distribution among individuals and groups, from the local to the global level of social organization. Capitals condition who is in a position to communicate, to and with whom, and with what outcomes and consequences; capitals are themselves reproduced, translated, and transferred by communication, day to day and generation to generation.

The first section lays out different forms of capital, as they relate to human communication, drawing on the seminal work of Pierre Bourdieu (1984/1979). In Chapter 1, we described communication as a process mediating human agency and social structure, lending orientation to agency and meaning to the structures that come to make up long-lasting communities, cultures, and civilizations. Here, we elaborate on what Bourdieu defined as economic, cultural, and social capitals, which constitute, at once, conditions and consequences

DOI: 10.4324/9781003057055-5

of communication over time. We add a fourth category of digital capital to specify how current communication systems interact with other social systems in extending and deepening a locally and globally unequal distribution of material and immaterial resources.

In the second section, we begin an empirical account of the complex process in which communication is capitalized, drawing on the Peoples' Internet (PIN) surveys to characterize the agency that people exercise daily online as parents, partners, citizens, consumers, patients, religious subjects, and more. How do our respondents do things *with*, but also *through* the internet, in collaboration and, sometimes, conflict with others? The third section offers complementary, contextualized perspectives on the interplay of communications and capitals from the qualitative fieldworks in China, Denmark, and the United States, exploring how internet users mobilize different capitals in their encounters with (more or less) digitalized institutions and infrastructures.

The fourth and longest section of the chapter broadens the perspective to consider digital, analog, as well as embodied forms of communication as resources in tackling both mundane choices and pressing dilemmas of everyday life. Across the three regions, and throughout private and public domains, different capitals place different social segments at a distinctive advantage or disadvantage as they articulate and enact plans and projects, ends and means of their lives, step by communicative step. If digitalization represents an ongoing revolution in the conduct of everyday life, it is, simultaneously, a highly uneven revolution with familiar winners and losers, and new manifest inequalities.

In the final section, we briefly reconsider the emerging digital media environment as a challenge for the development, at once, of theory and policy. The following chapter turns to a specific (and unprecedented) aspect of digital communication systems with additional, unforeseen, and still unforeseeable implications for the accumulation and distribution of capitals. For better or worse, we all leave behind bit trails as we speak into the system (Jensen & Helles, 2017), being subject not just to surveillance, but to an extraction of surplus value that is consolidating the production and distribution of economic, cultural, social, as well as digital capitals within entrenched social structures.

Communications and capitals

The sociology of Pierre Bourdieu, as noted, is particularly helpful in conceptualizing and specifying the classic, abstract duality of agency and structure as it operates throughout the mundane practices of everyday life, in private and in public. As such, his conceptual framework lends itself to empirical operationalization and to comparative studies, across space and time, of whether and how individuals live lives that they have reason to value, and how, in the process, larger communities and cultures are maintained and modified, and histories made. In addition to capitals, two concepts are key to the Bourdieusian framework: Fields and habitus.

First, different and delimited areas of social life are referred to as *fields*, recognizing that different resources (material and immaterial, more or less scarce) are key to different social domains, just as different rules apply to the administration of such resources and to the roles that people seek to occupy in the administration and control of resources and fields. While corporate CEOs and full professors occupy broadly comparable roles of privilege, the fields in which they operate and the resources they each command still differ in important respects. We return, later in this chapter, to different communicative practices as they unfold in different fields – for example, finding information about job openings or verifying controversial information about a politician. In each social playing field, people can be seen to variously compete and cooperate in achieving desired outcomes, for themselves and others. Fields, in sum, constitute 'objective' environments of social interaction in which individuals relate both to each other and to specific institutions, entering into shifting configurations, depending on their access to and deployment of relevant resources (Bourdieu & Wacquant, 1992).

The second concept – *habitus* – captures the process in which resources are embodied in individuals, enabling them to translate general resources into concrete *modus operandi*, for the business at hand and in the field in question. Like capitals, habitus represents a set of structural properties that condition how particular individuals conduct themselves within and across social fields. Habitus is understood by Bourdieu, more specifically, as a range of 'subjective,' intuitive dispositions that distinguish one group of people from another, manifesting in overt behavior, linguistic practices, and lifestyle preferences (Bourdieu, 1990). Akin to notions of identity in other social theory, a habitus is learnt, reproduced, and commonly thought of as 'natural' by the person experiencing and displaying it: Habitus is what a person is and does. The embodied, material, concrete nature of the habitus is suggested by the fact that it can be extended in tools and technologies. In the case of communication, habitus guides the uses, for example, of digital devices and infrastructures, thus enabling (and constraining) access to resources to get jobs done, to achieve material and immaterial gain (or not).

The concept of habitus has been applied in many studies of the socially patterned uses of information and communication technologies. Savolainen (1995, 2016), for one, contributed the insight that people's adoption of certain information-seeking strategies over others for problem solving follows neither from their general position in society nor from the available media in themselves; instead, strategies emerge in the encounter between the material equipment at hand and a person's habitus – between affordances and agency. (On the affordances of communication technologies, see further Chapter 4, p. 79.) With specific reference to the internet, Meyen et al. (2010) found that it is a complex conjuncture of personal dispositions, previous socialization, and current life circumstances (what Bourdieu referred to as the *opus operatum* – who people have become, or have literally made themselves) which accounts for their concrete *modus operandi* in approaching the latest medium of human communication: How and why the internet is increasingly embedded in everyday practices and personal lives.

For example, Robinson (2011) referred to the notion of habitus to explain the distinctive practices of information seeking that young people engage in when deciding on post-secondary education and engaging in career planning. And, to address broader questions of how life plans take (and change) shape, Cvetičanin et al. (2014) combined Bourdieu's concept of *strategies* (sequential actions towards achieving a goal) with de Certeau's (1984) notion of *tactics* (unpredictable actions that respond and adapt to given circumstances). Habitus, in sum, constitutes a general readiness to act that is given concrete orientation by the terms and conditions of moments and contexts.

A person's habitus works on and reproduces capital in concrete and consequential ways, as they engage in various domains or fields of social life. As defined by Bourdieu, capital has three fundamental forms: Economic, social, and cultural (Bourdieu, 1984/1979, 1986). *Economic* capital, first, is liquid, or what economists term 'most liquid,' which means that it consists either in money or in possessions that can readily be converted into money – which, in turn, enables individuals and groups to do and be a great variety of things. *Social* capital, next, refers to both actual and potential social relations, specifically long-lasting networks of relationships based in mutual acquaintance and recognition, which are the products of, but which also support continuing efforts of, securing material or symbolic benefits for oneself. *Cultural* capital, finally, covers a range of assets that put people in a position to demonstrate three broad types of competences: *embodied* (being able to interpret the meaning of selected artifacts and practices), *objectified* (owning objects that presuppose particular insight or background knowledge), and *institutionalized* competences (holding formal qualifications recognized by educational and other established institutions).

Cultural competences are familiar examples of resources that can be converted into economic value – for instance, a proven talent or a recognized education leading to gainful employment – and the point is a general one: Capitals are not just reproduced over time; they are transformed and translated in mutually reinforcing processes. Inherited wealth, old boys' networks, and distinctive lifestyles feed social synergies, which are articulated in agency and sedimented as structure. Bourdieu (1986), accordingly, directed attention to what he understood as the entire "structure of the social world" – the total configuration of the different forms of capitals that people experience and engage in a given time and place. Over and above the several social fields constituting it, this structure represents a common arena in which people must pursue their plans in life on multiply unequal terms. More than material possessions and monetary instruments, capitals include intangible, yet consequential resources that shape different ways of thinking and speaking about the social world in its present form – what *is*. More than preliminary end products of accumulation, capitals also condition communications about possible social worlds – what *could be*. Communication is key to both the accumulation and the translation of capitals and, hence, to imagined and imaginable futures.

Among the three forms of capital, Bourdieu (1986) referred to economic and cultural capitals as primary; he further noted how social capital fills a special role as a *bridging capital* that maximizes advantages or benefits deriving from these other capitals (see further Chen, 2013; Quinn, 2016a). In the case of media and communication, studies have shown, for instance, that having the right social connections may narrow digital divides (e.g., Chen, 2013; Pearce & Rice, 2017) and enhance digital skills (e.g., Correa, 2016), as well as serving to identify useful sources of information (e.g., Chen et al., 2014; Mowbray et al., 2018; Zimmer & Henry, 2017). In addition, digitalization can be seen to introduce a fourth form of *digital capital* (for an overview, see Ignatow & Robinson, 2017). Like social capital, digital capital serves a bridging function, including links across the online–offline divide, with implications for the kinds of agency that, increasingly, must be exercised in and across both realms.

Building from the work of Ragnedda and Ruiu (2020), we approach digital capital as a distinctive form of capital operating, most clearly and concretely so far, in the context of practical problem solving. Digital capital consists of accumulated knowledge, skills, and competences regarding relevant uses of digital technologies, in addition to necessary material resources (hardware, software, internet connections) (Ignatow & Robinson, 2017; Leguina & Downey, 2021; Ragnedda & Ruiu, 2020). We go on to elaborate how digital capital, on the one hand, bridges offline and online social spheres and, on the other hand, is translated into other forms of capital in ways that tend to reinforce the social positions of those already commanding other capitals (Bourdieu, 1984, 1986; Halford & Savage, 2010, Ignatow & Robinson, 2017). We also return to the implications for what has been referred to, since the 1990s, as digital divides. What began as scholarly and policy attention to first-level divides of basic access to the internet (e.g., DiMaggio et al., 2004; Zillen & Hargittai, 2009) has been shifted toward a second-level divide of skills, knowledge, and use gaps (Hargittai, 2002; Van Dijk, 2017), and, most recently, a third-level digital divide of outcomes (Mihelj et al., 2019): Unequal economic, social, and cultural consequences and benefits of internet use, locally and globally. We begin, however, by examining some of the mundane things that growing numbers of people around the world do online, and which, more or less directly, produce and reproduce economic, social, cultural, and digital capitals.

Getting things done online

It is easy to forget that, only 25 years ago, a wide range of everyday tasks could only be accomplished in person or through specialized media. In the 2020s, most people depend on the internet when making public and private appointments, finding a place to live, buying and selling things, transferring money, filing tax returns, and much more. As brought home by speech–act theory (Austin, 1962), humans do things with words; they also do things with media. Chapter 4 detailed how people continuously act *in* communication, in verbal language and other modalities, coordinating their social relations and networks and, in the process, contributing to the maintenance of wider communities and societies. But people also act *by* communication (Carey, 1989b/1975), accomplishing mostly trivial and, occasionally, remarkable things by exchanging bits and other signs and symbols in the context of specific social fields. Digital media are commonly termed interactive: Users interact *with* the internet, and in doing so, they also act *through* the internet.

As a first step, this section examines a selection of concrete activities which people typically engage in online as part of their everyday lives, across countries, regions, and sociodemographic segments. For clarity, we refer to these practices as 'instrumental' to distinguish them from other acts of media use and communication, even while recognizing that, for instance, finding a potential partner and seeking religious or spiritual guidance involves more than narrow means to specified ends. Table 5.1 lists the activities included in the PIN surveys. For each question, the national versions of the questionnaire included relevant examples to prompt respondents' reflection and recall, for instance, regarding different mobile applications (e.g., WeChat in China, Facebook in much of the rest of the world) as well as specific services such as national ride-hailing options and public transportation. All variables were dichotomized (1 = have done so, 0 = never done so). The second column in Table 5.1 indicates the share of all respondents across countries who have ever engaged in the activity in question.

To explore the relationship between these instrumental uses of the internet, its different users, and their social and cultural contexts, we ran a series of logistic regressions, summarized in Table 5.2. The first step of the regression included gender, age, education, and income as well as their overall contribution to the model (*Nagelkerke R^2*); the second step added countries to the regression. For the *sociodemographic* indicators, the general finding, as expected, is that younger respondents and those with higher levels of education and higher incomes are more likely to engage in instrumental uses of the internet. It is a well-documented pattern that the young, the well-educated, and the more affluent tend to adopt internet services earlier than other sociodemographic segments (e.g., Blank

TABLE 5.1 Instrumental uses of the internet

Instrumental activities (variable names in parentheses)	Share of total respondents (%)
Buying goods or services online (Buy)	87.3
Sending and receiving money (Money)	76.5
Contacting municipal or government offices (State)	63.1
Selling goods or services online (Sell)	55.8
Contacting a doctor or health service (Doctor)	52.1
Keeping track of health, diet, or exercise (Track)	46.3
Booking transportation (Transport)	42.1
Finding a place to live (Live)	41.8
Finding a potential partner (Partner)	20.4
Seeking religious or spiritual guidance (Guidance)	19.9

TABLE 5.2 Logistic regressions of instrumental uses of the internet

	Partner	Live	Track	Buy	Sell	Money	Transport	Doctor	Guidance	State
Gender (ref: Female)	2.048**	1.104*	.889**	.997	1.174**	1.249**	1.195**	.831**	1.261**	1.338**
Age (ref: 18–34)										
35–54 yr	.530**	.568**	.650**	.451**	.671**	.547**	.543**	.940	.685**	1.044
55–74 yr	.240**	.302**	.420**	.314**	.408**	.317**	.325**	.796**	.359**	1.013
Edu (ref: Primary)										
Secondary education	1.373**	1.485**	1.507**	1.891**	1.235**	1.519**	1.654**	1.315**	1.155	1.788**
Tertiary education	1.512**	2.237**	1.944**	3.771**	1.382**	2.509**	3.313**	1.984**	1.321**	3.021**
Income (ref: Below avg)										
About average	1.329**	1.243**	1.408**	1.265**	1.417**	1.143*	1.624**	1.346**	1.416**	1.350**
Above average	1.204*	1.422**	1.610**	1.612**	1.537**	1.518**	2.154**	1.588**	1.364**	1.761**
Nagelkerke R²	*.10*	*.91*	*.07*	*.09*	*.05*	*.08*	*.14*	*.05*	*.06*	*.08*
Country (ref: China)										
Germany	.560**	1.206*	1.203*	3.819**	2.401**	.389**	.271**	1.617**	.574**	2.029**
Denmark	.402**	.674**	.937	1.174	1.504**	1.198	1.423**	7.855**	.432**	9.192**
Hungary	1.140	3.420**	2.229**	2.703**	3.682**	1.432**	1.401**	2.930**	1.420**	4.769**
Italy	.723**	1.095	.926	2.972**	1.614**	.483**	.447**	1.646**	.836	1.808**
UK	.299**	.821*	.581**	3.870**	.875	.376**	.339**	1.773**	.406**	1.623**
US	.467**	.572**	.665**	1.793**	.664**	.175**	.341**	1.735**	1.109	.945
Nagelkerke R²	*.15*	*.17*	*.11*	*.14*	*.13*	*.18*	*.24*	*.14*	*.10*	*.20*

Individual logistic regression with internet activities as outcome variables and sociodemographic and country variables as predictors. Exponentiated beta values shown.

*p <.05.

**p <.01.

& Groselj, 2014). Gender, in comparison, plays a limited role, except for seeking to find a partner, which men appear to engage in online more than women.

It is at the level of *nations and regions* that the most interesting variations emerge. Perhaps surprisingly, the American and British respondents turn to the internet for fewer instrumental uses overall compared to their counterparts both in China (the reference category) and in the five European countries. Germans and Italians do engage in commercial uses (primarily buying things online), but they are less likely to send money or book transportation online. Danes cover most of the activities listed, apart from e-commerce. Indeed, Danes represent an outlier in some respects, that is, a distinctively digital group of respondents. For instance, for State ("Contacting municipal or government offices") – which presents the greatest variation among the seven countries overall – Danes are nine times more likely on average to communicate with public offices than their Chinese counterparts (the reference group). (A different sort of communication with the state – many-to-one (Jensen & Helles, 2017) in the form of surveillance – is not captured by the survey, but is taken up in Chapter 6 and in the concluding Chapter 7.) The Hungarians, like the Danes, represent an outlier (but likely, in part, because the Hungarian sample was skewed; see the Methodological Appendix in Chapter 8).

It is particularly noteworthy that our Chinese respondents do *not* come out as particularly active for commercial uses of the internet. In fact, they are less likely than any other nationality to buy things (except for Danes) and less likely (apart from US and UK nationals) to sell online. Compared to a common public as well as scholarly perception, that internet users in China have widely embraced e-commerce, the present findings offer a reminder that the Chinese population, including a rural segment of around 40% (World Bank, 2021), is still characterized by digital and other divides. The Chinese respondents are relatively more likely, however, to use dating apps (finding a partner), to book transportation, and to send money via the internet.

Alongside country of residence, age proved to be the second key background factor (technically speaking, the exponentiated beta values of these variables contributed most to improving the model, in addition to the 'Doctor' and 'State' variables, for which country, however, was itself the strongest predictor). Therefore, we explored the relationship between age and country further. Instrumental uses of the internet vary across age groups as well as countries, simultaneously and in theoretically interesting patterns (the interactions between these two variables were significant ($p < .01$) for all the instrumental types examined). Put most simply, 'young internet users' do not constitute any coherent global group (nor do middle-aged or older users, for that matter). Figure 5.1 lays out the relationship between country and age for the three most illustrative online activities: Sending and receiving money (Money), buying goods or services online (Buy), and booking transportation (Trans).

In the case of buying things online, almost everyone everywhere has done so – but not so in China, except for the youngest group (below 35 years of age).

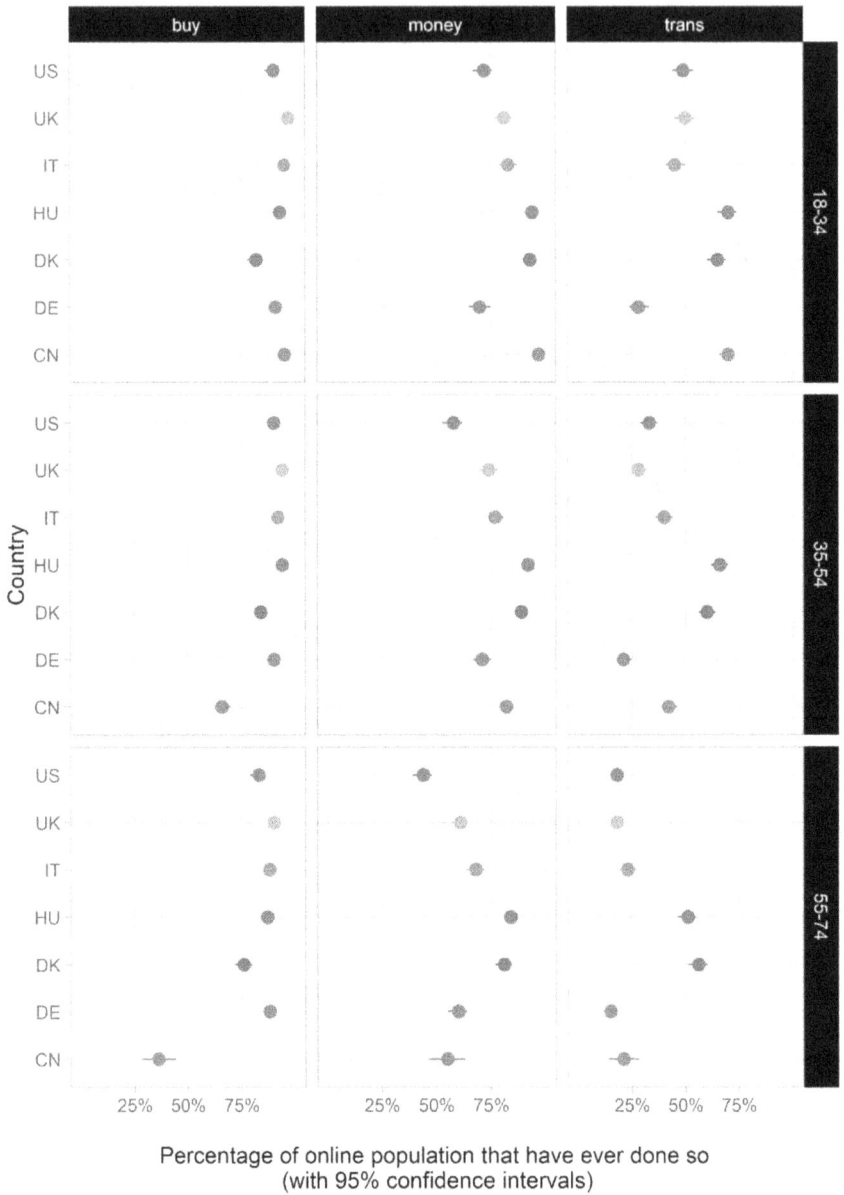

Percentage of online population that have ever done so
(with 95% confidence intervals)

FIGURE 5.1 Interaction between age and country for three instrumental internet activities

And, the older the Chinese respondents, the less likely they are to have bought anything online. In China, then, internet users are split into the young and the old. In Germany, by contrast, age does not entail substantial differences in instrumental uses of the internet. Either Germans across all age groups engage in the activity in question (sending and receiving money), or they do not (booking transportation online). And, for Denmark and Hungary, there is no noticeable age difference for any of the three illustrative instrumental online activities.

As an intermediate conclusion, this first step in analyzing respondents' exercise of (online) agency in different social fields (from buying and selling things to managing everyday logistics) has identified both substantial differences and distinctive similarities, between and within countries. To begin an interpretation of the structural forces circumscribing and the cultural sources informing communicative practices, consider the two extremes of the PIN project: China and Denmark. Their national infrastructures and social institutions, in fact, exhibit important similarities, even if they represent radically different traditions of political and economic governance. In both Denmark and China, as mentioned, internet users very actively send money and book transportation, enabled by high-quality mobile broadband in each setting. To send money, Danes can turn to an entrenched national infrastructure that competes with Silicon Valley alternatives (the native MobilePay vs. Apple Pay); in China, *de facto* monopolies fill this function (AliPay and WeChat Pay). To book transportation in China, Didi Chuxing and other ride-hailing apps get people moving, whereas in Denmark both public and private transportation systems provide popular apps for booking train and bus tickets and hailing rides (but, here, private taxi services like Uber are illegal). On the one hand, then, the internet has entailed convergence: The same mundane, yet essential everyday actions can now be carried out online by Chinese and Danish internet users alike. On the other hand, these and other communicative practices are given quite different and distinctive shapes, respectively, by the institutions of a centralized party state practicing "networked authoritarianism" (MacKinnon, 2011) and by a social welfare state that has invested massively in providing public services online as well as raising the digital literacy of its population (Agency for Digitization, 2016).

Up to a point, then, China and Denmark have made comparable strategic investments into strong and self-reliant national digital infrastructures and services. Both nation-states have taken up roles as "investors of first resort" (Mazzucato, 2018), ensuring variable measures of public control over critical IT infrastructure. These investments have provided a backdrop and an impetus, variously, to private-sector innovation (in Denmark) and to public–private collaboration on steroids (in China), including heavy state involvement in private-sector companies (Chen & Rithmire, 2020), complemented by policies keeping international competition out of the Chinese domestic market, notably in the tech sector.

Of course, both the historical trajectories and current configurations of China and Denmark as (digital) political economies also exhibit marked differences. The

Danish state and Danish society as such have been digital first movers, boasting almost universal internet access (see Table 8.1 in the Methodological Appendix in Chapter 8) and one of the most digitalized public sectors in the world (European Commission, 2019). China, in comparison, has witnessed a much slower process of internet diffusion, having only recently passed the 50% mark (notably not through PCs or laptops, but by mobile-first adoption of the internet), and representing, in addition, a considerable age divide: The older segments of the Chinese population lag well behind the young on most of the instrumental uses of the internet considered here. Moreover, whereas the Chinese party state has promoted especially basic access for the average user (and its own access to citizens through online surveillance), the Danish state has overseen the building of what amounts to a digital welfare state. Danes can, and in some instances must, access public services such as health agencies and tax offices through centralized digital access (the native NemID or "easy ID" system). This comprehensive system explains why, among the various instrumental uses of the internet, Danes are much more likely to book doctor's appointments and to interact with the state online – as digital-first, and sometimes digital-only, services.

Public debate in Denmark, as well, has noted how citizens are, in effect, being monitored through a centralized database of identifiable personal profiles, subject to a networked paternalism different from networked authoritarianism, but nevertheless an offer you cannot refuse; we return to some of the resulting normative issues in Chapter 6. Drawing on the qualitative fieldworks in China, Denmark, and the United States, we next detail some of the situated and localized ways in which people get things done online, as they navigate the internet – and mobilize several different capitals.

Navigating capitals

One common denominator for studies of how new technologies enter into societies and cultures has been the question of meaning: What is the meaning of the internet? In the terminology of Chapter 4, which *affordances* does the internet hold for 'me' or 'us,' at some social scale and in some sense of the word? In terms of agency and capitals, what can and do people *do* with the internet? To render technologies meaningful and relevant in the first place, people must *domesticate* them – make them their own – by embedding devices and applications into their lives and situating themselves in relation to the reconfigured worlds that the technologies mediate. In their landmark study of an American *Middletown* around the beginning of the last century, Robert and Helen Lynd (1929) tracked how a combination of two new (at the time) technologies – radios and cars – had transformed American everyday lives, bringing the wider world into the living room and families out and about beyond their immediate neighborhood. The tradition of domestication research (Silverstone, 2006) has elaborated on the social embedding specifically of information and communication technologies, first with reference to television within households and, since the turn of the millennium, on the internet as a medium and instrument, as well, of distance work, remote learning, and socializing all round (e.g., Bakardjieva & Smith, 2001; Bakardjieva, 2005; Haythornthwaite & Wellman, 2008; Thorhauge & Lomborg, 2016). The internet, in a sense, joins radio and cars in one medium, enabling both observation and interaction at a distance.

The 24-hour communication diaries from the fieldwork in each of the three regions bear witness to the complexities of accomplishing everyday life. To focus analyses and comparisons, we rely in this chapter on a subset of our informants: Young college students in China, Denmark, and the United States (18 out of 76 in total). For one thing, their life circumstances are broadly comparable, defined by similar institutions requiring particular communicative practices that, further, (re)produce different capitals in the long term, as well, for the individual and the collective. For another thing, college students are representatives of the younger segments of national populations, who illustrate the range of potential uses and wider implications of the internet for different professional and personal ends, from micro-coordinating a party with friends, to reserving a study room at the university, to ordering a late-night food delivery in the depths of exam season. As documented in Chapter 3 at a representative scale, the mass and networked communicative practices of our young respondents are remarkably similar across countries and regions; as indicated in Chapter 4, interpersonal communication constitutes another common denominator, across age groups as well as cultures. Here, we probe how different resources, backgrounds, and contexts condition various instrumental uses of the internet in each setting.

In *Copenhagen*, Kirsten, a 23-year-old woman, who shares an apartment with four other people, just finished her bachelor's degree, and is in the process of applying to a master's program. Figure 5.2 suggests her pervasive use of multiple media and applications throughout the day, from a desktop computer and a smartphone to face-to-face interactions, from voice calls and emails to social media (LinkedIn), a music service (Spotify), and a dedicated work portal at her student job. Her communications further crisscross economic (work), social (friends), and cultural (music) spheres, and while physically at her desk at work, from her desktop computer she searches for information about application procedures to various master's programs.

As reviewed in Chapter 2 and illustrated earlier in this chapter, Denmark is one of the most digitalized countries in the world (ITU, 2019), having pursued extensive public digitalization strategies and infrastructure projects over the past several decades. As a result, digital media and communication have become integral parts of public as well as private institutions, from national social services and municipalities to universities, hospitals, and commercial corporations. In the process, individual citizens have been primed, throughout the educational system and in a wide variety of job functions, for adopting diverse digital applications as everyday instruments. Kirsten's day of communication maps onto the institutional infrastructure of this digitalized Denmark. As a morning chore, she pays her rent on her mobile phone through online banking. Arrived at her

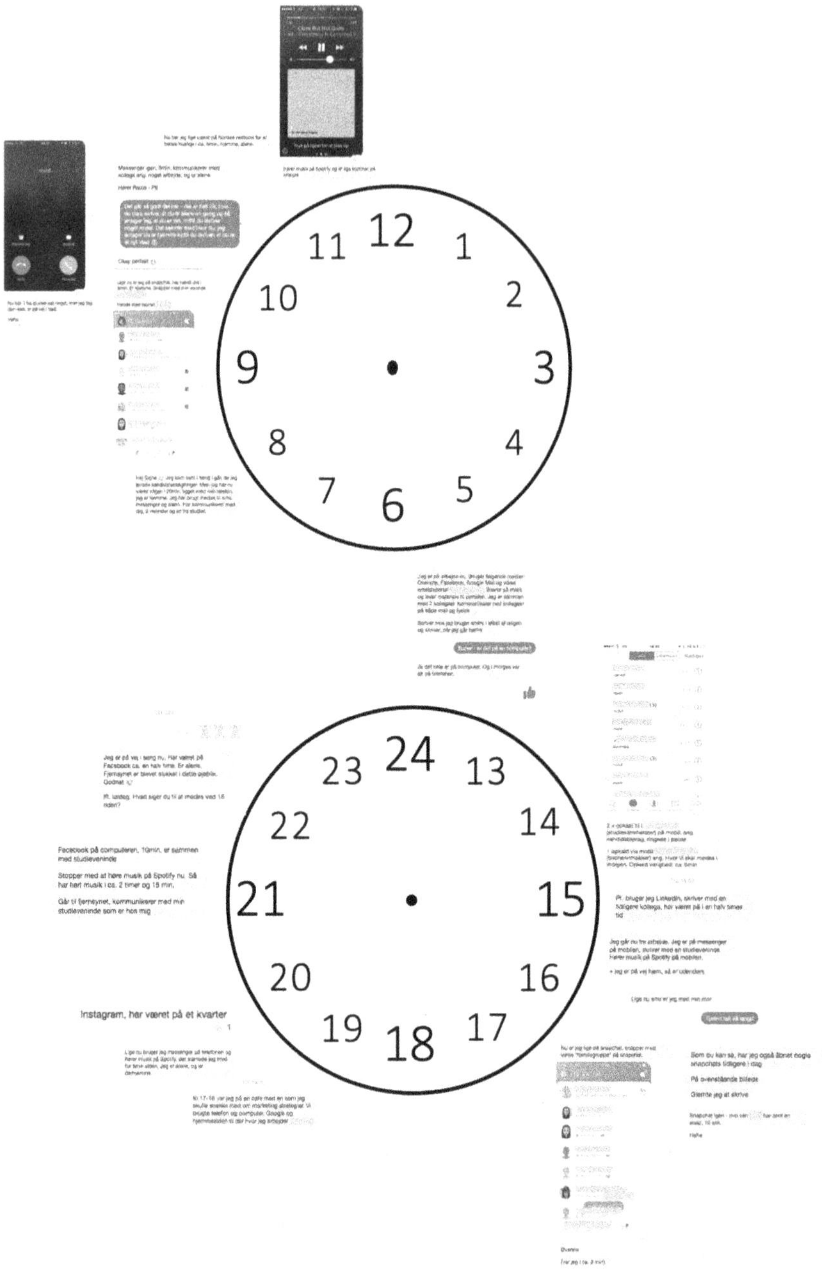

FIGURE 5.2 A day in Kirsten's life with media and communication

place of work, she refers to its (mandatory) communication app to communicate with her boss and colleagues, including setting up a face-to-face meeting later in the day. Blending the spheres of (current) work and (future) education (promising more and [even] better work), Kirsten has sufficient degrees of freedom to search for information on master's programs during working hours. At home again that evening, she turns to her own computer to apply for a newly advertised master's program through the university's online application system.

In *Beijing*, Chun, a 19-year-old woman, recently moved there from a small town in South China to attend university, where she lives in a campus dorm, sharing a room with three other female students. Figure 5.3, while overlapping with Kirsten's day of interacting with her professional and personal relations, highlights two additional and distinctive ways of managing digital and other capitals.

First of all, Chun depends on digital devices and applications both for classes and for her own self-directed learning. In an evening lecture, the professor required Chun and her classmates to perform an experiment via a mobile application, designed to form part of in-class activities. Later the same evening, she used her laptop to access the study materials for her class in Japanese, which had been uploaded by the instructor on an online portal.

Compared to Kirsten, however, Chun comes across as one representative of a mobile-first and, for many, mobile-only nation. Whereas, being a student, she enjoys the comparative privilege of having a laptop, as well, Chun's interactions throughout the day, including for academic matters, are centered in her smartphone and more specifically in WeChat, currently the leading mobile app in China. For instance, her instructor for the course in Japanese had formed a WeChat group for giving out assignments, and as the student assistant in the course, Chun was responsible for administering this function on behalf of the instructor. Also for wider communication and coordination through the internet, WeChat is her indispensable go-between – for keeping in touch with her family back home, chatting with her friends, conferring with her instructor, and clearing household issues with her roommates. WeChat even serves as a digital wallet, in the form of WeChat Pay, by which Chun pays for dinner in the university cafeteria.

Figure 5.4 spells out the place of WeChat in Chun's life in technical terms, accounting for almost half (43%) of battery usage on her phone during the preceding 24 hours. In the follow-up interview (held with all informants after their 24-hour diary-keeping), Chun responded to the invitation to imagine living without the internet for a day by referring specifically to WeChat, and with a hint of panic in her voice:

> Oh no! It will be problematic and extremely inconvenient if I cannot use the internet. I mean, without WeChat, I will be disconnected from the outside world. Worse still, I cannot survive outside of my dorm room. [Because] I feel that I do everything through WeChat: paying for food, using a shared bike, reserving a seat in the university library, ordering a taxi [...]

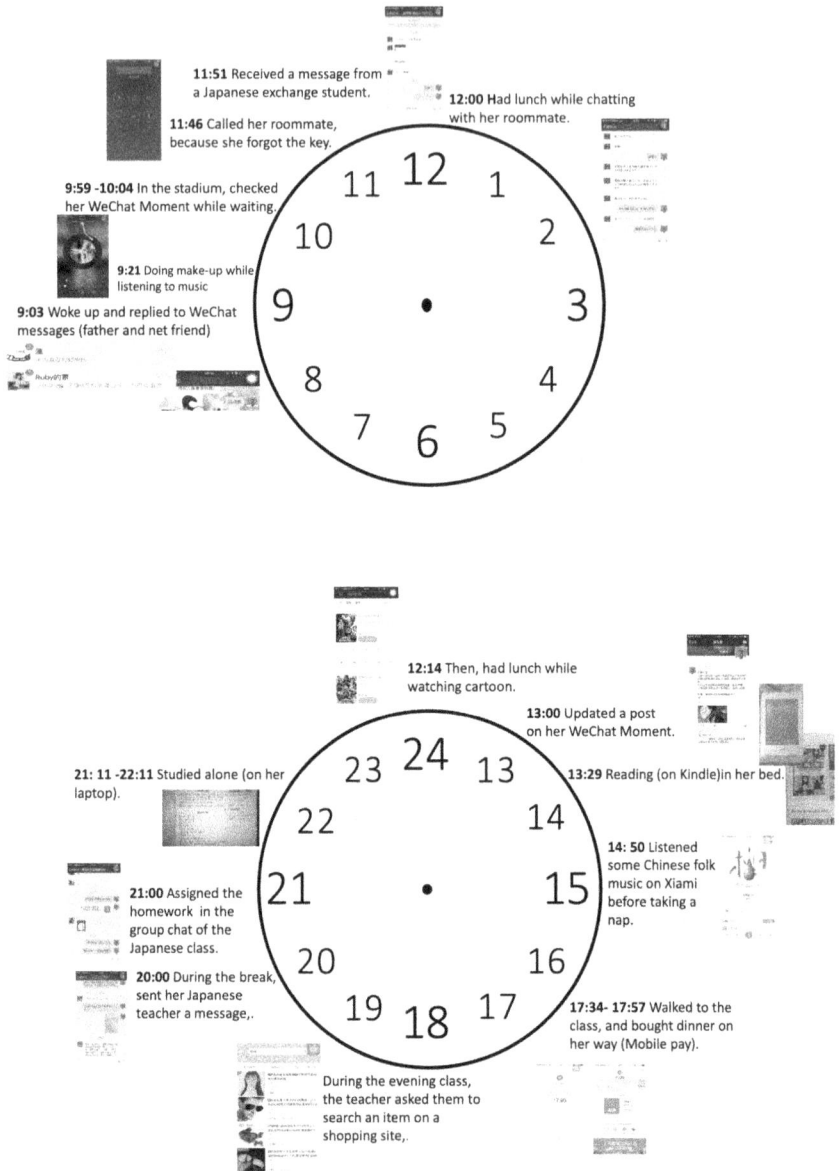

FIGURE 5.3 A day in Chun's life with media and communication

Chun's perspective on the internet might be thought of as that of a WeChat-first or even WeChat-only user.

In *Chicago*, finally, Ryan, a 19-year-old man, also lives in a dorm on campus. His diary (Figure 5.5 – informants were at liberty to choose the format for their diaries, whether screenshots or spreadsheets or other genres) adds further nuance

FIGURE 5.4   24-hour battery consumption on Chun's smartphone

regarding the communicative and other social uses of several different media and applications. Like Chun, Ryan relies on both his mobile phone and his laptop as part of the flow of everyday activities, but without one central and centralizing app. For example, texts, emails, and messenger messages all have their place in his personal communication ecology. His laptop serves as a resource in his social life as a student, as well. And, as noted in Chapter 3, mass communication remains a constitutive element of the lives of the young, including students: Ryan, for one, watches "baseball on tv with friends," and in a break from his studies before turning in after midnight, he relaxes with "web comics."

When it comes to professional and personal relations (and their many hybrids, as in college settings), Ryan's communicative practices point to two categories of interaction that were identified in early mobile communication research (Ling & Yttri, 2002). On the one hand, he stays in close contact with his girlfriend, Kate S. (who studies at another university in a different US state), multiple times throughout the day via Facebook and Snapchat. Personal and expressive, this category of communication recalls the classic fieldwork of Bronislaw Malinowski (1922), who coined the term *phatic* to capture communication primarily to be and stay in touch, to remain social together (the idea was integrated into Jakobson's (1960) classic communication model, which has retained its relevance for digital media and communication).

What	For how long	When	Communicating with	Note
Snapchatting girlfriend	2	9:30 AM	Girlfriend	Just woke up and checked in with the notifications on my phone. - Read and responded to a snapchat text from Katie S. (My girlfriend)
Checking Facebook messages	2	9:32 AM		Read through the few messages that happened in my fb group chat last night
Checking Facebook	2	9:34 AM	Friend (3.3)	Saw a facebook post in my dorm's group page about sports later today
Checking email (same content as above)	2	9:38 AM	Friend (3.3)	Also read an email about the same content
Archiving spam emails	2	9:40 AM		Read some other automated emails I got that I ignored and archived promptly
Texting	3	10:13 AM	Friend	Just texted back and forth about getting brunch with Katie.
Checking Facebook messages	2	11:05 AM		Read messages in the fb messenger group text
Snapchatting girlfriend	2	11:07 AM	Girlfriend	Responded to text from Katie S
Texting	2	11:09 AM	Girlfriend	Opened Snapchat from Katie S
Checking Facebook messages	2	11:36 AM		Briefly looked at messages in fb groupchat, people making plans for lunch, said nothing since I had just come back from lunch with Kelsey.
Texting	3	1:15 PM	Friend (3.3)	Brief texts back and forth with Katie K.
Watching video with friend	4	1:50 PM	Friend	Allie was in the room with me and showed me a video of a dog on Facebook.
Checking Facebook messages	5	1:50 PM		Brief run through of checking fb (liked the post on the top of my news feed but didn't read beyond that) and read the messages in the groupchat.
Archiving spam emails	1	1:55 PM		Also checked my email to archive a promotion about something I didn't care about. This time, those things were done on my laptop.
Watching online lecture	55	12:50 PM		This came after I finished watching lectures online and taking notes both on my laptop 12:55-1:50 (Note that this was interrupted by Katie K and Allie).
Watching YouTube videos with friends	60	1:53 PM	Friends	Am part of a jokey casual acapella group and we used my laptop 2-3 for playing youtube videos to sing over.
Tagging person in Facebook post	3	3:10 PM	Friend (3.3)	Just now. Tagged Katie K in a post on facebook about drinking water.
Google docs	15	3:12 PM	Study group	read and responded to some emails about the study group I lead.
Email	2	5:20 PM		Edited a google doc in prep for a meeting
Texting	2	5:35 PM	Friend (3.3)	and texted Katie K back and forth briefly.
Checking Facebook	2	5:00 PM		Read through some notifications on messenger, groupme, and emails.
Checking GroupMe	2	5:02 PM		Read through some notifications on messenger, groupme, and emails.
Checking emails	2	5:04 PM		Read through some notifications on messenger, groupme, and emails.
Texting	3	5:06 PM	Girlfriend	Another brief text back and forth with Katie S.
Email	2	5:09 PM	Student body	Responded to one email about formally going a student group on wildcatconnection (the northwestern site for clubs).
Googling information	15	5:11 PM		Briefly looked up a nutrition fact about snapple on google
Purchasing on Amazon	5	5:13 PM		and just bought a pair of headphones and a set of mechanical pencils on amazon.
Messaging on Facebook	5	5:49 PM	Friend (3.3)	Just now a brief fb messenger exchange with Katie K.
Fantasy football	5	5:44 PM		looked at my fantasy football lineup.
Checking Facebook	5	5:39 PM		and looked at a post in the dorm facebook group.
Checking Facebook	5	5:34 PM		Also checked the fb page of an environmental organization on campus to see when an event was and used the info to update the google doc I mentioned before.
School work	90	6:00 PM		Used my laptop for 1.5 (6:00-7:30) taking notes and reading off them.
Filling out form	30	7:45 PM	Dorm (as entity)	Submitted points on a google form for my dorm to record that I went to events 7:45-8:15
Checking Facebook	9	7:55 PM		7:55 checked fb
Watching YouTube video	24	8:06 PM		8:06 Watched the darth vader yule log
Filling out questionnaire	11	8:30 PM		8:30 answered a survey over email
Watching sports	10	8:30 PM	Classmates	Watched baseball on tv with friends 8:30-9:00
Snapchatting	5	8:45 PM	Friend (3.3)	Just had an exchange back and forth on snapchat with Katie K.
GroupMe	5	8:50 PM		Also briefly explained something to someone on my floor's group me.
Messaging on Facebook	45	9:10 PM	Friend	9:10-9:15 exchange with beth over fb messenger
Reading	45	9:45 PM		9:45-10:30 did some reading on my laptop and wrote posts and comments on a group forum for the class.
Checking Facebook (about work)	10	9:45 PM		9:45-10:30 did some reading on my laptop and wrote posts and comments on a group forum for the class.
Checking news	1	10:00 PM		Briefly looked some political news at 10:00
Snapchatting girlfriend	1	10:00 PM	Girlfriend	and answered some snapchats from Katie S.
Checking Facebook messages	3	10:06 PM	Friends	and fb messages from the group (worth mentioning the group has 23 people, 10 of whom talk regularly), but that took 5 minutes max.
Preparing for 'work' the following day	105	11:00 PM		11-12:45 prepping for study group I lead tomorrow
Texting	40	12:45 AM		12:45 break looking at webcomics.
Checking Facebook messages	5	12:45 AM	Girlfriend	sent a few texts to Katie S.
Webcomics	5	1:30 AM	Friends	checked facebook group for my dorm
Homework	60	2:00 AM		2:00-3:00 Doing HW on my laptop

FIGURE 5.5   A day in Ryan's life with media and communication

On the other hand, the internet also clearly has a variety of instrumental uses for Ryan, including coordination with friends and dorm mates on multiple social media. He texts back and forth to arrange a brunch, and he checks up on Facebook groups to coordinate activities both in his study group and at his dorm. Predictably, such interactions hold a social side, as well, building more or less strong ties, which may last a lifetime outside of college. Together, the two sides of communication and coordination align with Ling and Yttri's (2002) two categories: *Micro-coordination* takes care of (some of) the many practical details that make a day and a life go round, while *hyper-coordination* adds expressive and emotional dimensions to the communicative mix, obviously in the case of Kate S., Ryan's girlfriend, but also in the case of fellow students such as Kate K., Kevin, and others. With time, the resulting social capitals may translate into economic and cultural ones, as well.

The qualitative snapshots from the lives of Kirsten, Chun, and Ryan illustrate two comparative points concerning the communication systems in which they are each preparing for and anticipating careers and adult lives. First, social institutions such as universities are being pervasively digitalized around the world, requiring students to fit academic and (other) social aspects of their daily lives onto and into the internet (even while offline campus life and good old-fashioned television remain part of the three regional realities). Second, the national and regional infrastructures in which both universities and students are located lend distinctive shape to their situated communicative practices. The Danish digital welfare state, Chinese techno-nationalism, and US big tech circumscribe different ways of being students and becoming professionals, citizens, and more.

Across geographical distances and national borders, however, communicative micro-coordination accomplishes similar and essential tasks of administering and accumulating capitals, recently with digital capital in a bridging function. In Denmark, Kirsten has already acquired the cultural capital associated with a BA degree, which allows her to apply for a master's program, pending online access to more information on the academic contents and job prospects for different options, and requiring digital capital to navigate the application systems of different schools. A master's degree equals (even more) cultural capital equals (most likely) greater economic capital in a better and, perhaps, more intellectually (culturally) rewarding position. Along the way, Kirsten's student job as a social media manager, which she had landed in the first place, in part, because of her studies and BA degree within social science, in addition to helping fund her studies, further leaves her windows at work to invest her digital capital in the production of still more cultural and economic capital. And her present job in a domain with affinities to her formal qualifications likely generates social capital, as well, in the form of networks helpful in securing future positions.

In China, Chun, while still focused on student and campus life, deploys her digital capital, centered in WeChat, not just to participate in and facilitate the course in Japanese, but also to cultivate ties with a Japanese exchange student. Through the ability to converse in a foreign language, she thus accumulates cultural and social capital in tandem, further raising the prospect of later gaining economic capital from some form of employment relating to Japanese language and culture.

In the United States, Ryan's diary, finally, brings home both the quantity and the complexity of the (mostly online) communications that go into maintaining his social ties, from the strong one with his girlfriend to any number of semi-strong to weak ties with college friends and acquaintances, in addition to instructors and the university as an institution. While the cultural and social capitals being accumulated as a result may translate into economic capital down the line, the investments in terms of time and effort are broad, unspecific, and relatively uncertain. And yet, the communicative labor goes with the territory or field, in college as in other life stages and domains of activity. Humans cannot *not* communicate (Watzlawick, Beavin, & Jackson, 1967: 49) as they traverse diverse social fields.

The rest of this chapter returns to a representative scale of analysis, charting the relationship of economic, social, cultural, and digital capitals to different communicative practices, and suggesting how structure and agency come together in everyday problem solving. The opening analysis of selected instrumental uses of the internet focused on concrete communicative events or actions. The thick descriptions (Geertz, 1973), next, of the interplay of economic, social, cultural, and digital capitals in the student lives of a modern institutional setting, shared across political economies and cultural traditions, have begun to unearth some of the mechanisms enabling and constraining particular communicative practices. The following sections join the two perspectives – on communicative agency and conditioning structures, respectively – by asking what kinds of things people do with what kinds of media, in response to which personal and public trajectories, choices, and dilemmas.

Mapping capitals

Compared to the delimited instrumental uses of the internet, another section of the PIN surveys asked, more broadly, how respondents would access information and interact with others about five different aspects of their lives:

- finding information about job openings
- buying a new mobile phone
- verifying controversial information about a politician
- seeking guidance on a moral dilemma
- diagnosing an unknown illness.

While different practical and potentially problematic situations (Dewey, 1903) might have been chosen, respondents could be expected, across sociodemographic segments and national and regional settings, to want to know and communicate about each of these instances, in a recognizable context and relevant time frame. In a Bourdieusian perspective, moreover, the five questions addressed a range of social fields that practically any individual must navigate, occupying diverse roles as an employee or other economic agent, a consumer, a citizen, a moral agent, and a biological organism that lives and dies. To varying degrees and in variable combinations, economic, social, cultural, and digital capitals will condition communications about these roles and their existential consequences – for the individual's agency, survival, life quality, self-respect, and self-realization.

For each situation of problem solving, respondents were asked to indicate the different types (one or more) from a list of potential sources of information and communication that they would be most likely to turn to. The options covered four broad categories with additional specifications for each field or topic:

- traditional channels, typically with a physical location and involving face-to-face interaction (e.g., job agencies, doctors and hospitals, mobile phone shops)
- social networks (e.g., partners, friends, families, colleagues)
- legacy or established media institutions (e.g., newspapers, television, radio)
- internet (e.g., search engines, social media, specialist websites)

Extending the statistical analyses in Chapters 3 and 4, we first relied on multiple correspondence analysis (MCA). This is similar to the method used by Bourdieu (1984/1979) in his classic study of social differences and cultural distinctions in France, and we went on to conduct so-called ascending hierarchical cluster analysis (AHC) and multiple factor analysis for contingency tables (MFACT) to explore current digital communication systems (see further Leguina & Downey, 2021). These approaches, in combination, provided a robust framework for comparing communicative practices and user profiles across the seven national samples; we identified five clusters of respondents with consistent configurations of communicative practices and roughly similar sizes across countries. Table 5.3 first summarizes the distribution of these clusters in the seven countries.

To begin from the five different profiles, the largest cluster across all seven countries was labeled Traditionalist (in the United Kingdom, the Mostly Internet cluster is about the same size). Traditionalists make relatively limited use of all sources, and have no preference for any one particular source, except when it comes to strategies associated with solving specific problems (e.g., going to a store to ask about mobile phones, calling a doctor or hospital in case of illness). A second and much smaller cluster,

TABLE 5.3 Clusters of communicative practices for everyday problem solving (%)

Cluster label	China	Germany	Denmark	Hungary	Italy	UK	US
Traditionalist	40.8	43.5	30.9	37.8	35.6	27.7	39.2
Omnivore	12.5	6.1	7.1	10.9	10.9	7.8	9.8
Mostly Internet	22.0	31.6	17.4	29.1	25.5	27.9	24.3
Social Connection	24.8	18.9	21.1	22.2	28.0	14.2	26.8
Limited Resources	–	–	23.4	–	–	22.4	–

labeled Omnivores, in contrast, embraces a wide range of sources, combining traditional channels, social networks, legacy media, and the internet regardless of the issue requiring resolution. Two further clusters, both of substantial, if varied sizes, each have a more exclusive focus. On the one hand, Mostly Internet respondents will consult, in particular, specialist websites, review websites, search engines, and social media. On the other hand, Social Connection respondents will rely on their personal contacts to resolve everyday problems, asking friends, family, and colleagues for advice rather than referring to more established media and sources. In Denmark and the United Kingdom, a fifth cluster – Limited Resources – emerged. Whereas respondents in this formation mostly depend on their personal contacts, they make some limited use of websites, and otherwise turn to traditional sources for specific issues such as looking for a job, diagnosing an illness, and verifying controversial information.

Before we center on the relationship between these clusters and different kinds of capital, Figures 5.6–5.12 visualize the distribution of the full range of

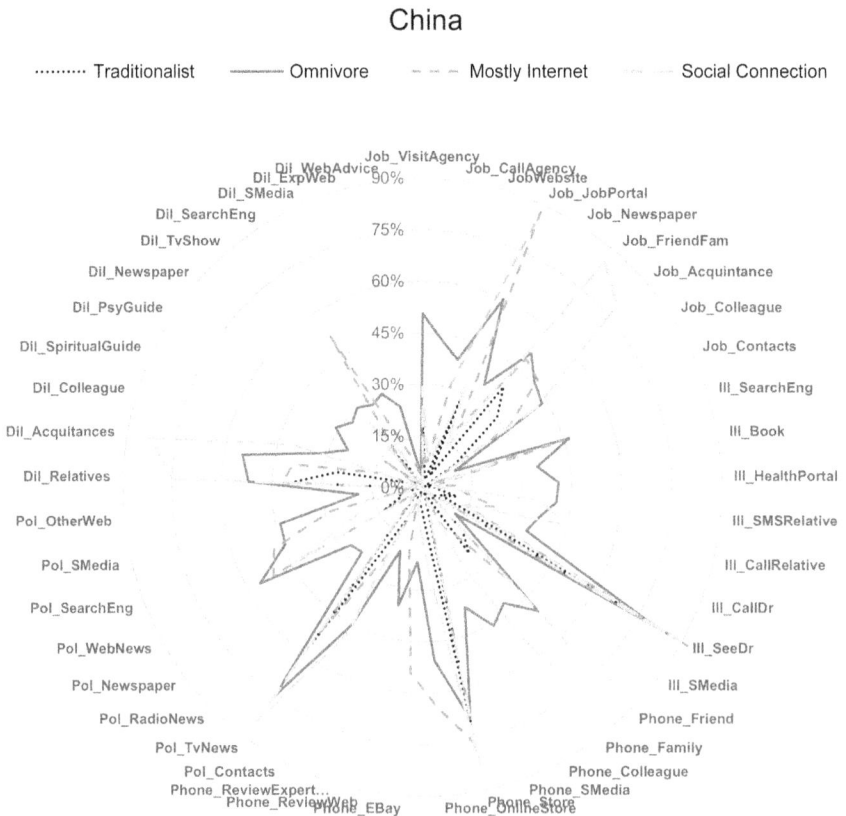

FIGURE 5.6   Information seeking for everyday problem solving, China. *Note*: Job: Finding information about job openings; Ill: Diagnosing an unknown illness; Phone: Buying a new mobile phone; Pol: Verifying controversial information about a politician; Dil: Seeking guidance on a moral dilemma

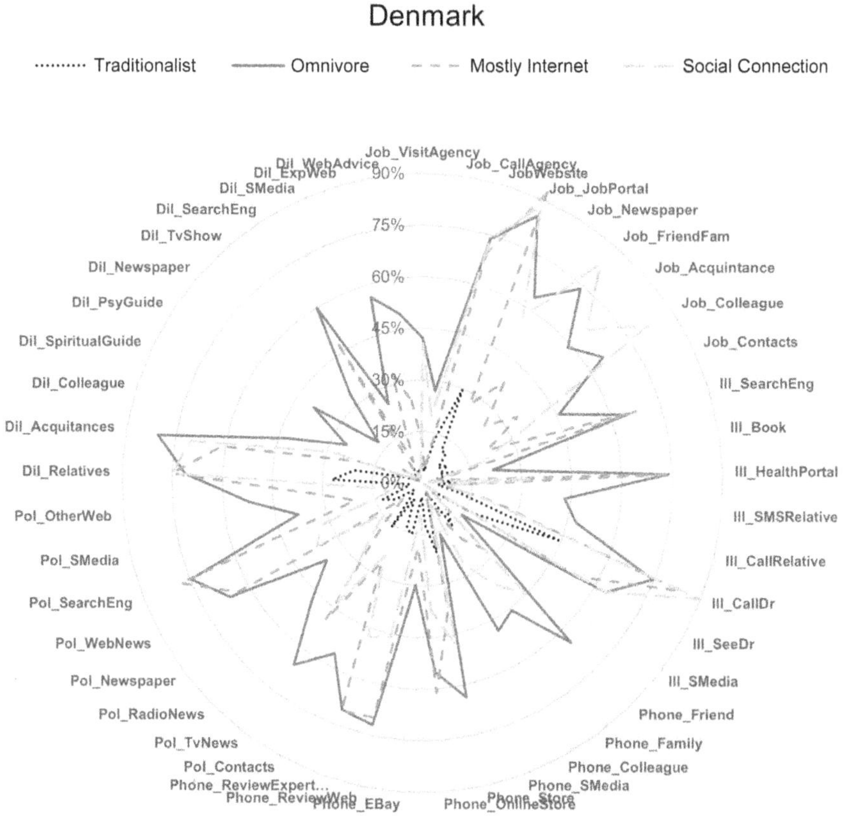

Denmark

········· Traditionalist   ——— Omnivore   – – – Mostly Internet   —— Social Connection

FIGURE 5.7   Information seeking for everyday problem solving, Denmark. *Note:* Job: Finding information about job openings; Ill: Diagnosing an unknown illness; Phone: Buying a new mobile phone; Pol: Verifying controversial information about a politician; Dil: Seeking guidance on a moral dilemma

information-seeking strategies for problem solving, across the five clusters, for each of the seven countries. In overview, a central finding is that the Omnivore clusters are very similar across countries. Indicated by solid lines in the figures, their members have the highest (or near highest) rates of engagement for all practices of information seeking. In particular, Omnivores stand out through their reliance on social media in combination with more official or traditional channels (e.g., job agencies, doctors and hospitals, mobile phone shops). The most noticeable exception is China, where Omnivores, similar to other clusters, appear relatively restricted in terms of access to strategies and resources both for resolving personal issues relating to health issues or moral dilemmas, and for clearing up controversial political information.

A key contrast to Omnivores, again across the seven countries, is represented by the Mostly Internet clusters (indicated by dark dashed lines). Mostly Internet

Germany

·········· Traditionalist ──────── Omnivore ─ ─ ─ Mostly Internet Social Connection

FIGURE 5.8 Information seeking for everyday problem solving, Germany. *Note*: Job: Finding information about job openings; Ill: Diagnosing an unknown illness; Phone: Buying a new mobile phone; Pol: Verifying controversial information about a politician; Dil: Seeking guidance on a moral dilemma

respondents will turn to search engines and specialist websites to solve everyday problems, perhaps as a way of compensating, in part, for limited access to other resources for problem solving. In comparison, the Traditionalist (indicated by dotted lines) and Social Connection (light dashed lines) clusters are more heterogeneous in their information-seeking practices. For example, while Traditionalists in China and the United States tend to rely, literally, on traditional or official channels for health problems and when buying mobile phones, in Hungary and Italy the Traditionalist clusters rather make use of websites and search engines for job hunting, health issues, and moral dilemmas. Similarly mixed strategies are illustrated by the Social Connection cluster in the United Kingdom, whereas in Italy Social Connectionists will turn to personal contacts if looking for a job, and to spiritual guides to resolve moral dilemmas.

Hungary

·········· Traditionalist   ——— Omnivore   – – – Mostly Internet   — — Social Connection

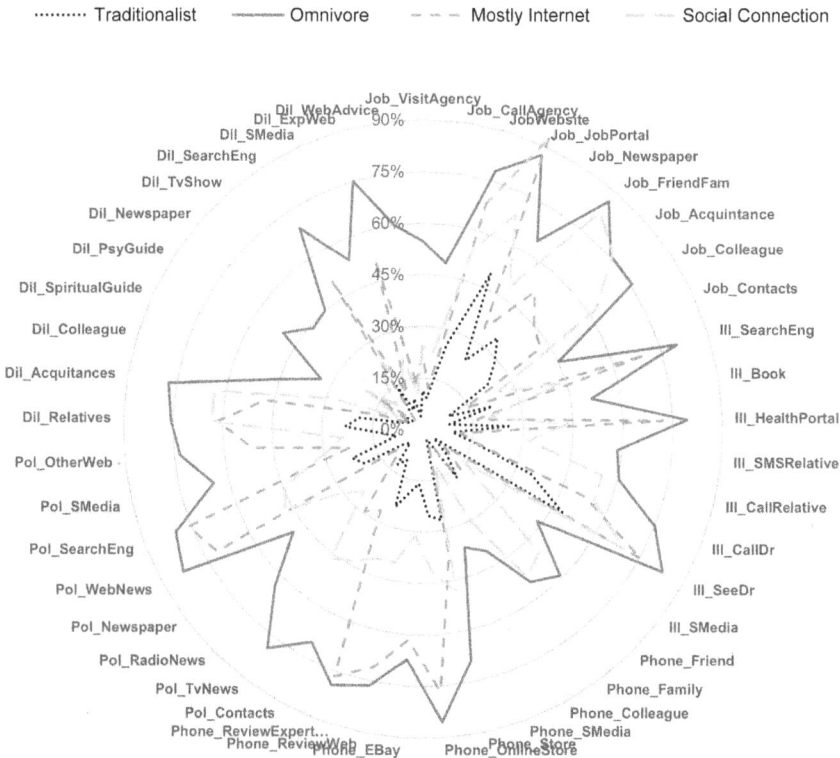

FIGURE 5.9   Information seeking for everyday problem solving, Hungary. *Note*: Job: Finding information about job openings; Ill: Diagnosing an unknown illness; Phone: Buying a new mobile phone; Pol: Verifying controversial information about a politician; Dil: Seeking guidance on a moral dilemma

We went on to relate the problem-solving clusters to the different forms of capital that their members command, noting variations both within and between countries. To operationalize and measure different capitals, we developed a metric from the following variables (for each country separately):

- **Economic capital**: Income (a lot above average, slightly above average, similar to the average, slightly below average, a lot below average), occupational class (service [professional, higher administrative and higher managerial occupations], intermediate [clerical and sales occupations], skilled and unskilled worker [skilled, semi-skilled, unskilled occupations, and farmworkers], non-labor [student and other occupations]).
- **Cultural capital**: Education (primary, lower secondary, upper secondary, vocational, bachelor's degree, master's degree, or above), parental education (same categories)

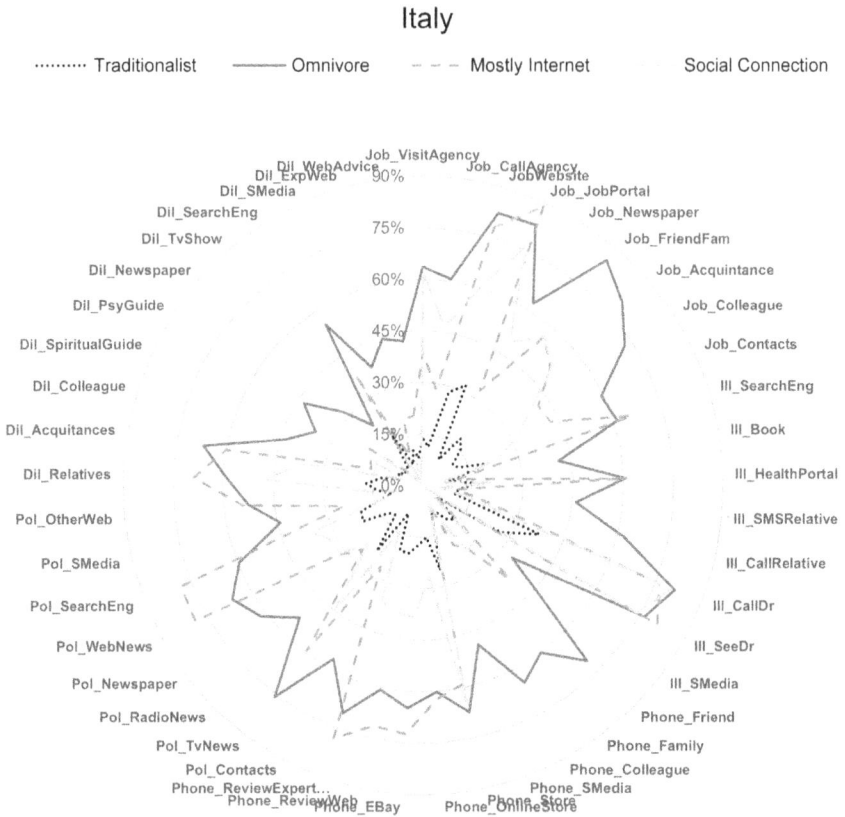

FIGURE 5.10 Information seeking for everyday problem solving, Italy. *Note*: Job: Finding information about job openings; Ill: Diagnosing an unknown illness; Phone: Buying a new mobile phone; Pol: Verifying controversial information about a politician; Dil: Seeking guidance on a moral dilemma

- **Social capital**: Membership in cultural, sports, religious, political, civil, and community organizations (none, one, two, or more), feeling connected to local community (no, weak connection, strong connection), feeling connected to ethnic/national group (same categories), feeling connected to religious/spiritual group (same categories)
- **Digital capital**: First time internet was used by respondent (5 or less years ago, 5–10 years ago, 11–20 years ago, more than 20 years ago), number of devices used to go online (1 or less, 2, 3, 4, 5, or more), using internet for work (regularly, frequently, rarely), using internet for practical purposes (regularly, frequently, rarely)

Through multiple correspondence analyses (MCA), we produced a single measure for each type of capital (Le Roux & Rouanet, 2004), effectively sorting

United Kingdom

········· Traditionalist ———— Omnivore – – – Mostly Internet ———— Social Connection

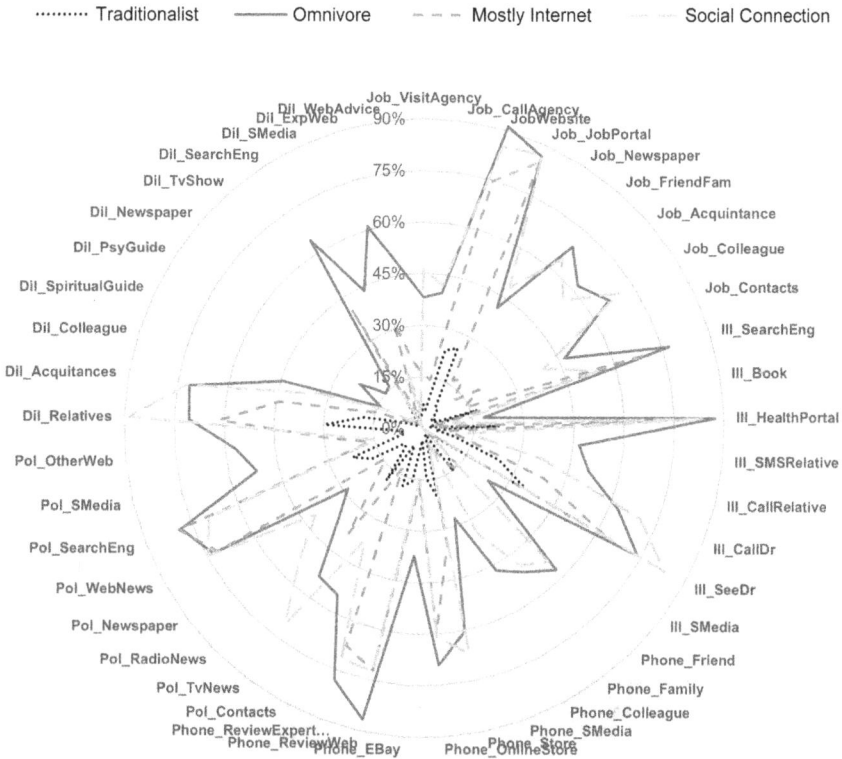

FIGURE 5.11 Information seeking for everyday problem solving, the United Kingdom. *Note*: Job: Finding information about job openings; Ill: Diagnosing an unknown illness; Phone: Buying a new mobile phone; Pol: Verifying controversial information about a politician; Dil: Seeking guidance on a moral dilemma

respondents from the lowest to the highest volumes of capital, and dividing each ranking into three levels of roughly equal sizes: Low (lower 33%), mid, and high (upper 33%) capital possession. And, in order to assess the over- and underrepresentation of individuals with different levels of capitals in each cluster, we performed a multinomial logistic regression (Agresti, 2013). In addition, the analysis noted standard sociodemographic background variables: age (18–34, 35–54, 55–74), gender (male, female), country (China, Germany, Denmark, Hungary, Italy, United Kingdom, and United States), place of residence (city, village/town), citizenship (local, other/multiple), and mastery of English (yes, no). (To allow for comparison not just within, but between countries, the Limited Resources cluster that was found only in Denmark and the United Kingdom was excluded from the following analyses.)

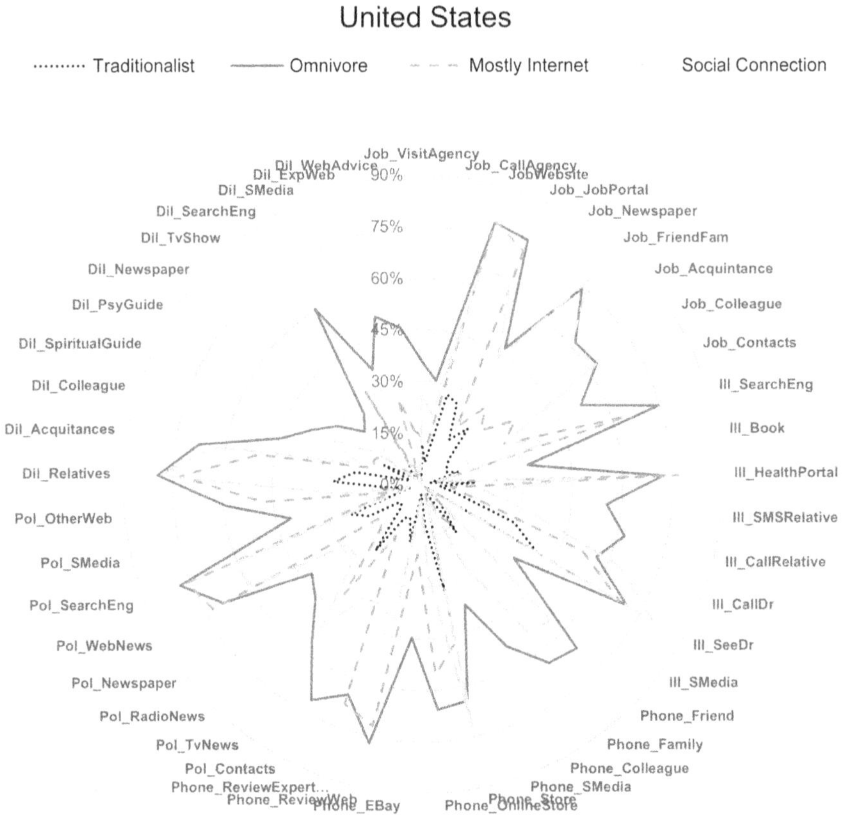

United States

FIGURE 5.12   Information seeking for everyday problem solving, the United States. *Note*: Job: Finding information about job openings; Ill: Diagnosing an unknown illness; Phone: Buying a new mobile phone; Pol: Verifying controversial information about a politician; Dil: Seeking guidance on a moral dilemma

Table 5.4 first relates the four forms of capital to the clusters of information-seeking and problem-solving strategies (i.e., the full set of clusters for each country). Given the mundane nature of everyday problem solving, it is not surprising that people's economic and, to a degree, also their cultural capital has a relatively modest influence on their communicative strategies (as expressed in comparatively low contingency coefficients in the table). Nonetheless, on both counts the influence is statistically significant, and the variations between countries are in line with the underlying structural mechanisms – political economies and technological infrastructures – outlined in Chapter 2 and illustrated in the qualitative accounts of students navigating the internet in China, Denmark, and the United States. For China in particular, Table 5.4 indicates that higher volumes of economic and cultural capital make more of a difference for respondents'

TABLE 5.4 Contingency coefficients for capital volume and clusters per country

Capital	China	Denmark	Germany	Hungary	Italy	UK	US
Economic	.211	.148	.147	.094	.087 (ns.)	.139	.178
Cultural	.289	.162	.108	.119	.125	.193	.191
Social	.259	.176	.219	.147	.179	.189	.222
Digital	.385	.376	.342	.232	.318	.391	.342

Note: All findings statistically significant at 95% unless noted (two-sided chi-squared test); ns., non-significant.

communicative strategies than in the other six countries. In addition to relatively lower internet penetration, alongside growing income and educational inequalities (Wu, 2019; Zou, 2015), this pattern is most likely explained by restrictions on access to and social uses of information in China. In other words, less informational and interactional freedom entails more polarization of citizens' potential communicative agency. In the United States and the United Kingdom, as well, despite greater communication freedoms and higher internet penetration rates, cultural capital has a stronger influence on problem-solving strategies than in the remaining Western countries, although less so than in China. Previous research confirms that, in developed countries with greater economic inequalities, such as the United States and the United Kingdom, also educational attainment has become more unequally distributed (Dorling & Tomlinson, 2016), so that cultural capital acquires a defining role in whether and how people seek information and solve problems. In contrast and by the same logic, in Denmark and Germany, both more egalitarian societies, while comparable to the United States and the United Kingdom for economic capital, people's communicative agency is less likely to be conditioned by (a lack of) cultural capital.

It is, however, the distribution of social and digital capitals that speaks most directly to differences and divides in communicative agency, both within and among the seven countries. Indeed, it is these findings that hold the most far-reaching implications, for theory as well as policy, since these are the capitals that facilitate access, most basically, to the comparative advantage that is associated with connectivity, as well as to a contemporary world without, in principle, economic, cultural, and other borders of any kind.

Regarding *social* capital, first, Table 5.5 bears out the great advantage of the Omnivore segment: High social capital goes together with more diverse information-seeking and problem-solving strategies (in the West, but at first glance not in China). Also the Social Connection segment has a substantial proportion of respondents with the highest level of social capital, across countries and regions, which follows logically from the centrality of personal contacts in their communicative strategies. Both of these segments will benefit from the 'bridging' function of social capital in securing other advantages, for example, through access to colleagues and other acquaintances for finding a new job, and to relatives when seeking to resolve a moral dilemma (see, further, Mowbray et al., 2018; Vitak and

TABLE 5.5 High social capital (top 33%) across clusters

Cluster label	High social capital (%)						
	China	*Germany*	*Denmark*	*Hungary*	*Italy*	*UK*	*US*
Traditionalist	35.5	23.6	27.8	30.5	32.8	25.3	23.0
Omnivore	8.4	66.3	59.8	50.6	52.1	49.2	48.0
Mostly Internet	29.0	33.4	35.6	29.5	32.3	27.1	28.3
Social Connection	26.7	36.0	34.4	39.7	26.2	46.7	40.6

TABLE 5.6 High digital capital (top 33%) across clusters

Cluster label	High digital capital (%)						
	China	*Germany*	*Denmark*	*Hungary*	*Italy*	*UK*	*US*
Traditionalist	15.8	50.8	14.7	23.9	21.3	15.2	17.3
Omnivore	54.0	26.1	50.5	45.1	49.7	51.6	53.4
Mostly Internet	54.4	22.8	53.4	43.6	46.3	49.9	48.1
Social Connection	32.2	14.3	42.2	30.7	29.2	45.9	36.2

Ellison, 2013). More surprisingly perhaps, the Traditionalist clusters hold a rather large percentage of respondents with the highest level of social capital; in China and Italy, the proportion is even greater than for the Social Connection cluster. Whereas Traditionalists are characterized by their limited range of information-seeking strategies, the finding is, in fact, in line with a primary reliance among Traditionalists on close social relations, and in the case of China specifically with a culture of *guanxi* (Qi, 2013): Figure 5.2 highlighted the importance of family and friends here in finding a job and talking about moral dilemmas. Chapter 4, further, noted a number of similarities between our Chinese and Italian respondents in terms of both the quantity and the quality of their interpersonal communication. Most striking, however, is the finding that, in China, the Omnivore cluster comes out with a very low level of social capital. Even if economic and cultural capitals may trump social capital in the Chinese context, the likely explanation is that the present social-capital metric does not capture well specific forms of public and private engagement against the background of Chinese history and culture (Li, 2013). We return, in the concluding chapter, to the challenges of developing comparative frameworks for studying communication systems that are, at once, cross-culturally sensitive and empirically operational.

Regarding *digital* capital, next, Table 5.6 indicates a clear pattern with the Mostly Internet and Omnivore clusters representing the highest level of digital capital: More diverse and more digital communication, unsurprisingly, goes together with more digital capital. The one exception is Germany, where Traditionalists represent the cluster with the largest proportion of respondents with the highest digital capital. Similar to Traditionalists in China and Italy for social capital, their German counterparts can be seen to only turn to the internet for dedicated purposes such as buying a new mobile phone from an online marketplace and finding job openings via job portals (as also borne out by Figure 5.8). The Social Connection clusters present further complications, particularly in Denmark and the United Kingdom, where this segment has a distinctively large proportion of respondents with the highest digital capital, compared to the other five countries representing all three regions of the present study. In contrast to German Traditionalists, Danish and British Social Connectionists rely on the internet for multiple purposes and at rates that are close to the Omnivore and Mostly Internet segments (as detailed in Figures 5.7 and 5.11). These complications serve as reminders, both that capitals interact, in part through bridging mechanisms, and that capitals constitute dispositions, not direct causes of actual communicative practices. As another intermediate conclusion, it is plausible that the complications relating specifically to digital capital bear witness to a historical situation in which ordinary users of the internet, like entrepreneurs and regulators, are still in the process of negotiating the ground rules for its potential and appropriate social uses.

As a final step in the analysis of capitals and communications, within and across the seven countries and three regions, we related both capitals and standard sociodemographic background variables to the different clusters of communicative agency through a multinomial regression model. The findings are laid out in Table 5.7. In technical terms, the model indicates the extent to which

TABLE 5.7 Multinomial regression of clusters according to sociodemographic features and capital volume (reference category: Traditionalists)

Exp(B) (Standard error)		Omnivore	Mostly Internet	Social Connection
Sex (ref: Male)	Female	1.065 (0.074)	1.063 (0.052)	1.185 (0.053)★★
Age (ref: 35–54)	18–34	1.297 (0.085)★★	1.036 (0.065)	0.918 (0.068)
	55–75	0.644 (0.099)★★★	0.964 (0.063)	1.028 (0.064)
Country (ref: UK)	CN	1.512 (0.171)★	1.147 (0.123)	2.601 (0.130)★★★
	DE	0.582 (0.160)★★★	1.020 (0.098)	1.142 (0.113)
	DK	0.868 (0.154)	0.676 (0.108)★★★	1.590 (0.113)★★★
	HU	1.309 (0.152)	1.285 (0.106)★	1.837 (0.118)★★★
	IT	1.442 (0.151)★	1.139 (0.107)	2.474 (0.115)★★★
	US	0.891 (0.141)	0.629 (0.098)★★★	1.324 (0.105)★★
Place (ref: Village/town)	City	1.422 (0.075)★★★	1.081 (0.054)	1.079 (0.055)
Citizenship (ref: Other/ multiple)	Local	1.148 (0.153)	1.672 (0.118)★★★	1.699 (0.127)★★★
Speak English	Yes	1.536 (0.103)★★★	2.304 (0.072)★★★	2.221 (0.074)★★★
Economic capital (ref: Mid)	Low	1.242 (0.091)★	1.016 (0.063)	0.918 (0.064)
	High	1.346 (0.093)★★	1.249 (0.066)★★★	1.320 (0.068)★★★
Cultural capital (ref: Mid)	Low	0.973 (0.097)	0.867 (0.067)★	1.059 (0.066)
	High	1.216 (0.091)★	1.252 (0.065)★★★	1.106 (0.068)
Social capital (ref: Mid)	Low	1.054 (0.095)	1.040 (0.062)	1.007 (0.064)
	High	2.071 (0.089)★★★	1.104 (0.064)	1.328 (0.065)★★★
Digital capital (ref: Mid)	Low	0.422 (0.099)★★★	0.402 (0.066)★★★	0.615 (0.063)★★★
	High	1.762 (0.087)★★★	1.485 (0.063)★★★	1.111 (0.068)

★Significant at $p = .05$. ★★Significant at $p = .01$. ★★★Significant at $p = .001$.
Log likelihood = 19010,141, pseudo-R^2 = 0.134, n = 10086.

differences in capital distribution and sociodemographic characteristics predict respondents' membership in a particular cluster; all variables have statistically significant effects.

In overview, younger respondents are more likely to belong to the Omnivore cluster, and female respondents to the Social Connection cluster, whose members, in turn, are likely to be younger than the Traditionalist cluster (our reference category). For country of residence, respondents belonging to the Omnivore cluster are more likely to be found in China and Italy than in the United Kingdom; Social Connectionists are more likely to be found anywhere but the United Kingdom and Germany; and Omnivores are more likely to live in cities. As expected, Traditionalists are the least likely to speak English, suggesting an affinity between level or breadth of education and a diversity of communicative strategies.

Pieces are falling into place as part of a global digital puzzle carried over from Chapters 3 and 4, which includes: privileged segments, across the three regions, of relatively more urban, globally oriented, young, omnivore media users and communicators; China and Italy as national backgrounds to distinctively expressive and engaging personal networkers; and women filling traditional roles as communicative caretakers for the social ties that really bind. At the same time, further complications are being added: Both the Mostly Internet and Social Connection clusters are more likely to have local citizenships (i.e., not dual) than our reference category, the Traditionalists. As digital capitals are being accumulated and configured in different national and cultural settings, it pays to still follow the money – the totality of capitals, their interactions, and their translation into communicative agency by people doing things with media.

In review, the Omnivore and Mostly Internet clusters command greater *cultural* capital than the other two clusters (as well as the fifth cluster found only in Denmark and the United Kingdom). Similarly, the Omnivore, Mostly Internet, and Social Connection clusters all hold higher levels of *economic* capital than the Traditionalists. To be sure, Omnivore respondents are also more likely to *temporarily* have lower economic capital at their disposal, being composed to a significant degree of young people (Table 5.7). With time, however, this subgroup will be in a position to transform their above-average cultural, social, and digital capitals into economic and other advantages through more versatile problem-solving strategies, in a life-long perspective, but also as they are being educated and socialized. Most significantly in comparative perspective, different historical legacies – and fundamental divides – emerge in the concrete communicative practices by which people manage their lives on a daily basis. To one side, in more egalitarian societies like Denmark and Germany, and despite differences in capital distributions here, as well, Omnivores are not alone in exercising more versatile forms of communicative agency; also the Mostly Internet and Social Connection clusters here more commonly rely on a range of sources comprising both online and personal relations (see Figures 5.7 and 5.8). To the other side, in China (Figure 5.6) and Hungary (Figure 5.9) (and to a lesser extent in Italy, the United Kingdom, and the United States), Omnivores can be seen to *de facto* monopolize certain communicative strategies covering both personal relations and legacy as well as social media. On a systemic and regional scale, not just *people*, but *peoples* are divided by communications and the capitals they carry and maintain.

Social and digital capitals, lastly, work in complementary ways in enabling communicative agency, as part of an ongoing digital reconfiguration of social interactions writ large. Whereas respondents in both the Omnivore and the Social Connection clusters are more likely to command high *social* capital, the Mostly Internet respondents do not differ markedly on this count from the Traditionalists (Table 5.7). A disposition toward online interaction, then, may neither replace nor equal traditional interactions as resources for accumulating and benefiting from social capital. Predictably, respondents from the Omnivore and Mostly Internet clusters both exhibit high levels of *digital* capital, which, in turn, feeds diverse digital communicative strategies (Table 5.7). As previously noted, however, the two groups approach the internet in distinctive ways, with Omnivores focusing on social media, Mostly Internets on specialist websites. The same volume or quantity of digital capital, thus, translates into different qualities of communication and, hence, different social uses of the internet, at least in the current stage of its embedding and consolidation.

Summary of findings

This chapter has examined the structural conditions and consequences of exercising communicative agency, across widely distributed contexts of social interaction and against the background of distinctive cultural and historical legacies. Relying on the theoretical framework of Pierre Bourdieu addressing economic, social, and cultural forms of capital, and adding the category of digital capital, we examined prototypical sets of everyday tasks and choices, their enactment in current communication systems, and the communication repertoires that different sociodemographic segments rely on as they do things with media. We conclude that, across these diverse national settings and regions of the world, people will do different things with different media, but in comparable ways, depending on their access to and command of different qualities and quantities of capitals. Even if economic and cultural capitals are not as strongly associated, in the quantitative terms of the surveys, with the clusters of communicative profiles as the social and digital capitals are, we identified characteristic patterns of utilizing and converting capitals that enable and enhance everyday information seeking and problem solving, in minimal acts of communication here and now, and which, over biographical and historical time, can be expected to reproduce and exacerbate multiple forms and levels of inequality within contemporary societies. Insights from the fieldworks in the three different world regions added qualitative grounding of and nuance to the mechanisms of capitalization which could be seen to operate not only across regions, but across social classes, as well, throughout public and private as well as economic, political, and cultural spheres of human existence.

Digital capital occupies a special bridging position in the ongoing global transformation of communication systems and their social uses. It supports the exercise of more substantial and diverse forms of communicative agency, privileging already advantaged individuals and allowing them to reap the benefits of their economic, cultural, and social capitals with comparative advantage. In this bridging role, importantly, digital capital resembles, overlaps with, but also differs from social capital. Whereas people may reach out to (potential) social relations and networks both offline and online, the present findings suggest that particularly younger respondents with more digital capital can compensate for relatively less economic and cultural capital through the exercise of a more diverse communicative agency. At the same time, several of the variations noted in this respect, for example, between otherwise comparable countries, hold the further implication that practices and conventions of how to attend to and administer one's social capital across the online and offline domains are still under construction and negotiation. By the same token, the relative roles of digital and social capital in maintaining or growing one's economic and cultural capitals appear likely to change, as well, as digitalization works out its incremental effects on human agency and social structure.

Like everyday communicative practices, theoretical frameworks and methodological designs remain subject to revision. Capitals and clusters correlate in the present analyses, to a significant degree, as one would expect from the interplay of social structures (or capitals) and human agency (or habitus, instantiated in particular problem-solving strategies). The global picture emerging is of a spectrum extending from relatively privileged and young Omnivores to less privileged and older Traditionalists, with variations and complications across the Social Connectionist and Mostly Internet segments, as well (and a Limited Resources segment beyond the spectrum). The findings, further, point to some gender-specific communicative strategies as well as some nationally distinctive communicative styles, as in the case of China and Italy, and as elaborated in Chapter 4. Most evidently, China represents not only a unique configuration of regulatory regime and cultural tradition, but a separate social field of sorts, which the present conceptual and analytical repertoires only partially capture. Social capital, at least in the case of China, may relate to economic, cultural, as well as digital capitals in ways that call not just for repeated empirical studies, but also for more sustained theory development on the mediating role of communication, across social fields and the offline as well as online domains. Before addressing this long-term challenge for media and communication research in the concluding chapter, we turn in the following chapter to additional forms of human capital that are being harvested as people do more with media than they might have thought.

6

WHAT MEDIA STILL DO TO PEOPLE

Rasmus Helles, Stine Lomborg, and Signe Sophus Lai

Tracking the trackers

In January 2020, Alphabet – the parent company of the Google family of internet applications – announced that its Chrome web browser would be abandoning the use of so-called *third-party cookies* tracking what people do on the web. While implementation has been postponed at the time of writing, the decision was cast as part of a wider corporate initiative to "make the web more private and secure for users" (Chromium Blog, 2020). What might appear as a small technological tweak, essentially dismantled the core of an ad tech industry that had been coming of age for more than a decade. Some commentators were quick to link Google's move to changes in the enforcement of legal regulations regarding personal privacy, for instance, through the 2018 General Data Protection Regulation (GDPR) of the European Union, with some pundits dubbing the shift a victory of legal rights over commercial powers. Others held that, rather than dealing a blow to Google's business model, the initiative demonstrated how a dominant player such as Google was able to circumvent and, in effect, replace or at least reconfigure the entire global ecosystem of small and medium-sized businesses trading in data, which had been built on top of a rather simple technology of third-party cookies (Bohn, 2021; Burgess, 2022).

Regardless of preferred perspective, the retirement of third-party cookies will likely consolidate the position of current market leaders within the global ecosystem of online advertising. At the same time, the events around 2020 suggest both the contingencies of the technologies and political economies of emerging communication systems, and the limited research into the mechanisms accounting for either stability or change in this strategic digital domain. In the present chapter, we look under the hood of infrastructures, where technologies and political economies come together to shape fundamental conditions of how humans

DOI: 10.4324/9781003057055-6

communicate. Compared to the more familiar media systems of the twentieth century (Hallin & Mancini, 2004), the digital communication systems of the twenty-first century bring back the question of what media and their operatives still do to people, even as people are enabled to do more things with more media. As noted by infrastructure and governance scholar Laura DeNardis, "arrangements of technical architecture are also arrangements of power" (DeNardis, 2020: 17). Embracing Langdon Winner's (1980) foundational question – "Do artifacts have politics?" – DeNardis (2020) responded with an emphatic yes: Far from being autonomous entities, technologies articulate social relations with contestable implications for the good life, locally and globally. Google's decision to block third-party cookies in its Chrome browser has been matched by decisions with comparable consequences by, for instance, Apple. Taken together, such rearrangements of technological infrastructures entail variable measures of control with communication systems and, hence, social control over who can say and do what, to and with whom (Beniger, 1986).

The first section of this chapter describes the basics of web tracking. Because it is constitutive of communication systems, and much less familiar than the mechanics of monetizing information and communication through either print or broadcast media, we provide a number of pointers to the embedding of deceptively simple technical features into grander dynamics of centralization and control. We go on to identify some of the key institutional factors that mediate the intersection of general technologies and specific political economies in different regions of the world. While web tracking in the United States and Western Europe displays distinctive patterns of centralization around familiar tech giants such as Alphabet (Google) and Meta (Facebook), in other regions of the world tracking has followed different paths – according to different principles of centralization, centered in different giants. In the last part of the chapter, we begin tracking the trackers in concrete detail, presenting findings from an empirical mapping of third-party trackers with special reference to the seven countries and three world regions of the Peoples' Internet (PIN) project. Outlining multiple cultures of tracking, the analysis refers back to the account, in Chapter 2, of different regulatory regimes around the world, and forward to the discussion, in Chapter 7, of some of the normative implications of the present and potential future infrastructures circumscribing the universal human practice of communication. The structure of the present chapter reiterates the three-way determination of communicative practices, outlined in Chapter 1, by material technologies, political economies, and cultural traditions.

Technologies of tracking

Infrastructures of tracking enable the exercise of considerable power, but depend, in a very concrete, very material sense, on quite basic technologies underpinning the entire online ecosystem of the contemporary world. Controlling if, when, and how tracking can be performed of web use and other communicative practices entails the wielding of significant *infrastructural power* (Mann, 2012; Weiss, 2006). Tracking (or not tracking) users within and across platforms determine, if only in the first instance (Hall, 1983), whether marketing and sales by corporations will be optimized, and whether states can engage in surveillance of their own citizens, and the citizens of other states. Such infrastructural power differs, to one side, from the *power of specific platforms* to regulate the freedom of expression, for instance, through algorithmic or human content moderation. To the other side, infrastructural power differs from the *epistemic power* to decide what will (not) be known, by either political authorities, commercial operators, or scientific researchers, about (segments of) the internet and (aspects of) its uses. Most important, *online* infrastructural power is categorically different from the infrastructural power traditionally associated with states, including the design and development of multipurpose transportation and communication systems (Frischmann, 2012). Online infrastructural power is wielded, instead, by private, commercial interests, which thus come to define and delimit the interests and agency of anyone else – what individual citizens, (other) private companies, but also public agencies can do to and with each other, online and with substantial offline ramifications. In sum, the infrastructural power of the Western Big Five and the Chinese Big Three online intermediaries, reviewed in Chapter 2, precedes and prejudices the exercise of other forms of power by public as well as private agents, in important ways that have remained surprisingly underresearched.

Because digital infrastructures are, at once, so basic and so pervasive, some research in this domain has highlighted the *invisibility* of the technologies at work (Bowker, Baker, Millerand, & Ribes, 2010). Third-party trackers may even be considered second nature by ordinary internet users. Debatable on its own terms, and restricting itself to the natives' perspective (Malinowski, 1922) on what is really going on online, any presumption of invisibility is decidedly misleading when it comes to the practice of surveillance by third-party tracking. From the onset of web tracking, it was *meant* to be invisible, a strategy and a feature, not a bug or a coincidence. In different jurisdictions, attempts at making the invisible visible, for example, through regulation introducing so-called cookie consent forms or, more recently, through outright banning of third-party-based surveillance, have been met with both explicit protest and behind-the-scenes lobbying by the ad tech industry (Corporate Europe Observatory, 2022). While certainly not unique to the digital realm – stakeholders in infrastructures from buildings to train lines have long sought to shift policy and regulatory regimes to their own advantage – the scale and scope of what had, until recently, been kept successfully under the digital hood are, indeed, remarkable. It took public scandals such as Edward Snowden's 2013 whistleblowing on National Security Agency surveillance of citizens and the Cambridge Analytica incident relating to the 2016 US presidential election, complemented by agenda-setting interventions by researchers such as Shoshana Zuboff (2019) on the underlying surveillance economy, to make visible the elephant online.

In the wake of events of the 2010s, researchers across several disciplines and domains of inquiry into digital computing and human communication could be heard asking themselves how it might come to this, to the present conjuncture of pervasive tracking. Despite contributions from computer science, media research, as well as legal studies on the development of the infrastructures aiding and abetting tracking (Braman, 2011; Christl & Spiekermann, 2016; Ermakova, Bender, Fabian, & Klimek, 2018; Libert, 2015; Roesner, Kohno, & Wetherall, 2012; Sargsyan, 2016; Veale & Borgesius, 2022), the reaction to the outcome so far as well as to future prospects is best described as one of interdisciplinary, intellectual shock. In retrospect, there has been a clear disconnect between practice and theory – an omnipresence of tracking and an absence of sustained public and policy debate informed by research on its technological foundations and social implications. The disconnect is explained, in part, by a distinctive conjuncture of simplicity and complexity: Simple technologies operating at scale have given rise to complex uses involving classic dilemmas of individual rights and social values – which motivates a further dive in this section into the mechanics and associated morals of tracking.

If a new kind or degree of surveillance society is, in fact, emerging, in different national and regional variants, the main vector of its infrastructural development, then, has been *web-based tracking*. Compared to other digital systems commonly used across public and private settings, web tracking represents a fairly simple technology (Liu & Chao, 2020). To track the activities of users, it is necessary, as a first step, to register their presence at the websites being visited. Registration is accomplished by the blocks of data known as *cookies* (and small programs called *scripts*) that are placed in the source code of websites and transferred to users' devices. The process essentially harnesses general features of the web as means to rather more specific ends: The experience of 'entering a website' follows from directing one's browser to establish contact with a remote computer (a server) by entering an 'address' or URL (Universal Resource Locator), which next delivers a file in HTML code (HyperText Markup Language) to the browser. This file contains lots of instructions and other information, so that the browser can generate a visual representation of interest in the browser window that the user is currently looking at, for example, the front page of a national or international news site. As users keep up with the news, the system keeps tabs on the users.

Most of the mechanics of rendering website content, as indicated, are invisible, unfolding unseen by the user, but providing the functional, seamless experience that users have come to expect as a discursive, cultural given. Key to this experience are the cookies – small files with strings of text, stored in a special folder, buried deep in users' hard drives – which serve many purposes beyond tracking. Cookies were originally invented and introduced to enable a server to ascertain the identity of users as they traversed different pages within the *same* website. In the early days of the 1990s web, once you left the front page of a news site (because you had clicked on a headline to read the rest of the story), the server had no technical way of 'knowing' or registering that the person (device) landing on the page with the full story was identical to the person who had been present at the frontpage a second or two earlier. Setting a cookie would give the particular web browser of a particular user a unique identifying code, which the server could then identify at a later time. So, the moment the proverbial user enters the front page of the news site, the server checks for a cookie from earlier visits, and if no cookie is detected, the server sets a cookie so that it may keep track of *this* user's future movements on *this* site.

It is noteworthy that cookies were not originally developed or designed to support tracking in the sense of surveillance; from the outset, the purpose of the technology was local and functional. As addressed in Chapter 5, keeping track of users became increasingly essential as the web and the internet as such brought home the point that communication, more than saying things, is also a way of doing things, for example, buying and selling material as well as immaterial goods. If you have placed an item in your shopping basket at an online store, cookies enable its server to register a likely upcoming purchase, even while you might still be browsing additional items, whether as virtual windows-shopping or as an addition to the commercial transaction; without cookies, you would lose your wares, because the server would lose track of you as soon as you clicked on another link within the site. This original category of cookies subsequently came to be known as *first-party cookies*: They are set by the server that also supplies the HTML file that the user is browsing, thus relating *two parties*, a server supplying what the user demands, within limits and with specifications.

The shift toward tracking as surveillance was marked by the introduction of *third-party cookies*. Transcending the local functionality of first-party cookies, these enable other servers, as well, to set cookies on users' devices: If you visit the website of *The New York Times* (nytimes.com), the HTML file that is sent to your browser contains additional code which initiates a further request by your browser for another cookie to also be sent, but from another server that is operated and controlled by, for instance, Google. (In fact, as we elaborate below, your browser will most likely request cookies from dozens of servers.) It was the introduction of these additional, networked functionalities, summed up as *third-party services*, which constituted the fundamental building block of the infrastructure of what has come to be known as surveillance capitalism (Zuboff, 2019). Third-party cookies, coupled with other digital technologies, offered the gateway through which so-called data broker companies such as Google could build extensive databases registering the activities of millions and billions of users. And it was the brokering of all this information – about who sends and receives which (other variants of) information, when, where, and in which networks – that built the currently consolidated data services aimed at websites as well as advertisers. It was and is in the clear and present interest of these central stakeholders and, of course, of the intermediaries brokering the data, to jointly monetize what people do with media.

It should be added that far from all third-party services are run as sources of data brokering. It is a generic feature of the HTML programming language that code can be embedded to call up external URLs, which add a whole range of functionalities to websites. To illustrate, the site called liveperson.com delivers chatbot functionality to support customers' interactions with many different websites. If you have queries about your subscription, for example, at the French website of the telephone company Orange or at the UK website of *The Times*, you will in both instances encounter a bot that is, in effect, a localized version of the same basic technology feeding into dedicated customer service operations. As specification of such third-party services, it may be more accurate to describe LivePerson as a company that evidently conducts a business above and beyond the tracking of the customers' chatting. The point is that a third-party service with a reasonable 'footprint' or extension on the web, such as LivePerson, simultaneously enjoys the opportunity, and has the capacity, to collect the same kind of information that data brokers will refine to develop user profiles. Whether a company chooses to also act as a data broker, or to wholesale its information to other companies as raw material for further processing, cannot be determined by tracking the trackers as we do in the last portion of this chapter, and requires additional methodologies exploring specific business models and modes of operation. But third-party services come with the potential for tracking, being integral parts of a networked infrastructure generating diverse forms of information with economic value for multiple stakeholders – which leads us to a final distinctive feature of the technologies of tracking: Third-party services depend on being part and parcel of an ecosystem with many parties.

We just noted that a third-party service needs to have a 'reasonable' footprint on the web if it is to produce a comprehensive and practically relevant file of any given user's online activities. Put differently, setting a third-party cookie *only* at nytimes.com will generate little information of value to advertisers and, hence, to data brokers. Third-party cookies serve, in a first step, as sensors, registering the presence of someone (a specific browser on a specific device) at a particular site. But, for data brokers to compile extended files on the browsing behavior of large numbers of users around the web, they need access to sensors on a similarly large number of sites that register *which* sites (some) users do (not) visit, typically including, as well, the particular pages within a site attracting more or less 'traffic.' Once again, the basic technological logic is simple, but significant: For the ecosystem to work, a large proportion of the owners and operators of the innumerable websites that make up the world wide web must agree to insert the code calling up the third-party services ('setting the cookie') as well as inserting the code in the HTML files that are sent from servers to website visitors. Data brokers, in short, cannot insert their code anywhere they want, even in an open architecture such as the web.

Fortunately for data brokers, websites have had an obvious shared interest in including the cookies of data brokers, which represent the coins of exchange for selling screen real estate to advertisers. In historical perspective, the negotiation of interests and arrangements entailed a decades-long, largely collaborative process, as data brokers and website owners joined forces to cultivate the world wide web as a suite of sensors (Hindman, 2018). With their cookies installed on a sufficient number of sites, data brokers will receive a steady stream of information about the trajectories of masses of identifiable users on the web – at least in principle. In practice, complex challenges have had to be tackled. For one thing, users are not immediately identifiable by name, but by code stored in cookies via browsers and on devices, which means that multiple sources of information must be combined to monitor a marketplace of attention populated by real people (Webster, 2014). For another thing, that basic building block – the cookie – can be deleted. Once members of the wider technological community understood the social implications of the technological logic, they began developing tools to prevent tracking, such as browser plug-ins deleting cookies. Individual users can also delete cookies via their browser settings, and many will use more than one browser, so that data brokers need to collate cross-browser portfolios in order to correctly aggregate multiple cookie identities into the same real-world user identity.

As highlighted at the outset of this chapter, solutions to these several challenges are still being developed and contested. While the details of ongoing developments fall outside the scope of the present analysis, the 2010s witnessed the consolidation of a practice and institution of *big data analytics* spanning not just media and communication, but private and public sectors of social life at large (Schroeder, 2016). As we elaborate in the following section, it was the mobilization of digital technologies as means of measuring and analyzing communication, as well – a medium for representing and communicating about how people communicate online – which enabled the monetization of the basic affordances of cookies and third-party services. To stay with the opening example of Google, this behemoth has learnt the lesson that digital technologies are generic and, literally, programmable, enabling the transfer, for example, of the principles and procedures of artificial intelligence from industrial manufacturing to communication services. In this last domain of human communication, a solution to the challenge of tracking people in an unambiguous and efficient manner was facilitated by the advent of smartphones as a new global normal, typically used by a single individual, thus bypassing the knotty issues of computers used by several people and single users traversing multiple devices. Having acquired and successfully expanded the Android operating system to around 70% of the world's current 6.5 billion smartphone users (Statista, 2022b), Google, through its mother company Alphabet, gained access to more and better information on what people do online.

Political economies of tracking

Cookies feed data into databases that amount to information assets with economic value. To monetize the available information, specialized software solutions have been developed on top, catering to the respective needs of the companies advertising, the agencies executing their campaigns, and the publishers displaying the advertising on their websites. Two main forms of display advertising have taken hold on the web. In an *advertising network*, first, the publisher of a website enters into an agreement with an advertiser, or group of advertisers, who will pay a fixed price for the display of ads a specified number of times on specified pages (or under specific conditions of exposure). A form of bulk selling, this variant is typified by a fixed price, in addition to a fixed location at a particular site (Choi, Mela, Balseiro, & Leary, 2020). As such, it constitutes a fairly straightforward extension of the pricing mechanism that had served stakeholders well for decades, even centuries, for the placement of ads in print newspapers, on radio, and on television.

It is the second, more complex way of allocating ads in digital times and spaces that represents the real innovation of online advertising: *Real-time bidding* is based on automated auctions, run without direct human intervention. In brief outline, the process has the following steps (for an overview, see Choi et al., 2020; Liu & Chao, 2020): The advertiser decides on a campaign, and stipulates a target audience. This audience is then defined and formalized in a digital system – a demand-side platform (DSP) – in terms of standard demographics and selected consumer preferences. DSPs, importantly and typically, interface with databases about consumers, held by data brokers and constructed over time through tracking, and they further allow advertisers to indicate an acceptable maximum price for different kinds of 'impressions' – the exposure of a particular user (browser and device) to the representation of a product or service in particular circumstances (timing, previous purchases, earlier trajectories). In many instances, the provider of the DSP software is itself the data broker. On the other side of the bargain, publishers will use comparable software tools – a supply-side platform (SSP) – which lists (parts of) their inventory, as characterized by a set of cookies installed at their site; the desired size and location of the display slot; and the minimally acceptable price. The middleman is the dedicated auction software, which interfaces with the systems to both sides, crucially their stipulated price ranges.

When a person visits a webpage, the cookie mechanism is activated, and the user entering the site is identified. So, before the page in question appears in the person's browser, their identifying information (a unique cookie ID) is relayed to the auction, which then interfaces with the data broker to establish the profile of the person in question. Next, the auction 'asks' a number of advertisers (with reference to the user profiles appearing in their DSPs) what they would pay to have a given ad displayed to a given person (which may involve prices relating to hundreds of campaigns run by dozens of advertisers), and on a given page (since advertisers may have preferences regarding sites where they want (not) to appear). In the end, the auction is 'won' at the optimal intersection of an asking price and a willingness to pay.

Whereas this outline brackets several technical and commercial details, including debates about the fairness and transparency of such auctions (Geradin

& Katsifis, 2019, 2020), it describes the basic mechanism of the second variant of display advertising, which accounts for about a third of all online advertising. And, again, from an engineering perspective, the functionality is relatively simple – deceptively simple. It is true that both the several software tools and the infrastructures linking them are accessible to multiple data brokers collecting information, mediating auctions, and, in principle, competing among themselves. The devil, this time around, is not in the technological detail, but in the big political–economic picture – which has been the outcome of market forces taking effect within a surprisingly short period of time.

It is not difficult to set up surveillance of traffic on a website, and it is just as easy to integrate site surveillance with the back-end systems translating traffic data into cash flows. The remarkable ease of tracking likely facilitated both the speed of the roll-out and the scope of the system as consolidated infrastructure. Thousands of website owners have, in a sense, crowdsourced the system, with little or no oversight by public authorities: 'Please place these cookies on your site, then link to our system, and you are in the business of tracking people.' The process stands out from traditional infrastructural development, even for other aspects of digital infrastructure, and is facilitated by the underlying structure of the web and by the networked nature of website operations, including content management systems and the increasing platformization of the internet as such (van Dijck, Poell, & de Waal, 2018). At an intermediate level, small cookies and large systems have been integrated through 'free' management tools, specifically Google Tag Manager. This software simplified the installation and management of trackers ('tags') for non-professional website administrators, and provided a user-friendly interface for gaining information from and managing trackers, including the installation of new ones and the removal of obsolete ones. Since its launch in 2012, Google Tag Manager has been redeveloped to conveniently handle practically all kinds of 'tags,' further offering reviews of various trackers and the testing of site load times, which are crucial to user experience.

The introduction of Google Tag Manager a decade ago marked the maturing of tracker infrastructures. At the level of the ecosystem, it normalized and accelerated the embedding of tracking technologies across the world wide web. As a corporate strategy, it helped Google attain a dominant position in the market for online tracking of users and their data. By streamlining tracking as a common practice, Google steered website development down a particular path, which, being simple, would appear preferable, even commonsensical. As a performative and potentially problematic infrastructure, tracking may be invisible not just to users, as mentioned, but to web managers, too, as they go about maintaining their site for other, personal or public, ends.

The normalization of tracking has gone hand in hand with an increasing standardization and modularization of web technologies, notably over the past decade too. The transition from stand-alone websites, written in HTML and run on individual servers, to networked packages has been a gradual one. Slowly but surely, a global migration of websites onto a comparatively small set of hosts has unfolded, with servers run as services out of data centers, and functionalities based on standardized systems, catering in equal measure to front-end (users) and back-end (advertisers and data brokers) interests. Users of the early web may remember a widespread GIF representing a roadworker frantically shoveling a pile of dirt, accompanied by the text "under construction." Alongside the migration, during the same period, of non-corporate uses of the web onto social media platforms, the disappearance of such iconography can be taken as a sign and a symbol that at least one phase in the infrastructuralization (Plantin, Lagoze, Edwards, & Sandvig, 2018) of the web, along with its tracking ecosystem, has been completed.

Our opening reference to Google's 2020 decision to abandon third-party cookies in its Chrome web browser may spell the beginning of the end of the current ecosystem. At the time of writing, there is no heir apparent, but several lessons to be learned from the past and present controversies to note. Google Analytics, launched in 2005, essentially gutted the existing market for web analytics at the time; complemented by other analytics outfits in its family, Google now accounts for around 75% of the web analytics market (Statista, 2022a). As replacement for the third-party regime, in 2021 Google floated a so-called FLoC solution (Federated Learning of Cohorts), an alternative purportedly guarding user privacy; but already in 2022, Google officially ended development of FLoC. Other big tech platforms, as well, may seek to host future infrastructures of tracking. All the while, political authorities have responded to the same concerns over privacy and criticisms regarding surveillance with which Google has motivated its changes of policy. In Chapter 2, we drew attention to the competing regulatory regimes of different world regions, most recently articulated by the Digital Markets Act and the Digital Services Act of the European Union. Taking stock of tracking in the context of the Peoples' Internet project, with third-party cookies still the rule, in the next section we ask how China, Europe, and the United States compare when it comes to the prototype of many-to-one communication – into the system (Jensen & Helles, 2017) – that communication systems have been soliciting from their users for more than a decade as a standard operating procedure.

Cultures of tracking

While research on tracking as a defining feature of digital communication is still in its infancy, studies have demonstrated that the intention to track and the competence of actually tracking citizens and consumers are both global: Scans of the one million most used websites in the world (in practice, in the West) indicate that thousands of distinct cookies are being set on users' devices (Englehardt & Narayanan, 2016). Even if a substantial proportion are ultimately controlled by the same handful of global companies (Alphabet, Meta, Twitter, and a few others), however, the majority are most likely operated by myriads of small businesses with national or regional orientations, as suggested by distinctive geographical and cultural clusters that we go on to examine. Tracker technologies may be global and generic, but the people being tracked, and therefore the third-party services, are locally and culturally situated.

A scan of top-50 websites in the seven PIN countries identified about 900 different trackers. With substantial duplication among the seven top lists, these trackers could be found at 201 sites in total. Many of the 900 trackers are, predictably, operated by global tech giants, but a substantial number occurs only at a handful of sites, and many only in one of the seven countries. For instance, the third-party service called "de17a" (operated by the Swedish ad tech company Delta Projects) only appears on a single, Hungarian site within our sample, and evidence from a wider scan, covering top 150 sites in all 27 European Union countries, indicated its presence in only 75 pages in all (Helles, Lomborg & Lai, 2020). Such a service may still be economically viable because not all websites within the footprint of a third-party service are created equal, as far as commercial logic is concerned: If a tracker is embedded in a range of sites with sufficiently large numbers of visitors, and if the contents and services provided by the individual pages that make up those sites, allow for a relevant and robust differentiation of target audiences, for instance, along various dimensions of consumer preference, then the tracker may compile and deliver user profiles with precision and value.

The size of the footprint of third-party services varies tremendously. The most common tracker in our sample was Google Analytics, at 55% of all sites. (Google Analytics is also the most common third-party service on the web overall (Statista, 2022a).) It is essential to specify, however, that most analyses of the footprints of trackers have departed from top lists deriving from traffic patterns, typically acquired from US-based (and US-centric) companies. Such lists do not reflect global traffic patterns in any even-handed manner, but prioritize Western countries, specifically the United States. This circumstance, of course, bears out the instrumental purpose and commercial knowledge interest (Habermas, 1971/1968) of tracking as technology and social practice. But, to begin an assessment of national, regional, and global variations in the prevalence and patterns of adoption for different (types of) trackers, it was necessary to select a different empirical approach. For the present analysis, we constructed a sample from the top 50 lists of the seven countries of the PIN project; all sites on those lists were scanned using the Lightbeam plug-in with a Firefox browser. The scan was conducted in 2018, overlapping with the times when survey data were collected, and ethnographic fieldwork was undertaken. The scan, further, took place six months before the introduction of the General Data Protection Regulation of the European Union, which could be expected to alter common practices of tracking. (The scan was repeated in 2020, but exhibited only minor variations, primarily due to sites closing down in the meantime.)

The network displayed in Figure 6.1 represents the scan data. The nodes of the network represent the sites in the sample; the distances between the nodes reflect the number of third-party services that sites have in common – the more shared

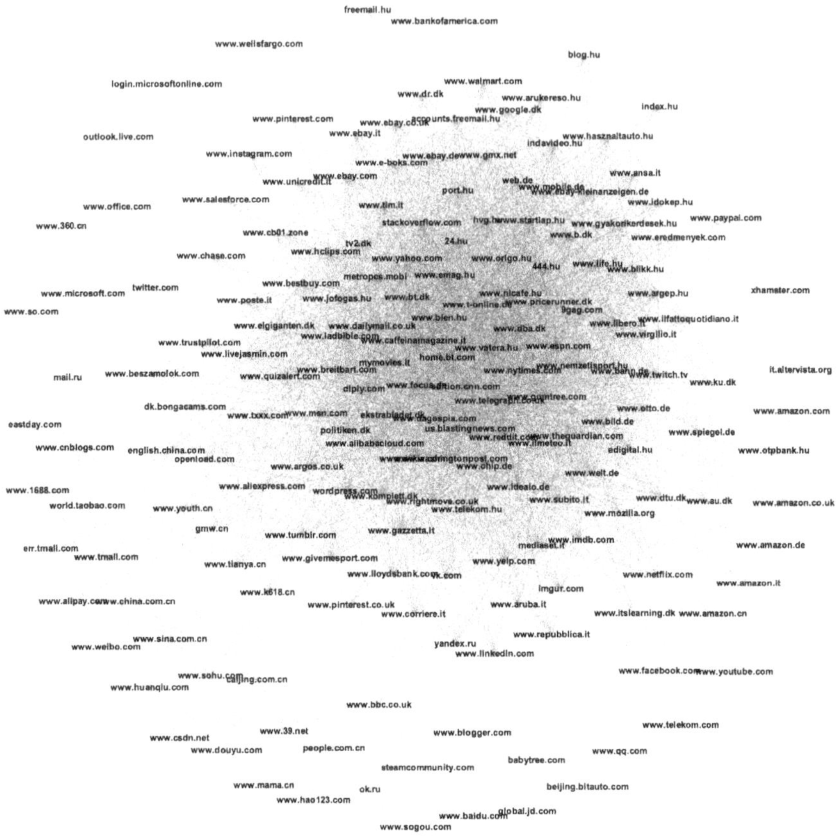

FIGURE 6.1 Network graph of third-party services in top websites of the seven PIN countries

third-party services, the closer the nodes (edges, or relations between nodes, left out for legibility). The network was projected from its original, bipartite form, omitting the eight most common trackers to avoid link inflation occurring in the transformation (Alupoaie & Cunningham, 2013).

Figure 6.1 brings out a distinctive pattern of regionalization, specifically for the Chinese and Hungarian sites in the sample. Looking at national affiliation (as indicated by country suffixes such as .cn and .hu), one detects toward the top right-hand part of the figure a Hungarian cluster of sites, comprising news, sports, and lifestyle content. Located toward the bottom-left of Figure 6.1, one finds a formation of Chinese sites, including tech giants such as the micro-blogging site Sina Weibo and the e-commerce platform Aliexpress. Considering regulatory regimes, Chapter 2 also identified China and Hungary as outliers, China much more so, Hungary relatively less so. While there is no necessary correspondence between regulatory regimes and tracker ecologies, it is plausible that, like different prototypes and practices of communication, third-party services may be structured, in homologous fashion, by the political economies and, perhaps, the cultural traditions circumscribing and inscribing them. A further interesting aspect of the network in Figure 6.1 is that, compared to China and Hungary, none of the remaining five PIN countries exhibit any clear pattern of regionalization for the national sites of their top lists. Sites with, for instance, a Danish (.dk), German (.de), or Italian (.it) suffix do not appear distinctively co-located. One might speculate, again, that the comparatively more open or globalized economies, political legacies, and cultural traditions of these countries invite less of a centering in and focusing on the matters and media of the nation-state.

Such a two-way split of the seven countries in terms of their relative regionalization is supported by a further cluster analysis of the network. Figure 6.2 lays out the findings of a so-called modularity analysis (Blondel, Guillaume, Lambiotte, & Lefebvre, 2008, resolution = 0.75). In summary, the analysis identified ten clusters, communities, or topical configurations in the graph, in addition to the two national geographical clusters already noted, the Hungarian cluster to the left, and the Chinese cluster on the right.

The cluster analysis, again, does not group any sites, apart from the Chinese and Hungarian ones, by geographical proximity, with the exception of a tiny set of two Italian news and entertainment sites (dagospia.com and caffeinamagazine .it). The analysis does, however, bring out a distinctive layout of 'communities' as defined by either the genre (typical form and content) of sites or their patterns of ownership. There is, for one, a cluster of news sites, such as *The New York Times* and *The Telegraph*. There is a further cluster of pornographic sites, which share trackers with the web versions of a range of tabloids, particularly from Italy and Hungary, and another small number of sites that host games and quizzes.

In overview, the topical clustering bears witness to commercial, cultural, as well as political logics, sometimes a combination of these, lending meaning to what users may be up to online – why they are available for tracking there in the first place. Most prominently, news sites are the main components of several clusters, being high-traffic and broad-interest sites located near the top of the lists we relied on for sampling sites. Because they see a lot of eyeballs and cookies, news sites can generate substantial incomes from advertising (if not necessarily enough to sustain quality journalism). They typically sell advertising space via advertising networks, or they enter into direct negotiations and arrangements with advertisers, which entails the installation of dedicated sets of cookies and scripts to document exposure to users and to measure campaign efficiency. But news sites also sell space for attention via real-time bidding, and because there is no natural limit to the number of auctions that can be held to sell (potential) impressions on users, many news sites exhibit a formidable array of cookies relating to multiple auctions and data brokers. One dilemma for news sites, including tabloids generating massive numbers of pageviews, is that they supply advertising space for which there may be no demand, at least not at an attractive price. Although data from web traffic is a key information commodity, and has been

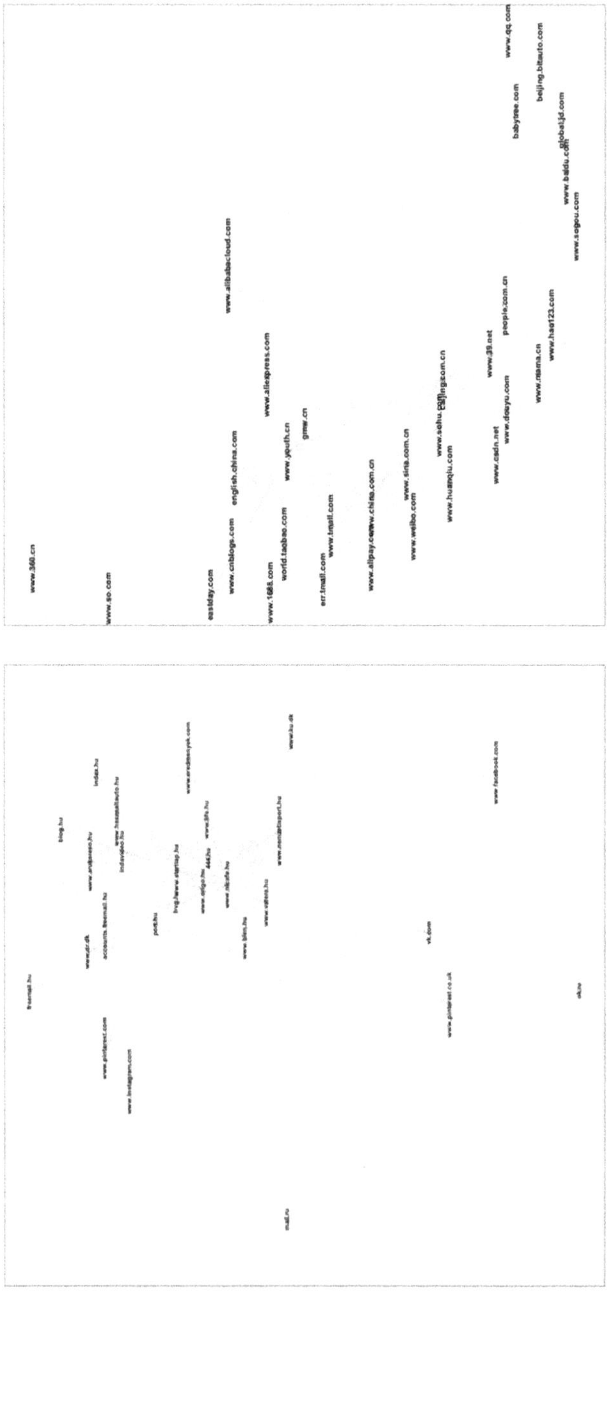

FIGURE 6.2 Chinese and Hungarian clusters from network analysis of top websites of the seven PIN countries

compared to gold and oil, excess inventory in the news media has come to be recognized and debated as a problem for a special industry with a fourth-estate, public-service remit (Agrawal, Najafi-Asadolahi, & Smith, 2020).

Other clusters, for example of game and quiz sites or pornographic sites, operate according to a more strictly commercial logic, but face challenges of a cultural and normative kind, as well. Pornographic sites have historically belonged at the top of web listings, like news sites, but without the same affinity to and engagement with advertisers. Indeed, pornographic sites were an early example of advertisers needing to take into consideration the contexts in which their ads would be placed. For mainstream advertisers, appearing next to highly popular content on, for example, Pornhub.com was and is not an attractive prospect. Accordingly, a range of trackers have been devised that almost exclusively serve pornographic sites (Vallina, Feal, Gamba, Vallina-Rodriguez, & Anta, 2019). Also beyond the domain of pornography, concerns over the contexts of advertising have been growing in recent years; contexts constitute cultures of meaning reflecting normatively back on the products and services being proffered. The issue has been brought to a head by real-time bidding systems that bracket the human middlemen. Examples of controversies arising from the automated placement of ads include the appearance of major companies in the context of the far-right Breitbart news and opinion site, as well as interventions by activist groups such as the Sleeping Giants initiative, which has succeeded in putting pressure on large advertisers by tagging their Twitter accounts in tweets describing where their ads had, in fact, been shown (Li, Bernard, & Luczak-Roesch, 2021).

When it comes to the national-geographical segmentation of third-party services, patterns of content and rates of traffic and exposure are trumped by culture and history. Previous research, centering on Europe, has shown that while tracking is indeed omnipresent on the web, not all trackers are present to the same extent in the same places (Helles, Lomborg & Lai, 2020). The wide world of the web is divided by trackers, just as the audiences being tracked will flow and converge on the web according to geography and culture (Taneja & Webster, 2016). The findings concerning the segmentation of trackers in the European setting are confirmed by the present network data from the seven PIN countries in three world regions, as illustrated by the Hungarian case: Cookies and scripts of third-party services originating from Eastern Europe are much more likely to be used on websites in that region than elsewhere (Helles, Lomborg, & Lai, 2020). Conversely, third-party services originating from Western Europe and the United States are less likely to appear (though far from absent) on sites in Eastern Europe. In addition, cookies from the Russian tech giant Yandex and its affiliates, as well as third-party services originating from the former Eastern bloc such as the Czech Republic, are found almost exclusively within the cluster of Hungarian sites. And, the pattern repeats itself for the cluster of Chinese websites: A number of trackers are found on these sites only, with several conglomerates apparently pursuing a strategy of embedding their own third-party services within the family of sites they operate. Trackers originating from other countries do appear on some of the sites in the Chinese top list, but their proportion is much smaller than for the other countries in the present study, suggesting the segregation of the Chinese internet in terms of both its regulatory regime and the actual communicative practices of Chinese users (Ng & Taneja, 2019: 485).

Summary of findings

The reviews and analyses of this chapter have suggested the strategic position and structuring function of third-party tracking within the infrastructure of contemporary communication systems, as they have taken shape over recent decades, and as they begin a process of restructuring. It seems clear that the geographical and regional variations we have identified cannot be ascribed to any single factor, whether technologies, political economies, or cultural traditions. For one thing, the configuration of trackers at websites in the United States and Western Europe, which follow topical and sectoral boundaries rather than geographical and linguistic-cultural lines, probably follows from the fact that this was where the web was first commercialized, giving rise to a more complex system of online advertising with a longer history (Wu & Taneja, 2019). For another thing, the global political economies of the diffusion of back-end as well as front-end digital technologies have been shaped over time by more local and specific market strategies, with geopolitical ramifications. The market for digital advertising developed against a background of monopolistic strategies, specifically Google's bid for hegemony through its acquisition of DoubleClick and a long string of other subsidiaries (Moore & Tambini, 2018), at a time when markets for online advertising were relatively more localized. In the meantime, the global shift from browser-based to smartphone- and app-based uses of the internet meant more communication in more territories, but by people with lower purchasing power than consumers in the West, which likely has made the Western Big Five less inclined to extend their infrastructures here, cookies and all. Other tech giants such as Yandex of Russia, further, have had time to establish a foothold in wider world markets. As of the early 2020s, then, the world, the web, and its trackers stand divided and diverse, driven by political economies, but with path dependencies writ large as cultures, unfolding across the *longues durées* of history (Braudel, 1980).

7
COMMUNICATION SYSTEMS AS SCIENTIFIC AND NORMATIVE AGENDAS

Klaus Bruhn Jensen and Rasmus Helles

Empirical findings

The cash value of empirical comparison

We begin this concluding chapter by synthesizing the empirical findings from the preceding chapters. Whereas the volume has outlined and advocated a theoretical and methodological framework for comparative research on communication systems, its explanatory and interpretive value must be assessed in practice – with reference to actual media and communicative practices in specific historical times and cultural places. The framework, further, invites consideration of potential or preferable alternatives to contemporary communication systems. It was the pragmatist philosopher William James (2013/1907) who emphasized the cash value of ideas – the practical relevance of theory and inquiry for human understanding and social action. Following the review of empirical findings, accordingly, we revisit and reassess the premises and models presented in Chapter 1, and we discuss the outlook for further comparative studies of communication systems. The final section of the chapter returns to some normative implications of the ways in which, and the extent to which, current communication systems enable and enhance the universal human capability of communication (Nussbaum, 2011; Sen, 1999). At the beginning of the 2020s, the *internets* of China, Europe, and the United States illustrate critical choices facing individual citizens and national publics as they go on communicating about what the internet is, ought to be, and could become.

The Peoples' Internet (PIN) project departed from prototypes of human communication – one-to-one, one-to-many, and many-to-many – as traditionally associated with specific media, and recently collected and configured on the internet as a meta-medium (Kay & Goldberg, 1999/1977). The empirical chapters have detailed how, in each case, these prototypes remain essential

DOI: 10.4324/9781003057055-7

elements of the everyday lives of different social segments in diverse national and regional contexts of the world, on the internet, through the full range of legacy or traditional media, and in the face-to-face interactions of embodied human beings. Communication systems constitute environments affording resources of representation and interaction, from which people build particular repertoires of media and communication, here and now, and in trajectories unfolding across biographical and historical time. Video did not kill the radio star; the internet lives and lets other media live, at least for the foreseeable future.

One-to-one communication

Interpersonal communication is a fundamental mode of coordination and coexistence across the *longues durées* (Braudel, 1980) of natural evolution and human history, part and parcel of the human condition. In and by communication with neighbors and next of kin, as extended from the local to the global level through material technologies and social institutions, people become and remain both persons with individual identities and members of communities. In digital media and communication environments, as well, we each occupy the center of a world in which some people are more significant than others (Mead, 1934).

Interpersonal interaction constitutes a common denominator for China, Europe, and the United States. Compared to mass and networked communication, interpersonal communicative practices are evidently more similar – in empirical terms, much more evenly distributed *across* the three regions. If people's one-to-many and many-to-many repertoires divide them into distinctive classes or profiles, their one-to-one (and few-to-few, as we elaborate below) interactions unite them around prototypical ways of being social and human.

Within regions and nations, however, some are more equal than others, also when it comes to interpersonal interaction. More resources – higher income and better education – enable more diverse and, hence, potentially more relevant and rewarding communications. Urbanization, similarly, facilitates the exercise of communicative agency, which should be kept in mind, not least, for comparisons involving China, where approximately 40% of the population still live in rural settings (World Bank, 2021). And gender, importantly, is associated with a distinctive pattern of interpersonal communication, with women shouldering primary responsibility for staying in touch with the ties that bind. On this count, more, and more diverse, communications may foster not more, but less equality of opportunity and obligation in the lives of families and households.

One-to-many communication

An implicit premise of much media and communication research over the last two decades has been that networked forms of communication might be replacing good old-fashioned mass communication as a mainstay of both everyday life and social life. A related distinction, commonly credited to Nicholas Negroponte

(1995), has referred to a shift from *push* communication, epitomized by broadcast television, toward *pull* communication, elected by users in accordance with their needs and interests. The outcome, in Negroponte's vocabulary, would be a 'daily me' – a personalized set of information resources that empowers the individual as the proverbial spider occupying the center of contemporary webs of communication. The present findings offer a reminder that, far from being dead or displaced, mass communication continues to flow through multiple media, online and offline, synchronously and asynchronously, across sociodemographic segments and cultural settings.

Respondents in the PIN surveys confirm that they will still go, if not necessarily with the flow as conceived by Raymond Williams' (1974) classic account of broadcasting, then certainly along with the many and widely available, continuous and continuing narratives of fact and fiction. As a modern cultural form, mass communication has put large publics in a position to stay updated on events and issues in a world far beyond personal or immediate experience. Even though the PIN questionnaire did not break down media use into different genres – news, documentaries, and reality shows; feature films; and television series – the summative measures for various media unequivocally bring home the continued centrality of mass communication in people's lives. For one thing, substantial majorities in the seven countries and three world regions will watch television and listen to radio in traditional fashion several times a week (with China as a partial exception, specifically for radio). For another thing, the internet consistently comes out as one more, complementary carrier of mass communication, alongside traditional broadcasting, again across national settings and sociodemographic segments.

It is especially noteworthy that, also in the youngest (18–34) age bracket, it is still a majority (indeed, in Italy more than 90%) who regularly turn to classic mass media. Research as well as public debate may have been tempted to exaggerate the digital uniqueness of young media users as the harbingers of a new historical era. We return, in the section on 'cultures of communication,' to the generational aspect of ongoing transformations of media and communication repertoires.

Many-to-many communication

Many-to-many communication, while prefigured by embodied and analog media as noted in Chapter 1 (Table 1.1), has been associated, above all, with the coming of digital media. And yet, there are practical, constitutive limitations to how much time and attention any individual can devote to communication, as either sender or receiver. As marketplaces of attention (Webster, 2014), communication systems are circumscribed by political–economic regimes, and equally by the evolutionary capacities and psychological inclinations of their human users. The more pertinent research question may be: How many (or few) do, in fact, communicate to and with how many (or few)?

For most people most of the time, the prototype of many-to-many communication is practiced few-to-few. Across regional and national settings and sociodemographic backgrounds, our respondents indicate that they will communicate much more frequently and diversely with a small and select set of friends and family. There is, in short, an inverse relationship between the frequency of communications and the size of 'audiences.' This is in spite of the fact that people do attend to public matters on social media – from political news to commercial brands – to variable degrees, but with nothing like the same intensity or involvement as for personal relations. It is noteworthy, further, that communications which presumably are primarily intended for, and of interest to, the few may end up incidentally addressing the many or the masses. In this respect, it is remarkable that the American and Chinese respondents in this study are *equally* likely to share comments on the internet for anybody to see, whereas the European respondents will reserve such comments for smaller audiences.

Beyond this centering of communication in the self and a relatively few significant others, there are important differences among the seven countries when it comes to respondents' interactions with the few and the many. Most distinctively, our Chinese respondents highlight the importance and value of being always-available for communication. They are joined, if not with the same intensity, by respondents in Hungary and Italy in actively sending to as well as receiving from their personal contacts. The other end of such a spectrum of communicative intensity is represented by Denmark and Germany, with the United Kingdom and the United States as intermediate cases. And, finally, communicative intensity or quantity goes together with communicative quality: Out of the various things that one might do online with others, internet users in China, Hungary, and Italy tend to 'do everything'; in Germany and Denmark, they will 'do nothing'; while the United States and the United Kingdom occupy a middle ground of many-to-many communication.

Many-to-one communication

Complementing the more familiar prototypes of human communication, we have introduced a terminology of many-to-one communication (Jensen & Helles, 2017) to refer to the interchanges that occur between digital systems and their users, in and of their interactions, and which are recorded for subsequent analysis with diverse and, in part, unanticipated applications and consequences. The trackers or third-party services (TPSs) that are in place around the world constitute an essential infrastructure that is a source of economic wealth and political influence, and which conditions the kinds of things that users will (not) be in a position to say, know, and do. A particularly noteworthy feature of this infrastructure is its combination of relative technological simplicity and political–economic complexity, which helps to explain why research as well as public debate have only recently begun to target the social implications of this distinctive affordance of digital technologies. Within a surprisingly short period of time, tracking has become a deceptively simple fact of life.

The political economies underpinning tracker infrastructures are still taking shape and being contested in different world regions, extending familiar models of advertising networks from print and broadcast media, while adding the digital practice of real-time bidding. In overview, so far the outcome has been a divided world of trackers, catering to markets that seek to attract the attention of geographically and culturally situated users and consumers. This is in addition to a more topical and sectoral segmentation of trackers in the United States and Western Europe, which may be attributed to the early and continuing commercialization here of the web as such. Although the diffusion of smartphones on a global scale has extended potential markets for advertisers and, hence, trackers, the growing numbers of smartphone users in the Global South likely will remain, for the foreseeable future, less attractive targets of tracking if one asks the corporate players pursuing global strategies in the digital domain.

All the while, public and policy responses to tracking as surveillance have been building over the past decade. During the same period, the regulatory regimes characterizing the three world regions of the Peoples' Internet project have increasingly come to stand out as competing visions of a future internet serving as the global, more or less common carrier of economy, politics, and culture. The qualitative fieldwork data from China, Denmark, and the United States did suggest respondents' awareness of the traces they leave behind in and through their many-to-one communication, but also their focus on interpersonal rather than infrastructural ramifications, on losing friends more than exposing themselves to unfriendly or indifferent others. We return, in the final section of this chapter, to some of the ethical and political implications of many-to-one communication.

Capitalizing on communication

Capitals or social resources are both conditions and consequences of communication. Economic, cultural, social, and, increasingly, digital capitals enable the communications by which people accomplish important ends in their lives; communicative practices, in turn, reproduce, and may enhance, these capitals. If capitals *circumscribe* more or less good lives, communications *inscribe* the ongoing reproduction and distribution of these same capitals in meaningful narrative and interactive patterns.

The empirical findings suggest two main conclusions in this regard, and a challenge for further research on communication systems. First, *within* each of the seven countries, respondents with greater capital volumes enjoy distinctive advantages in and through their communications: With more capital(s) come more rich or versatile communicative practices, which likely translate into further advantage. *Across* countries and regions, more egalitarian social systems, exemplified by Denmark and Germany, may compensate, to an extent, for this lawlike regularity of the resource-rich getting ever richer, also in and by communication.

Second, digital capital, like social capital, can serve both as a bridging capital and as a compensating capital, that is, as a means of gaining and accumulating economic and cultural capital, as well. Specifically, younger respondents can be seen to mobilize their digital capital to make up for less economic and cultural capital. At the same time, the relative efficacy of digital and social capitals as bridging mechanisms still appears under construction and negotiation in current communication systems.

Pierre Bourdieu's (1984/1979) analytical framework goes some way toward capturing the dynamics of privilege and power pervading communication and other social systems. The framework seems at a loss, however, to account for China as (a) social field(s) and, in particular, the administration of social capital in China through always-on communication. In the section considering future research, we return to this caveat as one of the challenges for theory development on communication systems.

Cultures of communication

In Chapter 1, we defined cultures of communication as distinctive combinations and configurations of communicative practices, enabled by the available material technologies, regulated by the predominant political economies, and articulating possible worlds in signs and symbols – which may be responded to and rearticulated, repaired and transformed, in the short, medium, and long term. A culture of communication can be understood as the sum of the affordances of a communication system, in a particular historical time and cultural place, a horizon of potential representations and interactions. For comparative research, it offers a middle-range conception (Merton, 1968) of the things that can be said and done with media overall, with the communicative prototypes as the empirical parameters subject to continuity and change.

Contemporary cultures of communication, in the three world regions of this study, variously incorporate the two most familiar prototypes of human communication: One-to-one (and few-to-few) interpersonal communication, online and offline, remains an essential condition and constituent of being human and being social; one-to-many mass communication, over the centuries, has proven its many attractions as one of the things that people can and will do with media. Digitalization, recently, has enabled two more prototypes, at scale, but with social consequences that are still emerging. On the one hand, many-to-many networked communication is being embraced most readily in China, whereas our American and European respondents are still negotiating the terms of its adoption (extending, as mentioned, from Hungarians and Italians doing close to 'everything' with so-called social media, via the British and the Americans doing 'something,' to Danes and Germans doing next to 'nothing'). On the other hand, many-to-one communication into the system has become a constitutive element of digital infrastructures over the past 25 years (Helles, Lomborg, & Lai, 2020), but is currently in flux, as trackers or third-party services (TPSs) are being replaced by other means of monitoring local and global marketplaces of attention.

We have identified a convergence of cultures of communication. The youngest age groups in the surveys are virtually indistinguishable across the seven countries and three world regions, even while older respondents variously retain, combine, or complement the new and the old in their media and communication repertoires. Also the young still go with the flow of mass *communication*, if less commonly than their elders through mass *media*. And, like their parents and grandparents, the young are active interpersonal communicators, to and with a select set of significant others, even more frequently and diversely so. Communication serves to define and negotiate both their 'others' and their 'selves,' in a formative life stage, by any and all media available. History and biography intersect: The young partly reproduce, partly remediate (Bolter & Grusin, 1999) established prototypes of communication, and they are, unsurprisingly, more adventurous than their elders in experiencing and experimenting with additional prototypes, as these are taking shape and gaining momentum. To assess the current state and future prospects of this ongoing process, we turn next from the empirical findings toward theoretical inferences and implications for further research.

Theoretical inferences

Technological momentum

Chapter 1 presented the theoretical framework of the Peoples' Internet project, summed up in Figures 1.1 and 1.2, laying out three types of determinants or mechanisms conditioning concrete communicative practices. The first of these – material technologies – begins to address the wider social process in which digitalization is reconfiguring contemporary communication systems. In Chapter 1, we referred briefly to Thomas P. Hughes' (1983, 1994) concept of technological momentum – the understanding that the social consequences of a new technology follow, not least, from its embedding in other social interactions and institutions. Once in place, the technology in question becomes a necessary condition of these interactions and institutions. In large parts of the world today, the internet has come to be taken for granted (Ling, 2012) as a resource for accomplishing any number of things, individually and collectively. Its consequences, accordingly, are best approached as processes that take effect over time, rather than as events occurring in particular moments and locations. Hughes specified, further, that technologies should be thought of as systems – complex structures in which both the parts and the whole intersect and interact with several other systems, some material, others immaterial. Hughes' (1983) case was electricity, as introduced into Western societies, 1880–1930. Communication technologies are another classic case of technological systems that interact with other social systems – and with each other.

Hughes (1994) was careful to note that technologies tend to go through various phases of implementation and consolidation, *en route* to achieving momentum and, in some instances, becoming critical infrastructures. Early on, a technology will be relatively open to multiple and sometimes conflicting social definitions (one early and key anticipated use of the landline telephone was music and other entertainments (Winston, 1998)); it later acquires standard forms and functions (voice calls by landline); and it may lend itself to adaptation (calling and texting by feature phone), perhaps in response to the introduction of comparable or competing technologies (digital smartphones in pockets, laptops in bags, work stations on desks). The chapters of this volume have documented one stage in an extended process through which single-purpose media and the internet as a multipurpose meta-medium have been emerging as parallel carriers of interpersonal and mass communication. The media and the meta-medium coexist as components of contemporary communication systems. The meta-medium, in addition, has supported digital-born media and has facilitated a measure of many-to-many communication, as typified so far by social media.

Beyond communication systems as generic forms of contacting others and representing cultures and worlds, the technological momentum of digitalization is evident throughout other social systems, as well. Even while Chapter 5 took up the internet as a resource for performing everyday tasks and resolving more or less pressing personal problems, most of the social consequences of digitalization fall outside the scope of this volume. The production and distribution of material and immaterial goods and services are being reconfigured, as are the conditions of labor and capital–labor relations (Baldwin, 2016). Health, education, and public services, being systems of social interaction, are increasingly premised on digital platforms and infrastructures, raising numerous issues of regulation and funding (van Dijck, Poell, & de Waal, 2018). And, for *media* systems, digitalization presents pressing issues of how to continue operations, at once, as businesses and as a fourth branch of governance (Hallin, 2020; Mancini, 2020). In the section considering further research, we return to the relationship between communication systems as generic front offices and their more specialized back offices, including but certainly not limited to news and other media as traditionally understood.

Capitalism with regional characteristics

Communication systems are, evidently, embedded in wider political economies – the second mechanism (Figure 1.2) circumscribing and determining (in the first instance (S. Hall, 1983)) which communicative practices may (not) unfold in particular contexts. As reviewed in Chapter 2, marketplaces of communication are shaped, at once, by supply and demand – for information, attention, mediating devices, and more – and by (mostly) national and (some) regional and global regulation by elected and delegated authorities. To one side, global political economies are thoroughly capitalized and marketized, with structures stimulating the social uses of information and communication through the diffusion of ever new consumer technologies (Rogers, 2003). The understanding that diverse social institutions and practices might be given special 'Chinese characteristics' has been associated with initiatives by Deng Xiaoping, from 1978, to introduce elements of a market economy in mainland China (Deng, 1984). It may be more appropriate, by now, to describe the three regions of the present study as instances of capitalism with special 'regional characteristics.' In all three settings, the development of technologies and services supporting one-to-one, one-to-many, many-to-many as well as many-to-one communication is being driven by market principles.

To the other side, the systems of political governance obtaining in China, Europe, and the United States are clearly distinctive. Chapter 2 (and parts of Chapter 1) reviewed the media and social systems of each of the seven countries, including the substantial differences in freedoms of information and communication, democratic participation, as well as digital capital or preparedness. With China as an outlier, there are significant distinctions to be made between the United States and Europe (and within Europe), as well, in terms of welfare systems and privacy and consumer protections generally, all of which enable and constrain communicative practices on the ground in each setting. The analyses in Chapter 2, further, noted the ambiguity of the divide between material and technological haves and have-nots: Whereas some regions of the world still await the diffusion of any widely accessible and applicable internet, in more prosperous parts digital technologies variously serve as means of either enhancing or restricting citizens' agency, with China effectively surveilling and filtering communication at home while exporting the required technologies to like-minded states. Regulatory regimes for the internet come with path dependencies on political and legal cultures. For better and worse, states cannot *not* regulate the communication systems under their jurisdiction.

Political economies leave further imprints on communication systems. Chapter 5 detailed how the unequal distribution of economic, cultural, social, and digital capitals relate to media and communication repertoires, with noticeable divides within, but also between, the seven countries of this study. Also for individual media and particular communicative practices, some are included, others mostly excluded. Most blatantly, the 'great firewall' cordons off China's online communication system from those of other political economies (even if it may be circumvented, to an extent, by Virtual Private Networks). Moreover, the findings regarding the uses of news and public affairs from legacy media indicate that, in China, as many as 27% of the present sample get updates less than weekly. If the present age is understood as one of monitory democracy and monitorial citizens (Keane, 2009; Schudson, 1998) – in which people will monitor their society and the world for when (political) action may (not) be needed – then citizens in China do have special characteristics. On the other hand, the analyses of media and communication repertoires in Chapter 3 found that, not just in China, but in Hungary and Italy, as well, people may be particularly active on social media, in part, to get alternative news from alternative sources beyond politically preconfigured media. And, as mentioned in Chapter 4, Chinese respondents are as likely as American respondents to post comments online for anybody to see (if only within the perimeters of 'their' firewall).

Trading cultures

The relative inclination of respondents in different cultural settings to either send or receive, both, or none of these things online, brings up the third and final factor determining communicative practices (Figure 1.2) – cultural traditions. In Chapter 1, we took our cue from Raymond Williams' (1975/1958) dictum that cultures are whole ways of life. Communication carries culture, which, in turn, configures communication in and about the lives being lived. Day to day and generation to generation, communication repeatedly inscribes what people do with each other into meaningful cultural traditions. And yet, culture is notoriously difficult to operationalize and interpret, by either quantitative or qualitative methodologies. We end this section of the chapter by noting some clues from the comparative analyses as to how cultural traditions are traded (*tradere*) in and by communication.

Chapter 4 highlighted a manifest inclination among our Chinese respondents to be, if not always-on, then always-available for communication, and we related this pattern to *guanxi* – the traditional emphasis in Chinese civilization on cultivating personal relations and networks (Yang, 1994). Both the quantitative evidence on the intensity of interpersonal interactions and the qualitative data identifying availability as a distinctive priority and a criterion of constant contact in China bear witness to a mechanism effectively generating (much more) one-to-one and many-to-many communication. Beyond China, several of the measures reported in Chapters 3 and 4 suggest a spectrum of communicative intensity on which, at one end, China is joined by Hungary and Italy, with the United Kingdom and the United States in a middle range, and Denmark and Germany occupying the opposite end. In one classic vocabulary of communication theory, this configuration aligns with two of Edward T. Hall's (1959) conceptions of the relationship between communicative practices and cultural traditions: high-context and low-context, and polychronic and monochronic culture(s). Taking China and Denmark as two extremes in these perspectives, in China multiple contexts of social relations (present and absent), and multiple interactions implicitly inviting attention all at the same time, likely motivate more frequent and diverse communications, whereas in Denmark delimited contexts with equally delimited interactions, one at a time, will be administered through more explicit and singular communications.

The point, of course, is not that these are essences of how the Danes, the Chinese, or any other nationality communicates, but rather that such mechanisms contribute to generating and patterning communicative practices across the *longues durées* of history (Braudel, 1980). Whereas some of the differences that culture makes are captured by quantitative measures of communication frequency and diversity, and other aspects by qualitative criteria of when (not) to communicate, further differences emerge from the three-way encounter of cultural traditions with political economies and the material technologies of the day. In Chapter 1, we referred to the idea of overdetermination – the complex interaction of several determining conditions to produce distinctive communicative practices. Intensive communicative interaction (China, Hungary, Italy) may be culturally prepared; it may, simultaneously, serve as a strategy of circumventing a communication system circumscribed by the political–economic powers that be in the present; and it may be afforded, even stimulated, by a specific historical technology supporting one-to-one as well as many-to-many communication. In comparison, more intermittent communicative interaction (Denmark, Germany) may, equally, be culturally prepared; it may bear witness to a relation of relative trust between the people communicating and relatively fewer, more or less official and established social sources of information; and it may persist even in societies with high internet penetration (Denmark, Germany, in Table 1.3) – which, in principle, had afforded and might be thought to promote both more, and more differentiated, communicative practices.

Opening a research agenda

This volume has presented a framework for the study of communication systems, pointing beyond *media* systems as traditionally conceptualized (Hallin & Mancini, 2004), and emphasizing the explanatory and interpretive value of *comparative* research, across cultural space as well as historical time. We have suggested and substantiated the validity and relevance of this framework through what may be taken as a case study of three world regions at the beginning of the 2020s, leaving most of the business of comparing communication systems unfinished, and raising additional questions of how to design and focus further research. In this section, we briefly identify four issues for future empirical studies, while noting, as well, an ongoing challenge of theory development regarding communicative practices at the intersection of long-standing cultural traditions, entrenched political economies, and innovative material technologies.

The first empirical issue follows from the necessarily limited scope of the Peoples' Internet project. Whereas the three regions covered in this book are of current strategic geopolitical interest, communication systems in other parts of the world call for similarly detailed studies in their own right. It may be taken as a sign of the growing maturity of a relatively young field that more culturally comparative studies are being published, also outside the specialization of intercultural communication research (Kim, 2018). The tradition of media systems research, for one, has begun to look beyond the Western horizons that framed its models from the outset (Hallin & Mancini, 2012). Another recent publication considered the culturally (and historically) variable meaning of being an audience, a public, and a user of media and communication services (Butsch & Livingstone, 2014). Building on earlier comparative classics (e.g., Blumler, McLeod, & Rosengren, 1992), more reference works are becoming available, too, as resources for further work in the area (Chan & Lee, 2017; Esser & Hanitzsch, 2012). Against the background of worldwide and society-wide digitalization, now is a good time to map not just media systems, but communication systems, as one contribution of the field of media and communication research to an interdisciplinary understanding of the contemporary world.

A second empirical task relates to comparisons across time. Despite a growing number of studies on (media and) communication history (for overview, see Simonson, Peck, Craig, & Jackson, 2013), the field has been, and still is, decidedly present-centered, in part responding to (perceptions of) constantly changing technologies and institutions and the associated demand for commercially and policy relevant knowledge. As suggested by the findings in this book, mass communication, for one, as shaped and reshaped over centuries, remains part and parcel of communication systems around the world. Three decades ago, Michael Schudson (1991) called for more *social* histories of the mutual constitution of communications and societies, beyond great-man institutional histories of mass media (and of digital upstarts), and beyond the-medium-is-the-message accounts of media and, recently, meta-media as revolutionizing social life as we used to know it so well. Social histories of either media or communication are still relatively few and far between (see, e.g., Peck, 2021). Another founder of the field, Kurt Lewin (1945: 129), had quipped that "nothing is as practical as a good theory." To inform theorizing and empirical research on contemporary communication systems, few things are as practical as a good history.

Third, different sectors of society, from the local to the global level, depend both on generic, (more or less) public communication systems, as emphasized in this volume, and on specialized, private, or privatized systems – from commercial platforms for goods and services to systems supporting healthcare and education (van Dijck et al., 2018). Media systems can be understood as one such sectoral system. A communication system might even be considered the sum of sectoral systems. But, as is often the case, the whole is more than the sum of the parts, and the parts have characteristic degrees of freedom, as variously asserted by owners, regulators, administrators, and other sectoral stakeholders.

Indeed, the demarcation of systems and subsystems – in technological, economic, and legal terms – is key to many of the normative issues pertaining to the organization and regulation of communication systems (which we take up in the final section of this chapter). Chapter 5 examined some of the many social sectors and roles in which people exercise communicative agency, crisscrossing divides between, for example, work and leisure, and between public and private domains of life. From cradle to grave – in terms of either survival and health or a meaningful existence informed through education, arts, and entertainments – communication systems condition what a person can do and be. At a time in history when digitalization is still gaining momentum, and when reconfigurations of state, market, and civil society are being negotiated within national and international institutions (Mansell & Ang, 2015), further and focused research on the junctures of strategic social sectors with communication systems is of evident public and normative interest.

A fourth and final set of empirical research questions arises from the fact that communication, more than providing representations *of* the world, constitutes a resource for human and social agency *in* and *on* the world. A case in point over the last decade has been the issue of misinformation and disinformation (Kapantai, Christopoulou, Berberidis, & Peristeras, 2021), which has reintroduced past notions of political propaganda, now by computational means (Woolley & Howard, 2019), to scientific and public agendas. If acting on misinformation or disinformation, publics might not serve their own interests in making their own histories. This widespread worry has been summed up in influential notions of echo chambers (Sunstein, 2007) and filter bubbles (Pariser, 2011), in which more or less erroneous information and extreme opinions will be promoted and reinforced, specifically on social media. Studies so far, however, do not support far-reaching conclusions concerning a polarization of public opinion by echo chamber and filter bubble. For one thing, empirical studies suggest that online news users and information seekers will encounter a diversity of viewpoints through incidental exposure and self-selection (e.g., Bakshy, Messing, & Adamic, 2015; Bruns, 2019b; Fletcher & Nielsen, 2017; Hosseinmardi et al., 2021). For another thing, as in media effects research generally (Jensen, 2021a), it is not clear that exposure to either misinformation or disinformation drives (a particular kind of) political opinions and actions: There is hardly any empirical evidence supporting this widespread assumption of so much contemporary public debate (Lazer et al., 2018).

Instead, the framework of communication systems invites a return to one of the foundational insights of the field, namely, that information flows in steps, across multiple media, including embodied human beings (Katz & Lazarsfeld, 1955; Lazarsfeld, Berelson, & Gaudet, 1944). To the classic two-step flow of mass and interpersonal communication has been added a third step of networked communication (Jensen, 2009), leading down further intermedial and intertextual paths. In order to assess and evaluate the difference that misinformation or disinformation, or any form of information, makes in different contexts of social action, many more qualitative, quantitative, as well as multimethod studies are needed to characterize and map the steps and trajectories of information throughout the communication systems in question.

Comparative research on communication and culture, predictably, presents issues for theory development. Chapter 5 specifically noted the limitations of Bourdieu's (1984/1979) analytical framework for capturing the category of social capital, and its relation to *guanxi*, in the Chinese context. Chapters 3 and 4, further, laid out culturally distinctive ways and means of being social that are only captured in the broadest of terms by Carey's (1989b/1975) definition of communication as the production, maintenance, repair, and transformation of realities, including individual and social identities. Chapter 6 also documented the emphatically regionalized nature of online tracking, what amounts to multiple dialects of many-to-one communication, as well. The field has long debated how to recognize the many local forms of the global, universal human practice of communication (e.g., Christians & Nordenstreng, 2014; Dissanayake, 1988; Goggin & McLelland, 2009; Kincaid, 1987; Wang, 2011). The comparative study of communication systems presents a welcome opportunity to revisit received models, of communication and of research; it also brings to the table practical, ethical, and political choices and dilemmas at a time of technological and institutional transformation.

Engaging public and political agendas

The capability of communication

Chapter 1 (and the Methodological Appendix in Chapter 8) introduced the premise that (communication) research is necessarily interested, in the specific sense that studies address not only what is, but also what could be, so as to inform public and political debate on what ought to be, and what should be done. Whereas culturally comparative studies generally facilitate such a weighing of ends and means, this section adds a second and more specific premise, defining communication as a distinctive human *capability*. Depending on the communication systems circumscribing people, particular communicative practices become possible (or not); depending on their communicative practices, individuals and collectives can (not) do and be certain things.

Pioneered by Amartya Sen (1999) and Martha C. Nussbaum (2011), the capabilities tradition has reinvigorated a positive understanding of human agency – freedom, in philosophical terminology – if only with occasional or implicit reference to communication as a human universal (for applications within communication studies, see, e.g., Birdsall, 2011; Britz, Hoffmann, Ponelis, Zimmer, & Lor, 2013; Coleman, Moss, & Martinez-Perez, 2018; Couldry, 2012; Garnham, 1997; Hesmondhalgh, 2017; Jacobson, 2016; Kleine, 2013; Mansell, 2002; Moss, 2018). Freedom, in this perspective, is not the original state of an individual in any natural or social circumstance, but a collective and historical accomplishment that must be maintained and reenacted on a continuous basis (Berlin, 1969/1958). Focusing attention on "enhancing justice and removing injustice" in specific social contexts and with reference to empirical alternatives, Sen (2009: ix) distinguished between freedom as an intrinsic value of human lives and as a set of instrumental rights designed to realize this basic value. On the one hand, freedom covers a set of means, of which he listed five: "(1) political freedoms, (2) economic facilities, (3) social opportunities, (4) transparency guarantees and (5) protective security" (Sen, 1999: n.p.). On the other hand, the capabilities approach treats freedom as an end in itself, "the freedoms of individuals as the basic building blocks. Attention is thus paid particularly to the expansion of the 'capabilities' of persons to lead the kind of lives they value – and have reason to value." In this understanding, capabilities manifest themselves as "functionings" or "the various things a person may value doing or being."

As illustration, Sen (1999: n.p.) has referred to the difference between an affluent person fasting and a destitute person starving. While both have the same functioning and are, in a sense, doing the same thing, each evidently has a different "capability set." There is an existential difference between what the first and the second person *could* do. Like the affordances of media, the capabilities of humans are to be assessed in relational terms, including the historical time and cultural space in which they are exercised. Also in more affluent countries, it is essential to ask what money can buy: "Being relatively poor in a rich country can be a great capability handicap, even when one's absolute income is high in terms of world standards."

One key implication of the capabilities approach is that the evaluation of potential and actual human flourishing (*eudaimonia*) around the world calls for more complex measures than standard ones such as income – whether personal or national. "For example, family income levels may be adjusted downward by illiteracy and upward by high levels of education, and so on, to make them equivalent in terms of capability achievement" (Sen, 1999: n.p.). Capability sets amount to life packages, beyond physical survival and material sufficiency. Capabilities, moreover, may be reinterpreted over time with reference both to ethically and politically motivated human rights, and to what was once inconceivable even as a human right, for example, personalized medicine or digital privacy. In sum, Sen's account of capabilities allows for a differentiated and processual understanding of what freedom – human agency – is, has been, and could become.

Among the contested issues in the capabilities literature have been how many capabilities there are, and whether a minimal standard applies to any given capability. Whereas Sen has refrained from judgment in both respects, emphasizing the importance of generally minimizing suffering, injustice, or lack of freedom through concrete social planning, Martha C. Nussbaum (2011) has proposed a list of ten central capabilities, ranging from life and bodily integrity to senses, imagination, and thought. For each of these, she has advocated a threshold or "ample social minimum" (p. 40) as a necessary requirement for social justice. Her summary question was, "among the many things that human beings might develop the capacity to do, which ones are the really valuable ones, which are the ones that a minimally just society will endeavor to nurture and support?" (p. 28).

Of special interest in the present context is Nussbaum's treatment of what Sen (1999: n.p.) had referred to as a "capability set," which she reformulated in terms of an interplay of capabilities that may be mutually reinforcing. In this regard, Nussbaum (2011) pointed to two capabilities that "play a distinctive *architectonic* role: they organize and pervade the others" (p. 39). First, *affiliation* refers to the ability to live with others and "to be able to imagine the situation of another," but also affiliation to oneself: "having the social bases of self-respect and nonhumiliation." Second, *practical reason* means "being able to form a conception of the good and to engage in critical reflection about the planning of one's life" (p. 34), which, in turn, entails the "opportunity to choose and order the functionings corresponding to the various other capabilities" (p. 39).

Each of these architectonic capabilities depends on the capability of communication, not listed by Nussbaum (2011) and only briefly gestured at by Sen (2009). Communication is a necessary condition of any affiliation with others and of the exercise of practical reason. Whereas, quantitatively, most communications belong to the innumerable interactions that inform the ongoing structuration of societies and cultures, some interactions address essentially contestable choices regarding decisive actions that have long-term and sometimes unforeseeable consequences. Individuals and communities discursively produce – hypothesize and anticipate – solutions to problematic situations (Dewey, 1903) by devising procedures, some of which are consolidated as institutions and practices of political governance. In both mundane and momentous interchanges, human beings find themselves in a communicative position, drawing on past experience and present interactions, and confronted by agendas for future action.

Rights and resources

Such a communicative position is part of the human condition: Humans "cannot *not* communicate" (Watzlawick, Beavin, & Jackson, 1967: 49), for survival and existence. But the communicative position is delineated by communication systems that are the products of collective decisions and social planning and, hence, open to regulation and reform. The present volume has mapped how people, within the contemporary communication systems of China, Europe, and the United States, do things with media. Given different communication systems, people can and will do different things. Deliberation on such differences presents fundamental normative questions of human rights, and the reform and redevelopment of these and related social systems pose practical challenges of how to secure the necessary and sufficient resources for realizing the human capabilities at stake.

The understanding of communication as a human right was incorporated into the Universal Declaration of Human Rights (United Nations, 1948) (UDHR), and has been reaffirmed by subsequent covenants and much national legislation. Most commonly cited regarding the two rights of access to information and of communication with others is Article 19: "Everyone has the right to freedom of opinion and expression; this right includes freedom to hold opinions without interference and to seek, receive and impart information and ideas through any media and regardless of frontiers." In addition, a right of participation was recognized in UDHR: "Everyone has the right to take part in the government of his [sic] country, directly or through freely chosen representatives" (Article 21), as was a right to privacy: "No one shall be subjected to arbitrary interference with his [sic] privacy, family, home or correspondence" (Article 12). It is these four rights that also current communication systems, in the end, ought to, and could, observe and uphold (see further Jensen, 2021b).

The rest of this section briefly considers the findings of the Peoples' Internet project against the background of these universally recognized rights: To access available *information*; to engage a few or many others, or the masses, in *communication*; *participation* in political governance and other aspects of local, national, and global community; and *privacy* protecting the communicative practices of individuals. Each of these rights depends on resources: Ways and means of translating the general human capability of communication into actual functionings. Also in matters of communication, freedom, as suggested by the capabilities tradition, is served by the presence, rather than the absence, of institutions regulating human actions and social interactions. In Figure 1.2, we laid out three forces and factors that condition communicative practices: political economies, cultural traditions, and material technologies. In an amended version, Figure 7.1 specifies three categories of institutions that enable and constrain – regulate – the operation of communication systems. First, the distinctive regulatory regimes of China, Europe, and the United States, make certain communicative practices more or less likely, possible or impossible. Second, institutions of knowledge and education condition, at once, the production and delivery of communication goods and services, and the cultivation of citizens' communicative competences. Third, as suggested by medium theory in Chapter 1, the infrastructures of communication that emerge over decades and centuries, constitute institutions in their own right – meta-institutions that frame the forms and functions of other institutions: sciences and arts, business models and state bureaucracies.

Institutions of communication and regulation

Starting from the institutions regulating the intersection of communication technologies and political economies, the availability of information is limited, most clearly, in China by 'the great firewall.' While mass communication and

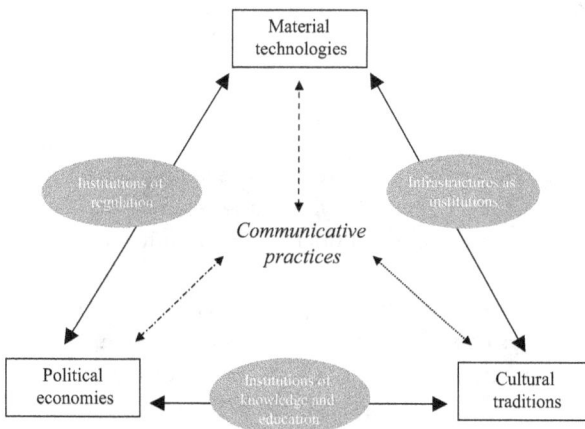

FIGURE 7.1 Institutions of communication and regulation

networked communication make information widely available here, as well, its selection and combination take place under the auspices of the party state's networked authoritarianism (MacKinnon, 2011). In comparison, Americans and Europeans are 'free' to search and access any information, but within communication systems that are configured in line with the production of surplus value from data, in marketplaces of attention (Webster, 2014), and, increasingly, premised on digital surveillance (Zuboff, 2019). Despite other significant differences between American and European communication systems, they share a relative absence of public regulation of the publicly available information. Citizens might even be seen to encounter a different sort of 'great glass wall,' akin to the glass ceiling identified by feminist theory and policy (Department of Labor, 1995): All the information in the world appears to be on offer, but on terms that are neither transparent to citizen-users nor subject to consequential, institutional regulation.

The regulation of digital privacy, in fact, moved to the top of the agendas of international public debate during the 2010s (Bräunlich et al., 2021). For example, a principle of *habeas data* has been advanced, by analogy to *habeas corpus*, to recognize the general, far-reaching implications of the more specific issue of privacy (for an overview, see Guadamuz, 2001). *Habeas corpus*, deriving from the English Magna Carta of 1215 and integral to modern jurisprudence around the world, literally means 'you may have the body.' The classic principle has served to protect individuals from unlawful imprisonment. *Habeas data* – 'you may have the data' – would, to begin, let individuals have personal information about themselves corrected or removed from relevant registers. It was first implemented in the constitution of Brazil in 1988 (Doneda & Mendes, 2014), and the European General Data Protection Regulation (GDPR), which took effect in 2018, included aspects of the principle. Chapter 6 illustrated how the tracking of online trajectories has become integral to communication systems across world regions; Chapter 4 noted fieldwork participants' awareness of their own many-to-one communication, but with concerns being expressed about the potential ramifications in interpersonal rather than systemic terms. Research has debated whether users approach digital systems through active or positive self-regulation, in terms of a privacy calculus of pros and cons (Trepte et al., 2017), or rather more passively, with a sense of digital resignation (Draper & Turow, 2019). As a minimum, because this is a feature, not a bug, of critical infrastructures, it calls for democratic oversight and public regulation. *Habeas data* belongs up there with the classic human rights of information and communication.

Institutions of research and education, further, inform what is said and done in and through communication systems; they cultivate knowledges, competences, and cultural traditions that are circulated by markets and regulated by states. Whereas research and development condition both the availability of information and the quality of communication services, the Peoples' Internet project has focused on the users of communication systems as persons and social agents.

Across the three regions, for interpersonal, mass, as well as networked communication, communicative and (other) social differences and divides go together, from education and income to urbanization and gender. As elaborated in Chapter 5, resources – capitals – accumulated in one domain carry over to other domains: Economic, cultural, social, and digital capitals are literally exchangeable, in and by communication. Also in the practical perspectives of public debate and political deliberation, the study of communication systems writ large is essential and urgent.

To conclude, we reiterate a premise from Chapter 1: Material technologies determine communicative practices, if only in the first instance (S. Hall, 1983), as infrastructures lending institutional form to human doings and beings. Writing, printing, broadcasting, and computing have each changed the conditions of human communication and social interaction, and there is every reason for publics and politicians to reflect and deliberate on the potentials as well as the limitations of each new technology of communication. Institutionalized as generic infrastructures, print media came to circumscribe and inscribe modern forms of life, from natural sciences and reformed religions to nation-states and public spheres (Anderson, 1991; Briggs, Burke, & Ytreberg, 2020; Eisenstein, 1979; Habermas, 1989/1962; Thompson, 1995). At the time of writing, the affordances of digital technologies are still being imagined and invented. For the time

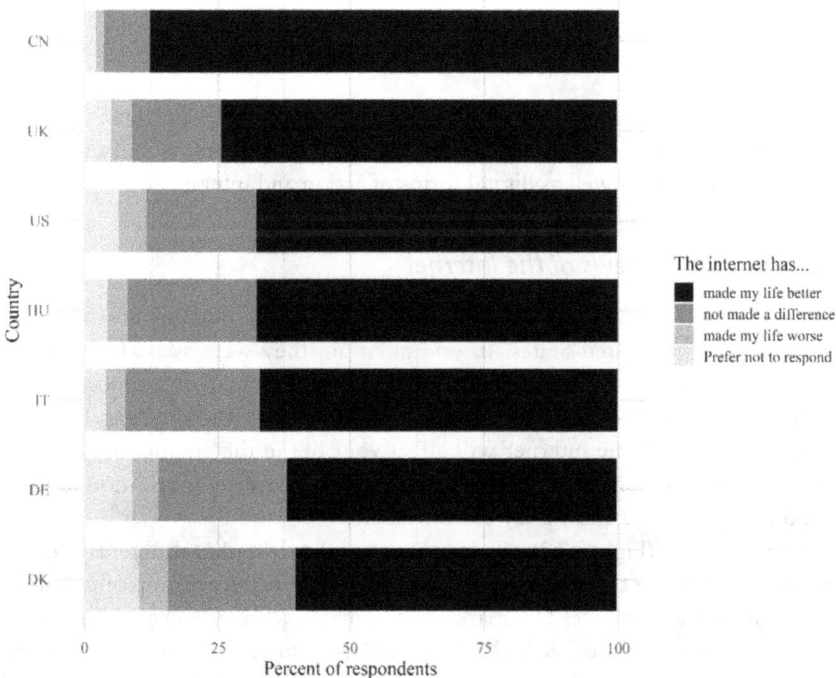

FIGURE 7.2   Reviews of the internet

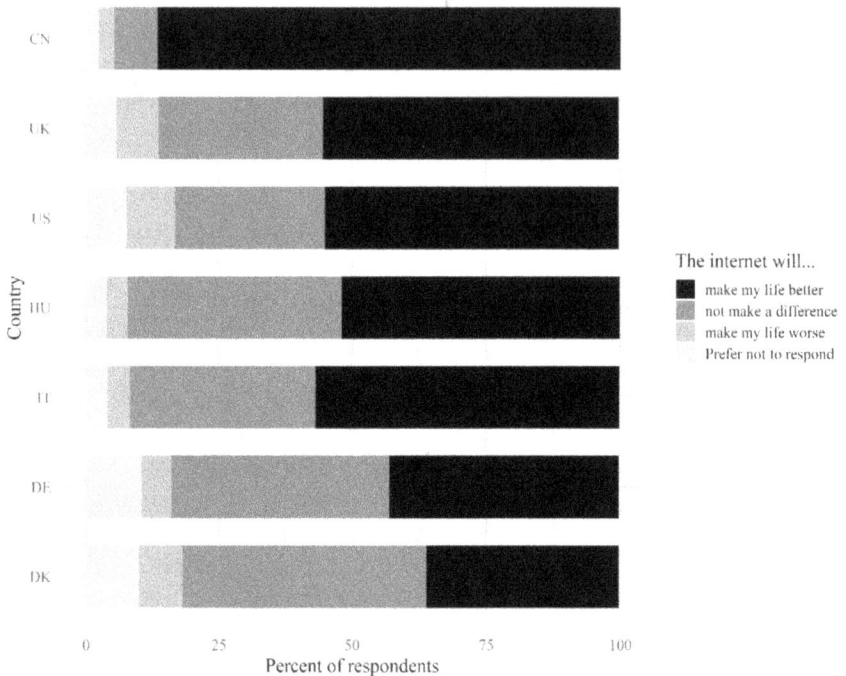

FIGURE 7.3   Previews of the internet

being, researchers, along with politicians and publics, exercise their capabilities and rights of communication within systems that combine and configure embodied, analog, as well as digital forms of action and interaction.

Reviews and previews of the internet

We leave the last word about the internet to our survey respondents in China, Europe, and the United States. In one question, they were asked to consider, "Since you started using the internet – to what extent has the internet affected your life?" The following question asked them to "Imagine the next 10 years. How do you think the internet will affect your life in the coming decade?" In both cases, the options were: Better, no difference, or worse, in addition to non-response. Figures 7.2 and 7.3 lay out the results.

Looking back (Figure 7.2), the internet is evaluated rather differently across, but also within, the three regions. A relatively more skeptical group of countries (national samples) includes Denmark and Germany, whereas especially in China and, to a comparable degree, the United Kingdom respondents consider the internet a valuable addition to their lives, with Hungary, Italy, and the United States occupying a middle ground.

Looking forward to the coming decade (Figure 7.3), respondents in China reaffirm their faith in the potentials of the internet, while Danes and Germans remain the most skeptical. In a wide middle ground, in the majority of the seven countries examined here, people may still be making sense of, and making up their minds about, what the internet is, ought to be, and could become.

8

METHODOLOGICAL APPENDIX

Klaus Bruhn Jensen and Rasmus Helles

Critical realism

We approach scientific research as a specific kind of social (and communicative) practice, anchored in time and place, and in particular interests as to how and why new knowledge could and ought to be produced in the first place. While critical realism as originally articulated by Roy Bhaskar (1979) has developed into a big tent encompassing a variety of approaches (for overviews, see Archer, Bhaskar, Collier, Lawson, & Norrie, 1998; Danermark, Ekström, Jakobsen, & Karlsson, 2019), we emphasize two premises of the tradition for present purposes: Critical realism is realist in that it presumes the operation of certain material and immaterial mechanisms as determinations or causes enabling, constraining, and bounding, in this case, human communication; the tradition is critical insofar as it proposes to question and shift such boundaries.

Following the science wars of the twentieth century (Ashman & Baringer, 2001; Labinger & Collins, 2001), critical realism has charted a third way and a middle road between two conflicting paradigms that had prioritized *either* the objects of inquiry as elementary and manifest (positivism, empiricism) *or* the inquiring subject as their origin and source (constructivism, postmodernism). Recognizing *both* a reality independent of human inquirers *and* their active role in comprehending reality, critical realists undertake the discovery of what they take to be underlying or generative *mechanisms*: Natural forces and social factors that explain why humans have particular *experiences* of reality and witness a certain range of *events*. How can and do people communicate, and how may research interpret and explain specific communicative practices with reference to their material circumstances, institutional conditions, and cultural contexts?

As illustration, consider how social networks are built, maintained, and modified in and by communication, in part, via what has come to be referred to since the

DOI: 10.4324/9781003057055-8

2000s, simply, as social media. In a first step, researchers *experience* – describe and document – the verbal and visual expressions by which people present themselves to others: family, friends, acquaintances, and anonymous others. Next, quantitative and qualitative analyses serve to characterize these data as evidence of particular kinds of *events*: Personal life transitions or participation in public–political manifestations. In a third step, the presence (or absence) of specific experiences and events, and the patterns of particular individuals and groups (not) having certain experiences and (not) participating in certain events, are explained theoretically by *mechanisms*, from the diffusion (or not) of digital networks and devices (Rogers, 2003) to the political (de)regulation of communication markets (Radu, 2019) and the cultural conventions of (not) presenting oneself to (more or less significant) others (Goffman, 1959). Mechanisms as conceived by critical realism represent operationalizations of the three sets of basic conditions circumscribing communicative practices that we identified in Chapter 1 (Figure 1.1): Material technologies, political economies, and cultural traditions.

For the concrete planning and conduct of empirical studies, critical realism departs from three complementary positions:

- *Ontological realism.* Critical realism approaches reality as a limit condition – a working hypothesis enabling further inquiry into the specifics of what is, but also what could be. Ontological realism reverses the burden of proof that science and scholarship have sought to lift since the modern turn associated with René Descartes's *cogito*: Doubts arise in concrete instances, in practice, not as any theory-driven or blanket skepticism. The proof of reality is in the interactions we have with it – as researchers, communicators, informants, and much else – and in its resistance to some kinds of interventions (Hacking, 1983). Social media users in mainland China cannot access Facebook (at least not without workarounds such as Virtual Private Networks (VPN)); social media users in Europe and the United States cannot communicate through WeChat (at least not without substantial language and some intercultural training).
- *Epistemological relativism.* Critical realism, further, assumes that human understanding of reality depends on a range and sequence of perceptions, cognitions, and inferences, all of which may be questioned, rejected, or revised, by individuals upon reflection or through deliberation by communities. Relativism here does not imply that "anything goes" (Feyerabend, 1975), but rather that different levels and aspects of reality call for different types of inquiry and analysis. Where surveys address (some aspects of) *what* people do on social media, qualitative interviewing help to articulate responses as to *why*: What are the experienced motivations and outcomes of being always-on and staying in touch on Chinese and American (equaling European) social media? The harvesting of third-party trackers on websites produces evidence of additional qualities and quantities of online communication that neither surveys nor in-depth interviews can capture.

- *Judgmental rationality.* Finally, all research involves an exercise of rationality which, at some point, must end in (fallible) judgments about what is the case, and what to do next, whether concluding that further research is needed, or acting on the insight that the line between online community standards and the public policies regulating social media may need redrawing. In both cases, it is analysis at the level of theoretical frameworks and epistemologies, rather than the measurements and discursive meanings emerging from data collection and analysis (as conceived by the analytical levels of Figure 1.4), that motivates either continued reflection or concerted action. As a communicative practice, scientific research is itself a form of human and social action, circumscribed by material, institutional, and discursive conditions, and inscribing knowledge interests (Habermas, 1971/1968) into both empirical study designs and normative inferences and implications drawn from findings. In Chapter 7, we discussed some of the political and ethical issues that comparative studies bring into focus, and which came to the fore in international public debate, too, during the 2010s. We return, at the end of this appendix chapter, to some of the choices facing future comparative communication studies regarding their practical applications and policy implications. First, however, the following sections present additional design and technical information on the three key empirical elements of the study, further situating each approach in relation to critical realism, and explicating the knowledge interests guiding their combination in the study as a whole.

Quantitative surveys

Critical knowledge interest

It was Jürgen Habermas (1971/1968) who coined the concept of knowledge interests. While he subsequently changed his position, instead prioritizing disinterested communicative action as the source of empowering and emancipatory knowledge (Habermas, 1973) (for an assessment of Habermas's shifting positions, see Jensen, 2021b: chap. 3), his original statement holds continued explanatory value for contemporary research practice. In brief summary, Habermas (1971/1968) identified three basic knowledge interests. First, a *technical* knowledge interest is associated with "the empirical-analytic sciences" that concern themselves with the production of "possible predictive knowledge" (p. 308), with natural sciences as the prototype. Importantly, a technical knowledge interest may spill over into the study of humans, cultures, and societies as part of a scientistic perspective emphasizing social control. Second, the *historical–hermeneutic* sciences engage in "the interpretation of texts" and "the understanding of meaning [and] tradition" (p. 309f.). Again, if one approaches meaning – the understanding of self, others, and tradition – in an "objectivist" perspective, Habermas suggested, this "locks up history in a museum" (p. 316). The third, *emancipatory* knowledge interest was the hopeful element of the typology. Here, Habermas was careful to distinguish "the systematic *sciences of social action,* that is economics, sociology, and political science" from "a critical social science" that targets "ideologically frozen relations of dependence that can in principle be transformed" through a process disseminating knowledge – communication – what other social theory has referred to as a process of double hermeneutics (Giddens, 1979). A critical knowledge interest, in this perspective, considers less what *is* than what *could* be and what perhaps, on reflection and deliberation, *ought* to be *different*.

As moving targets still taking shape around the world, communication systems invite critical comparative research on what they could be in practice, or might become at least in principle, departing from the things that states and markets, citizens and consumers, have, in fact, been doing to and with them so far. In order to examine and evaluate communication systems, it was essential to include in the research design a broad variety of communicative practices, covering not just the uses of different media, new and old, for news and entertainment, but as importantly the myriad ordinary (and sometimes extraordinary) actions that people carry on in and by communication. To assess who does (not) do certain things with media, in which contexts, and with what consequences, it was equally essential to document the distribution of all these communicative practices across sociodemographic segments within the different national and regional settings. Surveys, accordingly, presented themselves as the baseline method of choice. As noted in Chapter 1, amid an ongoing digitalization of research infrastructures, as well, surveys remain a necessary instrument for comparative studies covering multiple media forms and communicative practices.

Questionnaire

The Peoples' Internet (PIN) project developed a standardized questionnaire, which was translated into the major language of each country, using identical wordings and scales of measurement. The selection and combination of questions emerged from an iterative process with contributions from project participants in all seven countries – mainland China, Denmark, Germany, Hungary, Italy, the United Kingdom, and the United States – so as to make each question meaningful and relevant across national and cultural settings. Relying on English as the common working language of the project, this process produced a baseline questionnaire in English, which, next, was translated into local versions by native speakers and reviewed by project participants as quality control. In each case, illustrative examples, for example, of television channels, online services, and mobile applications were included with the various questions to facilitate respondents' recognition of the topic in question. In addition to a standard range of background variables (e.g., age, gender, ethnicity, education, income, marital status), the surveys addressed four sets of topics:

- *media use* (frequency of use and time spent, for traditional as well as digital media, from books and newspapers to websites and streaming services)

- *interpersonal communication* (who respondents communicate with, through which media, from face-to-face interaction to instant messaging)
- *online activities* (from using social network sites, selling/buying things, and banking to dating, contacting health services, and interacting with state agencies)
- uses of particular media and communicative practices to perform *everyday tasks* and to clarify situations involving *choices* (e.g., looking for a new job, weighing controversial information about a politician, resolving a moral dilemma)

Survey modes

In order to secure valid data sets from all seven countries, it was necessary to employ two different survey modes or procedures of data collection. The two modes represent standard practice for the settings in question. On the one hand, in all countries except China, the surveys relied on samples deriving from non-probability sampling through internet panels (Dillman et al., 2014). In recent years, online panels have provided a common and efficient way of surveying the population of countries with high internet penetration rates. As people self-select into internet panels and further choose which surveys to take part in, this approach could be considered closer to convenience sampling than to a classic random sampling approach. However, reviews of the quality of such non-probability procedures suggest that the resulting samples appropriately reflect the parameters of populations when post-stratification measures or similar forms of weighting are applied (Salganik, 2018). Accordingly, the present panel surveys were carried out by an international provider, YouGov (during the summer of 2018), and then weighted by age, gender, education, and geography.

In China, on the other hand, internet penetration remained comparatively low at the time of this study (Table 8.1). Thus, in order to cover internet users across the country, specifically including both rural and urban areas, a face-to-face survey mode was chosen. CTR Market Research carried out the face-to-face interviews with a sample deriving from multistage cluster sampling (from December 2018 to March 2019). Also this sample was weighted by demographics to represent the entire population of mainland China. And, because the Chinese sample was taken from the full population, it was necessary to further subsample the internet population (those who have used the internet and continue to do so). This entailed removing the 32.6% of the Chinese sample who were non-users (a slightly smaller percentage than what would be expected from internet penetration rates in China as indicated in Table 8.1). As a last step, and to enable relevant comparisons between and among countries, the resulting sample of Chinese internet users was randomly subsampled to be of equal size to the samples from other countries.

The two survey modes suggest a classic methodological dilemma for comparative research, namely, how to balance identical research procedures and approximated comparable outcomes. Evidently, respondents may answer questions

TABLE 8.1 Survey baseline statistics (compared to the general population per country)

Country (listed by population size)	Internet penetration[1]	Percent 18–35 yr Sample (Pop.)[2]	Perc. Tertiary Educ. Sample (Pop.)[3]	Perc. Urban Sample (Pop.)[2]
China	54.3% (2017)	45.5% (39.9%)	11.4% (9.7%)	50.3% (52.1%)
United States	87.3% (2017)	29.3% (37.0%)	33.7% (48.3%)	80.7% (80.5%)
Germany	89.7% (2018)	27.7% (29.8%)	19.0% (29.9%)	80.3% (80.3%)
United Kingdom	94.9% (2018)	26.4% (35.4%)	39.7% (47.2%)	81.1% (81.1%)
Italy	74.4% (2018)	26.8% (27.6%)	26.8% (19.6%)	N/A
Hungary	76.1% (2018)	29.3% (30.5%)	38.6% (26.0%)	70.5% (51.3%)
Denmark	97.3% (2018)	30.0% (33.7%)	22.3% (40.4%)	N/A

[1] International Telecommunication Union (ITU, 2019). Years in parenthesis refer to the latest available data for each country.
[2] United Nations – Statistical Division (United Nations, 2019). Share of the population 18–35 years of the adult population of 15–74 years. Data from 2017, China from 2010.
[3] Organisation for Economic Co-operation and Development (OECD, 2020). Population 25–64 years. Data from 2018, China from 2010.

differently in face-to-face interactions and online by themselves (Dillman et al., 2014). Since an online sample was unlikely to deliver the same coverage of the internet population in China as in the other countries, however, the combination of survey modes seemed the least worst option for the present study.

Samples

The procedures produced a total sample of 10,772: China (n = 1,617), Denmark (n = 1,510), Germany (n = 1,511), Hungary (n = 1,505), Italy (n = 1,514), the United Kingdom (n = 1,610), and the United States (n = 1,505). In addition to the different survey modes, a few caveats merit attention. First, between 88% (in China) and 95% (in Denmark and the United Kingdom) of respondents use the internet on a daily basis. Analyses and inferences, then, are based on a particularly (digitally) active segment of populations. Second, the internet populations differ from the overall populations in distinctive ways, which we consider next.

Table 8.1 sums up key differences between our survey samples and overall populations (the latter numbers in parentheses). The numbers bear witness to various stages of internet diffusion. For Denmark, Germany, the United Kingdom, and the United States, where nine out of ten use the internet, the internet population likely mirrors the general population; for Italy, Hungary, and especially China, the picture is different. In the case of China, the sample likely is subject to a first-mover effect, dominated by a relatively more tech-savvy segment. In more internet-saturated countries, samples likely tap a more diverse set of communicative practices encompassing a wider range of user backgrounds. It is important to keep these differences in mind when interpreting the various analyses and to remain cautious when inferring present and potential future trajectories of communication systems in the three regions.

More specifically, Table 8.1 indicates variations on three parameters: The share of young persons (18–35 years) in the population 15–74; people with tertiary educational backgrounds; and people living in urban settings. It is reassuring to note that, in China, the sample largely reflects the general population across these parameters; we take this as testament to the careful sampling procedures employed in China. In comparison, the online sampling procedures for the rest of the countries present issues of interpretation and comparison. In the United States, the United Kingdom, Germany, and Denmark, samples have a somewhat lower share of well-educated respondents than expected; the sample is also slightly older than expected. By contrast, in Hungary, and to a lesser extent in Italy, the sample is both more well-educated and more urban than the general population, representing more elite segments. The lesson is that an online sampling strategy, while not producing consistent biases, may affect samples in various respects, depending on geographical settings (e.g., regions of the world) and social systems (e.g., levels of internet penetration). In the end, however, all samples did manifest substantial variations across key sociodemographic variables, which made them suitable for comparative analyses, while keeping in mind the caveats noted here.

Analyses and inferences

To analyze survey responses, we relied, in particular, on the statistical technique of latent class analysis (LCA). We first comment on technical aspects of LCA, and conclude the treatment of the surveys by returning to their explanatory value and critical potential.

LCA is basically a clustering approach that assigns cases (e.g., respondents) to clusters based on their scores on several indicator variables (e.g., survey questions). Like other clustering techniques, LCA seeks to maximize differences between clusters (heterogeneity across clusters), while minimizing them inside clusters (homogeneity within clusters) (Uprichard, 2009). In contrast to standard clustering techniques (such as K-means or hierarchical clustering), LCA relies on probability scores rather than measures of distance (e.g., Euclidean distance). In this way, each case receives a probability score for each cluster, rather than being assigned to one separate cluster. A good reason for preferring probability scores is that cases rarely fit perfectly within one cluster, but will share similarities with the members of other clusters, so that a unique assignment of cases to clusters will introduce classification errors into the statistical model (Bolck et al., 2004). Probabilistic approaches mitigate such errors (Magidson, 2002; Vermunt and Magidson, 2002). LCA, further, relies on standard measures of model fit (such as log-likelihood estimates and information criteria) to aid in selecting the most appropriate cluster solution. LCA, lastly, allows for the use of categorical variables as indicator variables, and for including covariates to describe the clusters through secondary variables, i.e., describing clusters through a range of sociodemographic characteristics, including national and cultural affiliations.

To explore the relationship between communications and capitals in Chapter 5, the analyses further incorporated multiple correspondence analysis (MCA), the method pioneered by Pierre Bourdieu (1984/1979). Here, to capture relevant nuances, we went on to conduct ascending hierarchical cluster (AHC) analysis and multiple factor analysis for contingency tables (MFACT) (see further Leguina & Downey, 2021).

Taken together, the survey analyses served to map a broad range of communicative practices, online and offline, and to identify their distribution and variation across sociodemographic segments as well as national and regional settings. As data points, individual survey responses bear witness, in the terminology of critical realism, to *events* (acts of representation and interaction), as expressed by respondents in response and with reference to an *experience* of familiar categories of doing different things with media (e.g., sending an email, streaming a television series, searching information on best buys). As accumulated and interrelated in several analytical steps, these data points support the inference and interpretation of *mechanisms*, for instance, regarding inequalities of access to information and communicative resources, and additional mechanisms regulating the preferred or expected places, times, and frequencies of engaging in one-to-one, one-to-many, and many-to-many communication, respectively. Mechanisms, such as capitals (Chapter 5) and the distinctive affordances of humans and technologies for communication (Chapter 4), are elaborated and substantiated, in the other chapters of the book, in the terms of relevant theoretical frameworks.

Qualitative fieldworks

Critical knowledge interest

Qualitative fieldwork in each of the three world regions (represented by China, Denmark, and the United States) complemented the quantitative surveys. If quantitative studies focus on *what* people do with media, with each other, and with social institutions – the distributions and variations of different communicative practices – qualitative studies shift attention toward the *how* and the *why* (*not*): How, for example, do different forms of capital enter into the structuration of communication in specific social contexts and segments, and why do people persist in (or refrain from) joining, for instance, political debates, whether in face-to-face encounters or through online fora? What, in any event, is a 'political' debate or a 'personal' dilemma calling for resolution? Qualitative research is generally recognized as a form of thick description (Geertz, 1973) of human *experiences* and social *events* in their concrete contexts and, thus, a resource for probing the *mechanisms* at work, their delimitations and interrelations. What kind of social event did, in fact, take place; how did the experiences of participants relate to the event, as a condition, a consequence, or both; which material forces and immaterial factors might be inferred from these events and these experiences; and why did *other* events and experiences *not* take place or precedence?

The qualitative component of the PIN project primarily explored the embedding of communicative practices into the diverse everyday lives of different informants in the three regions (on details of the qualitative design, see further Lai, Pagh, & Zeng, 2019). In this way, qualitative data served to pinpoint instances of the intersection of material technologies, political economies, and cultural traditions (the three aspects of communication systems, Figure 1.1) in concrete communicative practices, their forms and contents, presence or absence. Whereas the conclusion in Chapter 7 discusses qualitative–quantitative complementarities with reference to the present findings, we reiterate here the conception of qualitative approaches as different, but equal to quantitative approaches for examining and evaluating communication systems. Qualitative and quantitative data are both necessary, but insufficient sources of insight into the structure of communication systems and the communicative agency of their users.

Sampling for networks and maximum variation

While sometimes treated as an aside in the methodology sections of qualitative publications, sampling is a key consideration for the validity and explanatory value of qualitative work. A legacy of classic anthropological and sociological ethnographies, and an important component of media and communication studies (Jensen, 2021c; Lindlof & Taylor, 2019), qualitative research has increasingly embraced the requirements of systematic empirical data collection and analysis. A central challenge has been how to define and motivate variants of what remained, for a long time, a negatively defined remainder category of *non-probability* sampling. A related challenge has been how to move beyond a still common conception of qualitative fieldwork as the study of a geographically or organizationally bounded site, its members, and what (the devil they think) they are up to (Geertz, 1974). In a world increasingly connected by communication, transportation, and migration, the fields of theoretical as well as practical interest frequently constitute more than one site. We took our cue from George E. Marcus (1995), who called for *multi-sited* ethnographies, in part, to allow for the establishment of macrocosms or encompassing realities through reference to multiple distributed microcosms. To find out what people do with media, and along with others, we followed *people* moving *across sites*, physically and virtually, in and by communication.

In sampling terms, we combined *network* sampling and *maximum variation* sampling. The main strength of network sampling, on the one hand, is that it taps into already existing social networks of relations, rather than hypothesizing or tracking such relations in a large and heterogeneous universe. Networked samples, accordingly, afforded naturalistic perspectives on communications and other social interactions; simultaneously, they offered multiple perspectives by different social agents on the *same* interactions or issues. On the other hand, maximum variation sampling ensured a measure of diversity across age, gender, ethnicity, educational level, religious beliefs, marital and parental status, and place of residence. While, in a small *n* qualitative study design, such diversity is necessarily illustrative rather than representative, the resulting samples had a robust range in these respects in all three regions. In practice, the point of departure for sampling was maximally varied individuals, who, in the next step, constituted the first node of a network, and who suggested and provided access to other members of the network.

Table 8.2 summarizes the samples that entered into the fieldwork in China, Denmark, and the United States, respectively, including the number of networks and geographical sites, and the key sociodemographic characteristics of individuals. The total number of informants was 76, each of whom was interviewed twice for a data set of 152 interviews, as two parts of a three-step data collection procedure, which we describe in the following section.

Combining interviews and diaries

A classic challenge of qualitative fieldwork is how to document events and experiences for later analysis, as they take place or as soon as possible thereafter. In media and communication studies, additional complications follow from the parts played by multiple people and by contents and forms of communication which, literally, are spoken into the air (Peters, 1999) or into systems (Jensen & Helles, 2017) that may remain closed to inquiry. To address the inherent difficulties of fieldwork, we opted, again, for triangulation (Denzin, 1970), this time by integrating spoken and written, found as well as made (Jensen, 2013) qualitative evidence: Two varieties of interviewing as well as diaries in several modalities.

The first step in data collection consisted of *semi-structured introductory interviews*. The general aim was to elicit narratives and perspectives from informants on their lives, with communicative practices as the thematic anchor. We asked about people's everyday routines, their personal networks, the issues and events they found important, and the media they would use. As communicative points of reference, we asked for (and were granted in confidence) 'guided tours' of

TABLE 8.2 Fieldwork informants (networks and key sociodemographics)

		China	*Denmark*	*US*
Sites		7	9	5
Networks		9	5	5
Respondents		39	20	17
Gender	Female	21	13	11
	Male	18	7	6
Age	≤20	6	1	8
	21–35	19	7	1
	36–50	10	4	3
	51–65	4	3	4
	≥66	0	5	1

their smartphones, tablets, and computers. We also had the opportunity to pose clarifying questions, for instance, regarding the settings they had chosen (or left as default) for sounds and other notifications, and concerning any principles of organizing applications and folders on their various devices. In this way, we are able, in a sense, to peek into the past – identifying earlier actions or events – and to ascertain present consequences and experiences. Communicative practices are, to a considerable degree, routinized and implemented into the media that be, in a taken-for-granted everyday present. These insights from the first round of interviewing, next, were enriched throughout a second step and type of data collection.

To gain a deeper understanding of participants' everyday routines and communicative practices, without our presence or intervention, the second stage of data collection turned to *diaries* – records in text, image, or sound – about communicative events and experiences. Toward the end of the introductory interview, informants were given both oral and brief written instructions on how to keep a communication diary. We basically asked each person to register any media uses throughout one to two full days, as soon as possible after the event:

1. When did it take place, and for how long?
2. Where were you, and who were you with (if anyone)?
3. What were you using media for (e.g., texting, social network sites, email, apps, TV or radio programs, phone calls)?
4. Who were you communicating with (if anyone)?

For each event, participants were entirely free to decide on how to report it, both regarding the medium or platform (e.g., social media, email, a phone call to the researcher, a paper record) and regarding modality (text, audio, video). Informants were also offered information on automated data collection apps and other software that they might prefer to use. In effect, participants chose a wide variety of formats, contributing rich records of their contextualized communicative practices.

The communication diaries served a dual aim. In addition to characterizing communicative events and the associated experiences, sometimes with explanatory comments, the diaries constituted a point of departure for the third step of data collection: *Elicitation interviews*. This form of interviewing serves to elicit elaboration and further reflection on another data source, in this case the diaries, but also on topics from the introductory interview. The methodological combination of interviews and diaries goes back at least to the 1970s, when Zimmerman and Wieder (1977) proposed this strategy to avoid some of the logistical challenges of participating observation. In media and communication research, for example, the tradition of media repertoire studies that we draw on in Chapter 3 has relied on this approach (Hasebrink & Domeyer, 2012).

In the present study, a preliminary semi-structured interview guide was adjusted for each informant to incorporate aspects of both the person's diary and the first interview. This brought out many additional points on the backgrounds and contexts – the how and the why – of their communicative practices, including unnoticed (in diaries) aspects of the ubiquitous and pervasive practice of communication. Furthermore, the elicitation interviews gave specific attention to face-to-face communication, which for simplicity had not been included in the diary instructions, but which could now be targeted among the blanks or periods of no media use or other communication, according to the diaries. Last but not least, the second round of interviewing was an opportunity to address an issue that tends to fall between the qualitative and quantitative chairs of empirical communication studies – not the what, how, and why of communication, but its *absence*: Why *don't* people communicate, at all or in specific ways, given the conditions and contexts in which they find themselves?

Analyses and inferences

Unlike quantitative surveys, qualitative fieldworks typically do not lend themselves to synthesis in tables, figures, and other summative representations. Full documentation from the three settings is given in three Ph.D. dissertations, available online (Lai, 2021; Pagh, 2020; Zeng Skovhøj, 2020). In the present methodological appendix, we include characterizations of the 76 informants and 19 networks, a commentary on qualitative data analysis, and an indication of some of the inferences and conclusions deriving primarily from the fieldworks.

Figures 8.1–8.3 lay out the 19 networks in China, Denmark, and the United States, respectively. In each case, the network is described through the names (pseudonyms) of its members, with arrows indicating the nature of the social relation as well as the lines of referral from one person to another for interviewing, and dotted lines suggesting mutual acquaintance (without explicit referral for interviewing). Other notations indicate different types of networks, for example, occupational or family-based ones and, in the case of China, networks centered in either Beijing, Shanghai, or Tibet, with additional rural nodes. In overview, the networks comprise a diversity of individuals across age, gender, ethnicity, educational level, religious beliefs, marital and parental status, and place of residence.

An Achilles heel of qualitative research has been data analysis: How to move beyond interesting, sometimes striking statements or images, to more systematic empirical substantiation of inferences and insights. Two resources for qualitative data analysis have recently been gaining ground. On the one hand, a variety of software packages for qualitative coding, analysis, and visualization are now available (Silver & Lewins, 2014), facilitating explicit and detailed comparisons within and between data sets, and supporting dual coding and other collaborative research endeavors. Such practices of intersubjectivity have long been standard in quantitative research, and they were integral to the comparative analysis of the three qualitative data sets from very different national settings. On the other hand, a number of reference works have specified linguistic and thematic approaches to language

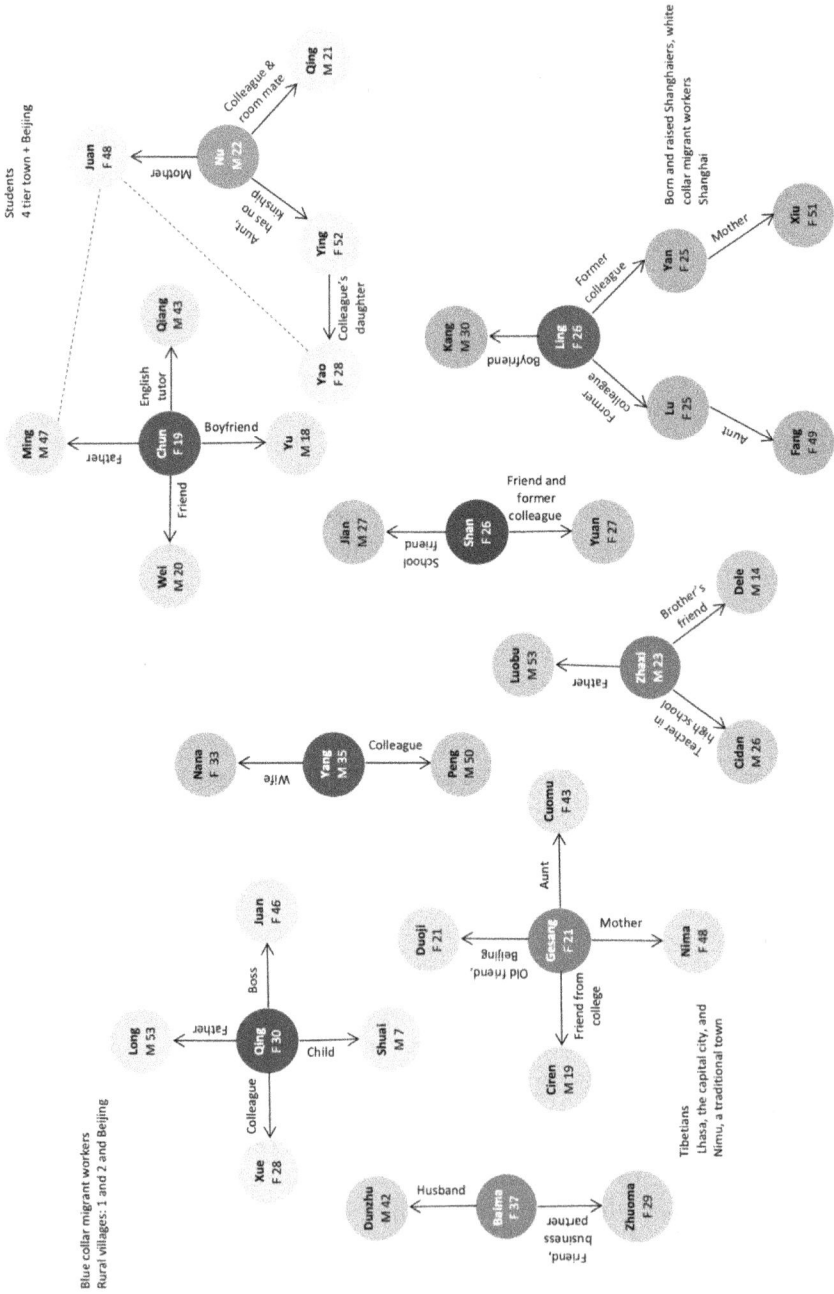

FIGURE 8.1 Networks of informants in China

Kai
M 84

Immigrants
country wide

Sofia
F 28   Sister   Fatma
F 24

Colleague
& friend

Birgitte
F 52

Hedda
F 78   Mother   Marie
F 36

Students
Copenhagen & Funen

Kirsten
F 24

Louise
F 28

Mother

Friend

Sister

Stine
F 23

Friend & business partner   Miriam
F 49

Sanne
F 42

Noah
M 28   Friend

Friend from masonry's wife

Tim
M 57   Daughter   Hanne
F 22

Johnny
M 34   Anna
F 72

Father in law

Nephew

Husband

Jørgen
M 71

Jens-
Otto
M 75

Families
Central Jutland & North of
Zealand

Friend & former neighbor

Liam
M 52   Wife   Ena
F 43

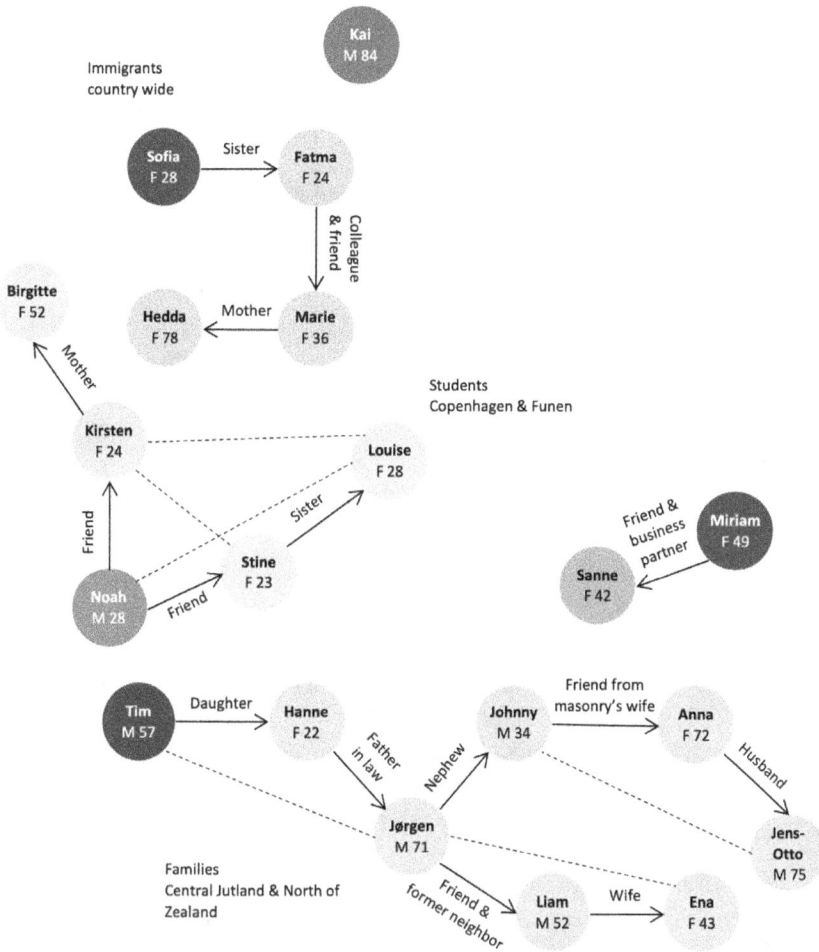

FIGURE 8.2   Networks of informants in Denmark

and other signs and symbols as key objects of analysis in qualitative studies (for an overview, see Jensen, 2021a). For this study, all 152 interviews were transcribed, coded, and iteratively and comparatively analyzed by the three fieldworkers.

The qualitative fieldworks, in addition to instantiating and specifying the *experiences* associated with diverse communicative *events*, served to clarify some of the *mechanisms* operating in and through communication systems, including the persistence of political economies, the contextual affordances of material technologies, and the gradual uptake of new cultural traditions. In China, for example, Chun mentioned having different online personalities on two social media. On the first one, WeChat, everyone knew her real identity, and here, she would only share positive content. On the other platform, Fanfou, where she remained anonymous, she could pour out her negative thoughts without fear of

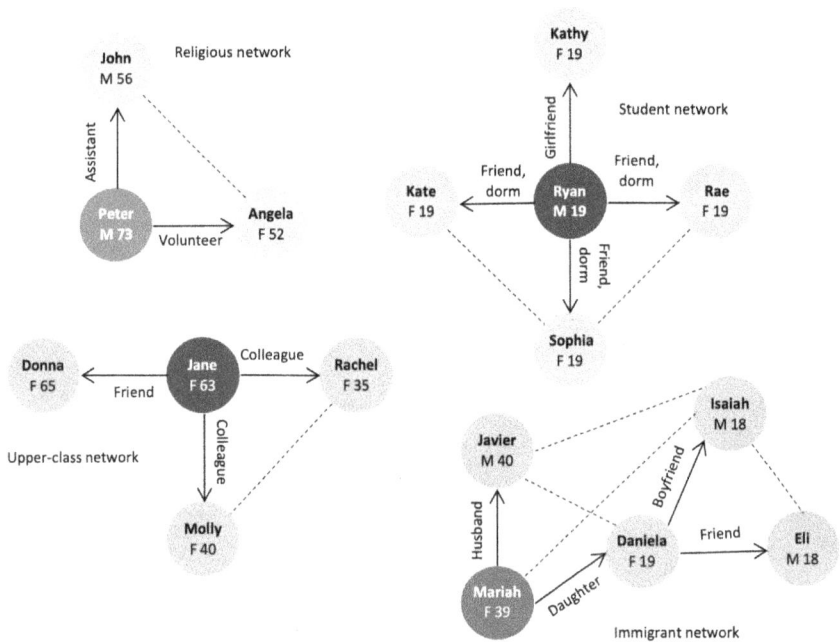

FIGURE 8.3 Networks of informants in the United States

repercussions. In Denmark, Ena had abruptly shifted from writing to a friend in Eastern Europe on Facebook Messenger to instead calling her via FaceTime, as the conversation turned to a difficult topic. When they could hear each other's voices, Ena managed to console her friend. In the United States, John had a business selling religious paintings, and he used to rely entirely on exhibitions and word of mouth. But, after friends had encouraged him to utilize digital platforms in order to enhance his business, he would now multitask throughout the day, replying to inquiries and checking incoming orders on both his email and his personal Facebook profile.

Tracking the trackers

Critical knowledge interest

The most evident critical implications of studying communication systems follow from their implementation of many-to-one communicative practices as a standard operating procedure (Jensen & Helles, 2017). If early internet studies of the 1990s frequently focused on cyberspace and online communities, and research from the 2000s gradually turned toward the social media emerging and gaining momentum, during the 2010s surveillance by state as well as commercial agents became a key agenda of both research and public debate. It is only recently, however, that the interactions between ordinary users and various systems and institutional agents have come to be conceptualized as communication that lends itself to empirical analysis (e.g., Jensen, 2013; Lomborg & Frandsen, 2016). This form of communication has far-reaching implications for the understanding and regulation of human agency and social structure, locally and globally. Compared to media systems, which equally monetized audience attention (Webster, 2014), communication systems entail a new degree of integration into the core of different political economies, through generic technologies spanning other systems of material and immaterial production and distribution, as well.

Like digitalization as such, tracking is still working itself out and making itself felt as a social and communicative practice. As Chapter 6 elaborates, a key element of digital infrastructures has been so-called third-party services (TPSs), some of which track usage and users, and which, to an extent, can be reverse-engineered to identify their operating principles (and to develop circumventing measures and appropriate regulation). Many-to-one communication, including subsequent repurposing of the resulting data in several steps, typically unfolds within closed systems, as illustrated by the Cambridge Analytica scandal relating, in part, to the 2016 US presidential election. And, beyond the white to grey areas of ethics and law, national intelligence agencies are at the receiving end of a range of black data flows, from the 'great firewall' of China's party state to the US National Security Agency, as documented by Edward Snowden's whistle-blowing in 2013. Tracking the trackers represents one important point on an emerging agenda developing critical methodologies for computational communication science (Domahidi, Yang, Niemann-Lenz, & Reinecke, 2019).

Sampling big data

Media and communication research has been importing analytical methods from computer science to account for the specificities of digital communication systems, including the operation of trackers (see further Helles, Lomborg, & Lai, 2020). To sample and collect data for the present comparative purposes, we drew, among others, on the work of Timothy Libert (2015), Marjan Falahrastegar and colleagues (2014, 2016), and Reuben Binns et al. (2018) about web infrastructures. We used the Lightbeam plug-in for the Mozilla Firefox browser to collect data on TPSs relating to the seven countries of this study. Whereas the promise of 'big data' has sometimes been referred to as doing away with sampling and "getting everything: $N = all$" (Mayer-Schönberger & Cukier, 2013: 26), sampling remains essential to procure relevant data sets for specific analytical and critical purposes.

The data set used here comprises the TPSs identified on the top 50 sites for each of the seven countries. The candidate list of trackers was constructed by traversing the top lists and harvesting metadata about all TPSs that were loaded by each site during January of 2018. The aggregated top lists were derived from the Alexa database (https://www.alexa.com) and nominally comprised $N = 350$

sites with a total of more than 900 different trackers. However, considering site duplication between some (e.g., imdb.com appeared on four lists) or all lists (e.g., google.com), we arrived at a sample of unique sites, $N = 201$.

Analyses and inferences

The information harvested about the sites and their constituent TPSs made it possible to first extract a network structure. In this network, both websites and third-party services represent nodes, making it a bipartite network with two types of nodes. In Figure 6.1, a link between two nodes indicates that two websites are connected in that they both embed a given (number of) TPSs. And, the more shared third-party services, the closer the nodes.

To produce a more focused analysis, the full network structure was subsequently subdivided into clusters through a modularity analysis (Blondel et al., 2008). We identified 12 clusters, with a median size Mdn = 14. In a preliminary analytical step, the structures of the network and its clusters could be considered features of the material technologies of the web. For the understanding of communication systems, the more pertinent questions were, first, how these structures relate to (other) social systems and mechanisms (political economies, cultural traditions) and, second, how structures and systems enable and constrain particular communicative practices. Whereas trackers in themselves only outline a probability space – being one set of determinations of how communicative practices may unfold – their massive presence and manifest institutionalization suggest both intended outcomes (by systems) and likely trajectories (for their users).

Logistics, ethics, and politics

Lessons of state and market

Comparative studies of communication systems face a number of distinctive challenges, in addition to generic tasks of securing funding and organizing the logistics of global research collaborations. Chapter 7 discusses implications for further studies of communication systems, including other regions of the world and the constituent elements of such systems as they relate, for instance, to national and international political governance, e-commerce, education, and health. By way of concluding this methodological appendix, we briefly offer lessons from the Peoples' Internet project concerning some of the *preconditions* for research examining and evaluating the changing conditions of human communication.

Generously funded by the Carlsberg Foundation and greatly facilitated by collegial networks in the three regions, the project itself had to communicate and navigate via the material technologies, political economies, and cultural traditions that were also its objects of analysis. Perhaps not surprisingly, in view of the fact that information (and communication) is power, political economies presented the most immediate complications.

Quantitative surveys in mainland China, first, had been prepared through earlier contacts and collaborations with a key research institution there. As planning of data collection progressed, it became increasingly difficult to obtain comments from the original collaborator on draft questions and other aspects of the empirical design; communication slowed, then stopped entirely. While we cannot know the precise reason for this turn of events, interpretations of the relevance and legitimacy of international research collaborations might have changed. Most importantly, the solution to the problem reemphasized the centrality of personal relations in Chinese (academic) culture: Thanks to other collegial contacts, who ensured that the survey complied with local examples, norms, and guidelines, and in conjunction with another study already underway, it proved possible to administer data collection in mainland China in the same format as in the other six countries.

Another component of the original plan had been to use data on web traffic as a complement to surveys, fieldworks, and tracker analyses. Departing from earlier subscriptions to a US-based service provider, we had an ample budget for acquiring the relevant data sets during specified periods for the present comparative purposes. And, for a while, we were able to access data and to prepare further analyses; then, access was terminated and proved impossible to restore. Despite numerous contacts with different individuals and sections of the service provider's organization, for more than a year, and despite having more than enough funds for subscription, we had to realize that, at least for the present volume, these data were not forthcoming. We cannot know whether the contract, in the end, had proven too small to be commercially interesting, or whether other circumstances affected negotiations; we do conclude that, like state-supervised research entities, the infrastructures of markets may get in the way of data being communicated, bought and sold, so as to enable more research on how communication systems work.

Habeas data

The buying and selling of data have moved to the top of research and public-debate agendas over the past decade, rightfully so, specifically when it comes to the understanding and administration of personal data. Digital technologies have brought home the point that data are not personal in and of themselves; data *become* personal, depending on the contexts in which people and systems place them. Given a sufficient number of data points, it is increasingly possible to establish the identities and activities of individuals without traditional identifying information (e.g., Rocher, Hendrickx, & de Montjoye, 2019). Digitalization is presenting a new order of ethical challenges for research on communication systems.

The Peoples' Internet (PIN) project was approved by the relevant institutional review board at the University of Copenhagen, Denmark. Most of the data collected and analyzed have been represented and stored in aggregated formats, including survey data from YouGov and the tracker data harvested via webxray.org; the potentially more sensitive qualitative data from fieldworks have been kept on secure university servers in accordance with legislation following from the EU General Data Protection Regulation (GDPR). The project has also observed professional guidelines of empirical research from international associations such as the Association of Internet Researchers and the International Communication Association (Franzke, Bechmann, Zimmer, Ess, & Researchers, 2020; ICA, 2019). As such, the study has aspired to contemporary best practices and to scientific social responsibility.

In a future perspective, empirical studies of communication systems present additional questions of principle. The issues can be stated in terms of what *can* (not) and what *ought* (not) to be known, particularly about persons. Communication researchers have sometimes been frustrated by limitations on access to data, for example, from social media, which deprive critical studies of much knowledge about their operations and implications (Bruns, 2019a). Data monopolies may entail other forms of monopoly or inequality. We just noted our relatively banal trials of gaining access to web traffic data for this particular project. In effect, certain very important things *could not* be known about contemporary communication systems, even if interested scholars and readers may refer to other valuable studies in this domain (e.g., Taneja & Webster, 2016). It is less common, but timely to reflect on what *ought not* to be known about persons – what researchers should not do to or with people, even with their informed consent in the present, given unpredictable trajectories of information in future communication systems. More than an academic question, such concerns may stimulate further deliberation on the interaction of technologies, methodologies, and ethics, and on research as a public and human service.

Communication systems will not stand still. Already, an internet of things (IoT) (Howard, 2015; ITU, 2005) is gaining momentum (Hughes, 1983), implementing new varieties of many-to-one communication into everyday life along with the flows of one-to-one, one-to-many, and many-to-many interactions. IoT entails a broader and deeper integration of communication systems into the core of other social systems, touching on questions of survival and quality of life, in public and in private. IoT, further, places in doubt the received understanding of media as objects with interfaces, and of communication as interactions, broadly speaking, with other entities, including institutions, organizations, and their human representatives, as extended in technological artifacts. With this volume, we have called for more (comparative) studies of communication systems, shifting attention beyond media systems, and approaching the latter as constituents of communication systems. It may be that IoT, or its sequels, will motivate reinterpretation and reconceptualization of communication systems, as well. For each stage and system to come, technologies will occasion both methodological and ethical choices.

As a subset of human ethics, research ethics involves issues of rights – rights of communication, but also of not being communicated *about* and, perhaps, acted *on* in certain ways by others. A terminology of *habeas data* has been proposed as a way of articulating what is at stake (Guadamuz, 2001; Jensen, 2021b). Where the classic legal principle of *habeas corpus* points to and prioritizes the integrity of embodied individuals, *habeas data* suggests that not only do people have and hold information; they *are* information: Persons with lives and biographies represented in more or less durable media. It is a right that can be violated, in public communication, but also through multistep scientific communication with unforeseen or inadvertent consequences. Far from advocating either less research or less communication, we do call for more communication by researchers on the contingencies of (what may become) personal information – what *we* ought (not) to do with media and their users as persons and publics.

Do communication systems have politics?

In his classic article addressing the question, "Do artifacts have politics?", Langdon Winner (1980) responded in the affirmative, further distinguishing two ways in which technologies entail politics. In the broadest sense, technologies represent "ways of building order in our world" (p. 127), being material means of human actions and social interactions, which become embedded in society as institutions and infrastructures that envelop people. Winner's first point, thus, had a family resemblance with the theoretical landscape in which we situated our analyses in Chapter 1: Determination in the first instance (Hall, 1983) and the overdetermination of communicative practices at the intersection of material technologies, political economies, and cultural traditions (Figure 1.1). Also Winner's (1980) second, more specific, point aligns with the perspective we have pursued in the intervening chapters, namely, that some artifacts are more political than others, "inherently political technologies" (p. 128). A case in point is communication systems: Ways of building order in local and global worlds, even while such systems leave the definition of order and the delimitation of worlds essentially contestable (Clarke, 1979), subject to empirical examination, normative evaluation, and practical contestation along long lines of double hermeneutics (Giddens, 1979).

Whereas we discuss specific political implications and normative evaluations further in Chapter 7, we end this methodological appendix by returning to a premise in Chapter 1: Epistemologies imply knowledge interests, or politics in Winner's sense. Communication systems can and should be examined and evaluated for what they empower humans to do and be, as individuals and collectives, locally and globally. As importantly, communication systems should be studied comprehensively, at least from time to time, to explain their intersections and interactions with other systems and artifacts that condition the good life. This book has presented a framework in which the interpretation and reinterpretation of communication systems may proceed. The point of double hermeneutics, in Anthony Giddens' (1979) summary statement, is that research reinterprets reality as part of a dialectic of theory and practice. Unlike natural and material sciences, like other human and social sciences, media and communication research studies a reality that has already been interpreted by the people being studied. And when a Darwin, a Marx, or a Freud reinterprets how reality works, it also changes people's interpretations of themselves and others, sometimes in fundamental ways and with long-term consequences. Less grandly, but with an eye on the *longues durées* of history (Braudel, 1980), we invite other media and communication researchers to revisit communication systems to consider what people do with media, and what researchers, along with other people, can and ought to be up to.

REFERENCES

Abbate, J. (1999). *Inventing the internet*. Cambridge, MA: MIT Press.

Agency for Digitization. (2016). *A stronger and more secure digital Denmark: The digital strategy 2016–2020*. Copenhagen: Agency for Digitization.

Agrawal, N., Najafi-Asadolahi, S., & Smith, S. A. (2020). Optimization of operational decisions in digital advertising: A literature review. In S. Ray & S. Yin (Eds.), *Channel strategies and marketing mix in a connected World* (pp. 99–146). Cham: Springer.

Agresti, A. (2013). *Categorical data analysis* (3rd ed.). Hoboken, NJ: Wiley.

Alupoaie, S., & Cunningham, P. (2013). *Using tf-idf as an edge weighting scheme in user-object bipartite networks*. Retrieved from arXiv:1308.6118.

Anderson, B. (1991). *Imagined communities: Reflections on the origin and spread of nationalism* (2nd ed.). London: Verso.

Archer, M., Bhaskar, R., Collier, A., Lawson, T., & Norrie, A. (Eds.). (1998). *Critical realism: Essential readings*. London: Routledge.

Ashman, K. M., & Baringer, P. S. (Eds.). (2001). *After the science wars*. London: Routledge.

Austin, J. L. (1962). *How to do things with words*. Oxford: Oxford University Press.

Bakardjieva, M. (2005). *Internet society: The internet in everyday life*. London: Sage.

Bakardjieva, M., & Smith, R. (2001). The internet in everyday life: Computer networking from the standpoint of the domestic user. *New Media and Society, 3*(1), 67–83.

Bakshy, E., Messing, S., & Adamic, L. (2015). Exposure to ideologically diverse news and opinion on Facebook. *Science, 348*(6239), 1130–1132.

Baldwin, R. (2016). *The great convergence: Information technology and the new globalization*. Cambridge, MA: The Belknap Press.

Baron, N. S. (2008). *Always on: Language in an online and mobile world*. New York: Oxford University Press.

Bateson, G. (1972). *Steps to an ecology of mind*. London: Granada.

Behre, J., Hölig, S., & Hasebrink, U. (2020). Combining old and new: Patterns of media use across legacy and online media in Germany. *Comunicazioni Sociali, 1*, 8–21.

Bell, D. (1973). *The coming of post-industrial society*. New York: Basic Books.

Beniger, J. (1986). *The control revolution: Technological and economic origins of the information society*. Cambridge, MA: Harvard University Press.

Beniger, J. (1992). Comparison, yes, but – The case of technological and cultural change. In J. G. Blumler, J. M. McLeod, & K. E. Rosengren (Eds.), *Comparatively speaking: Communication and culture across space and time* (pp. 35–50). Newbury Park, CA: Sage.

Berlin, I. (1969). Two concepts of liberty. In I. Berlin (Ed.), *Four essays on liberty* (pp. 118–172). Oxford: Oxford University Press. (Original work published 1958).

Berners-Lee, T. (1999). *Weaving the web: The original design and ultimate destiny of the world wide web by its inventor.* San Francisco, CA: Harper.

Bhaskar, R. (1979). *The possibility of naturalism.* Brighton: Harvester Press.

Binns, R., Zhao, J., Kleek, M. V., & Shadbolt, N. (2018). Measuring third-party tracker power across web and mobile. *ACM Transactions on Internet Technology, 18*(4), 1–22.

Birdsall, W. F. (2011). Human capabilities and information and communication technology: The communicative connection. *Ethics and Information Technology, 13*(2), 93–106.

Blank, G., & Groselj, D. (2014). Dimensions of internet use: Amount, variety, and types. *Information, Communication and Society, 17*(4), 417–435.

Blondel, V. D., Guillaume, J.-L., Lambiotte, R., & Lefebvre, E. (2008). Fast unfolding of communities in large MetWorks. *Journal of Statistical Mechanics: Theory and Experiment, 2008*(10), P10008.

Blum, R. (2005). Bausteinen zu einer Theorie der Mediensysteme [Constituents of a theory of media systems]. *Medienwissenschaft Schweiz, 2,* 5–11.

Blumer, H. (1954). What is wrong with social theory? *American Sociological Review, 19*(1), 3–10.

Blumler, J., McLeod, J., & Rosengren, K. E. (Eds.). (1992). *Comparatively speaking: Communication and culture across space and time.* Newbury Park, CA: Sage.

Blumler, J. G., & Katz, E. (Eds.). (1974). *The uses of mass communications.* Beverly Hills, CA: Sage.

Bohn, D. (2021). Google delays blocking third-party cookies in Chrome until 2023. *The Verge.* Retrieved from https://www.theverge.com/2021/6/24/22547339/google-chrome-cookiepocalypse-delayed-2023.

Bolck, A., Croon, M., & Hagenaars, J. (2004). Estimating latent structure models with categorical variables: One-step versus three-step estimators. *Political Analysis, 12*(1), 3–27.

Bolter, J. D., & Grusin, R. (1999). *Remediation: Understanding new media.* Cambridge, MA: MIT Press.

Bourdieu, P. (1984). *Distinction.* Cambridge, MA: Harvard University Press. (Original work published 1979).

Bourdieu, P. (1986). The forms of capital. In J. G. Richardson (Ed.), *Handbook of theory and research for the sociology of education* (pp. 241–258). New York: Greenwood Press.

Bourdieu, P. (1990). *The logic of practice.* Stanford, CA: Stanford University Press.

Bourdieu, P., & Wacquant, L. (1992). *An invitation to reflexive sociology.* Cambridge: Polity.

Bowker, G. C., Baker, K., Millerand, F., & Ribes, D. (2010). Toward information infrastructure studies: Ways of knowing in a networked environment. In J. Hunsinger, L. Klastrup, & M. M. Allen (Eds.), *International handbook of internet research* (pp. 97–117). Dordrecht: Springer.

Braman, S. (2011). Privacy by design: Networked computing, 1969–1979. *New Media and Society, 14*(5), 798–814.

Braudel, F. (1980). *On history.* Chicago, IL: Chicago University Press.

Bräunlich, K., Dienlin, T., Eichenhofer, J., Helm, P., Trepte, S., Grimm, R. D., … Gusy, C. (2021). Linking loose ends: An interdisciplinary privacy and communication model. *New Media and Society, 23*(6), 1443–1464.

Briggs, A., Burke, P., & Ytreberg, E. (2020). *A social history of the media* (4th ed.). Cambridge: Polity.

Britz, J., Hoffmann, A., Ponelis, S., Zimmer, M., & Lor, P. (2013). On considering the application of Amartya Sen's capability approach to an information-based rights framework. *Information Development, 29*(2), 106–113.

Brüggemann, M., Engesser, S., Büchel, F., Humprecht, E., & Castro, L. (2014). Hallin and Mancini revisited: Four empirical types of western media systems. *Journal of Communication, 64*(6), 1037–1065.

Bruns, A. (2019a). After the 'APIcalypse': Social media platforms and their fight against critical scholarly research. *Information, Communication, and Society, 22*(11), 1544–1566.

Bruns, A. (2019b). *Are filter bubbles real?* Cambridge: Polity.

Bucholtz, I. (2015). Media use among social networking site users in Latvia. *International Journal of Communication, 9*, 2653–2673.

Burgess, M. (2022). Google has a new plan to kill cookies: People are still mad. *Wired.* Retrieved from https://www.wired.com/story/google-floc-cookies-chrome-topics.

Butsch, R., & Livingstone, S. (Eds.). (2014). *Meanings of audiences: Comparative discourses.* New York and London: Routledge.

Carey, J. W. (1989a). *Communication as culture.* Boston, MA: Unwin Hyman.

Carey, J. W. (1989b). A cultural approach to communication. In J. W. Carey (Ed.), *Communication as culture* (pp. 13–36). Boston, MA: Unwin Hyman. (Original work published 1975).

Castells, M. (1996). *The rise of the network society.* Oxford: Blackwell.

Castells, M. (1996–98). *The information age: Economy, society, and culture.* Oxford: Blackwell.

Castro Herrero, L., Humprecht, E., Engesser, S., Brüggemann, M., & Büchel, F. (2017). Rethinking Hallin and Mancini beyond the west: An analysis of media systems in Central and Eastern Europe. *International Journal of Communication, 11*, 4797–4823.

Cattell, R. B. (1966). The scree test for the number of factors. *Multivariate Behavioral Research, 1*(2), 245–276.

Certeau, M. de (1984). *The practice of everyday life.* Berkeley, CA: University of California Press.

Chadwick, A. (2013). *The hybrid media system: Politics and power.* Oxford: Oxford University Press.

Chan, J. M., & Lee, F. L. F. (Eds.). (2017). *Advancing comparative media and communication research.* New York and London: Routledge.

Chen, H., & Rithmire, M. (2020). The rise of the investor state: State capital in the Chinese economy. *Studies in Comparative International Development, 55*(3), 257–277.

Chen, W. (2013). The implications of social capital for the digital divides in America. *Information Society, 29*(1), 13–25.

Chen, W., Lee, K., Straubhaar, J. D., & Spence, J. (2014). Getting a second opinion: Social capital, digital inequalities, and health information repertoires. *Journal of the Association for Information Science and Technology, 65*(12), 2552–2563.

Choi, H., Mela, C. F., Balseiro, S. R., & Leary, A. (2020). Online display advertising markets: A literature review and future directions. *Information Systems Research, 31*(2), 556–575.

Christians, C. G., & Nordenstreng, K. (Eds.). (2014). *Communication theories in a multicultural world.* New York: Peter Lang.

Christians, C. G., Glasser, T. L., McQuail, D., Nordenstreng, K., & White, R. A. (2009). *Normative theories of the media: Journalism in democratic societies.* Urbana, IL: University of Illinois Press.

Christl, W., & Spiekermann, S. (2016). *Networks of control: A report on corporate surveillance, digital tracking, big data & privacy.* Retrieved from https://crackedlabs.org/en/networksofcontrol.

Chromium Blog. (2020). *Building a more private web: A path towards making third party cookies obsolete.* Retrieved from https://blog.chromium.org/2020/01/building-more-private-web-path-towards.html.

Clarke, B. (1979). Eccentrically contested concepts. *British Journal of Political Science, 9*(1), 122–126.

CNNIC. (2019). 43rd statistical report on internet development in China. *Statistical report on internet development in China 43.* Beijing: China Internet Network Information Center (CNNIC). Retrieved from http://cnnic.cn/hlwfzyj/hlwxzbg/hlwtjbg/201902/P020190228510533388308.pdf.

Coleman, S., Moss, G., & Martinez-Perez, A. (2018). Studying real-time audience responses to political messages: A new research agenda. *International Journal of Communication, 12,* 1696–1714.

Coppedge, M., Gerring, J., Knutsen, C. H., Lindberg, S. I., Teorell, J., Altman, D., … Ziblatt, D. (2019). V-Dem codebook v9, varieties of democracy (V-Dem) project. Retrieved from https://www.v-dem.net/vdemds.html.

Corporate Europe Observatory. (2022). How corporate lobbying undermined the EU's push to ban surveillance ads. Retrieved from https://corporateeurope.org/en/2022/01/how-corporate-lobbying-undermined-eus-push-ban-surveillance-ads.

Correa, T. (2016). Digital skills and social media use: How internet skills are related to different types of Facebook use among 'digital natives'. *Information, Communication and Society, 19*(8), 1095–1107.

Couldry, N. (2012). *Media, society, world: Social theory and digital media practice.* Cambridge: Polity.

Couldry, N., Livingstone, S., & Markham, T. (2007). *Media consumption and public engagement: Beyond the presumption of attention.* London: Palgrave Macmillan.

Craig, R. T. (1989). Communication as a practical discipline. In B. Dervin, L. Grossberg, B. J. O'Keefe, & E. Wartella (Eds.), *Rethinking communication* (Vol. 1, Paradigm Issues, pp. 97–122). Newbury Park, CA: Sage.

Craig, R. T. (2018). For a practical discipline. *Journal of Communication, 68*(2), 289–297.

Crawford, K. (2009). Following you: Disciplines of listening in social media. *Continuum: Journal of Media and Cultural Studies, 23*(4), 525–535.

Cvetičanin, P., Spasic', I., & Gavrilovic', D. (2014). Strategies and tactics in social space: The case of Serbia. *Social Science Information, 53*(2), 213–239.

Danermark, B., Ekström, M., Jakobsen, L., & Karlsson, J. C. (2019). *Explaining society: Critical realism in the social sciences* (2nd ed.). London and New York: Routledge.

DeNardis, L. (2020). *The internet in everything: Freedom and security in a world with no off switch.* New Haven, CT: Yale University Press.

Deng, X. (1984). Building socialism with a specifically Chinese character. Retrieved from https://web.archive.org/web/20180703103947/http://newlearningonline.com/new-learning/chapter-4/deng-xiaoping-socialism-with-chinese-characteristics.

Denzin, N. (1970). *The research act: A theoretical introduction to sociological methods.* Englewood Cliffs, NJ: Prentice-Hall.

Department of Labor. (1995). *Good for business: Making full use of the nation's human capital.* Retrieved from https://web.archive.org/web/20140810033848/http://www.dol.gov/oasam/programs/history/reich/reports/ceiling.pdf.

Dewey, J. (1903). *Studies in logical theory.* Retrieved from http://www.gutenberg.org/files/40665/40665-h/40665-h.htm.

Dillman, D. A., Smyth, J. D., & Christian, L. M. (2014). *Internet, phone, mail, and mixed-mode surveys: The tailored design method* (4th ed.). London: Wiley.

DiMaggio, P., Hargittai, E., Celeste, C., & Shafer, S. (2004). Digital inequality: From unequal access to differentiated use. In K. Neckerman (Ed.), *Social inequality* (pp. 355–400). New York: Russell Sage Foundation.

Dimmick, J., Kline, S., & Stafford, L. (2000). The gratification niches of personal e-mail and the telephone. *Communication Research, 27*(2), 227–248.

Dissanayake, W. (Ed.). (1988). *Communication theory: The Asian perspective.* Singapore: Asian Mass Communication Research and Information Center.

Divers, J. (2002). *Possible worlds.* London: Routledge.

Domahidi, E., Yang, J., Niemann-Lenz, J., & Reinecke, L. (2019). Outlining the way ahead in computational communication science: An introduction to the IJoC special section on "computational methods for communication science: Toward a strategic roadmap". *International Journal of Communication, 13,* 3876–3884.

Doneda, D., & Mendes, L. S. (2014). Data protection in Brazil: New developments and current challenges. In S. Gutwirth, R. Leenes, & P. de Hert (Eds.), *Reloading data protection: Multidisciplinary insights and contemporary challenges* (pp. 3–20). New York: Springer.

Dorling, D., & Tomlinson, S. (2016). The creation of inequality: Myths of potential and ability. *Journal for Critical Education Policy Studies, 14*(3), 56–79.

Draper, N. A., & Turow, J. (2019). The corporate cultivation of digital resignation. *New Media and Society, 21*(8), 1824–1839.

Dutton, W., & Reisdorf, B. (2019). Cultural divides and digital inequalities: Attitudes shaping internet and social media divides. *Information, Communication and Society, 22*(1), 18–38.

Edgerly, S. (2015). Red media, blue media, and purple media: News repertoires in the colorful media landscape. *Journal of Broadcasting and Electronic Media, 59*(1), 1–21.

Eisenstein, E. L. (1979). *The printing press as an agent of change: Communication and cultural transformation in early-modern Europe.* Cambridge: Cambridge University Press.

Englehardt, S., & Narayanan, A. (2016). Online tracking: A 1-million-site measurement and analysis. *Proceedings of the 2016 ACM SIGSAC conference on computer and communications security.* Retrieved from https://doi.org/10.1145/2976749.2978313.

Ermakova, T., Bender, B., Fabian, B., & Klimek, K. (2018). Web tracking – A literature review on the state of research. *Proceedings of the 51st Hawaii international conference on system sciences.* Retrieved from https://scholarspace.manoa.hawaii.edu/handle/10125/50485.

Esser, F., & Hanitzsch, T. (Eds.). (2012). *The handbook of comparative communication research.* London and New York: Routledge.

Esser, F., & Vliegenthart, R. (2017). Comparative research methods. *The international encyclopedia of communication research methods,* 1–22. Retrieved from https://onlinelibrary.wiley.com/doi/full/10.1002/9781118901731.iecrm0035.

European Commission. (2018). *The digital economy and society index (DESI) report 2018.* Bruxelles: European Commission. Retrieved from https://ec.europa.eu/digital-single-market/en/desi.

European Commission. (2019). *The digital economy and society index (DESI) report 2019.* Bruxelles: European Commission. Retrieved from https://ec.europa.eu/digital-single-market/en/desi.

Falahrastegar, M., Haddadi, H., Uhlig, S., & Mortier, R. (2014). The rise of panopticons: Examining region-specific third-party web tracking. Paper presented at the International Workshop on Traffic Monitoring and Analysis. Retrieved from https://link.springer.com/chapter/10.1007/978-3-642-54999-1_9.

Falahrastegar, M., Haddadi, H., Uhlig, S., & Mortier, R. (2016). Tracking personal identifiers across the web. Paper presented at the International Conference on Passive and Active Network Measurement, Heraklion, Greece. Retrieved from https://link .springer.com/chapter/10.1007/978-3-319-30505-9_3.

Fei, X. (1939). *Peasant life in China: A field study of country life in the Yangtze valley*. London: Routledge & Kegan Paul.

Feyerabend, P. (1975). *Against method: Outline of an anarchistic theory of knowledge*. London: New Left Books.

Finnemann, N. O. (1999). *Thought, sign, and machine: The computer reconsidered*. Retrieved from http://www.hum.au.dk/ckulturf/DOCS/PUB/nof/TSM.

Flensburg, S., & Lai, S. S. (2020). Mapping digital communication systems: Infrastructures, markets, and policies as regulatory forces. *Media, Culture and Society, 42*(5), 692–710.

Fletcher, R., & Nielsen, R. K. (2017). Are news audiences increasingly fragmented? A cross-national comparative analysis of cross-platform news audience fragmentation and duplication. *Journal of Communication, 67*(4), 476–498.

Flew, T. (2021). *Regulating platforms*. Cambridge: Polity.

Forster, M. (2008). Johann Gottfried von Herder. Retrieved from http://plato.stanford .edu/archives/fall2008/entries/herder/.

Fourcade, M., & Healy, K. (2017). Seeing like a market. *Socio-Economic Review, 15*(1), 9–29.

Frankopan, P. (2019). *The new silk roads: The present and future of the world*. London: Bloomsbury.

Franzke, A. S., Bechmann, A., Zimmer, M., Ess, C., & Association of Internet Researchers. (2020). *Internet research: Ethical guidelines 3.0*. Retrieved from https://aoir .org/reports/ethics3.pdf.

Freud, S. (1911). *The interpretation of dreams*. Retrieved from http://www.psywww.com/ books/interp/toc.htm.

Frischmann, B. M. (2012). *Infrastructure: The social value of shared resources*. Oxford: Oxford University Press.

Garnham, N. (1997). Amartya Sen's "capabilities" approach to the evaluation of welfare: Its application to communications. *Javnost – the Public, 4*(4), 25–34.

Geertz, C. (1973). *The interpretation of cultures*. New York: Basic Books.

Geertz, C. (1974). "From the native's point of view": On the nature of anthropological understanding. *Bulletin of the American Academy of Arts and Sciences, 28*(1), 26–45.

Geradin, D., & Katsifis, D. (2019). An EU competition law analysis of online display advertising in the programmatic age. *European Competition Journal, 15*(1), 55–96.

Geradin, D., & Katsifis, D. (2020). "Trust me, I'm fair": Analyzing Google's latest practices in Ad Tech from the perspective of EU competition law. *European Competition Journal, 16*(1), 11–54.

Gibson, J. J. (1977). The theory of affordances. In R. Shaw & J. Bransford (Eds.), *Perceiving, acting, and knowing: Toward an ecological psychology* (pp. 67–82). Hillsdale, NJ: Lawrence Erlbaum Associates.

Gibson, J. J. (1979). *The ecological approach to visual perception*. Boston, MA: Houghton-Mifflin.

Giddens, A. (1979). *Central problems in social theory*. London: Macmillan.

Giddens, A. (1984). *The constitution of society*. Berkeley, CA: University of California Press.

Gillespie, T. (2010). The politics of 'platforms'. *New Media and Society, 12*(3), 347–364.

Gilligan, C. (1982). *In a different voice*. Cambridge, MA: Harvard University Press.

Goffman, E. (1959). *The presentation of self in everyday life*. New York: Anchor Books.

Goffman, E. (1974). *Frame analysis*. Cambridge, MA: Harvard University Press.

Goggin, G., & McLelland, M. (Eds.). (2009). *Internationalizing internet studies: Beyond anglophone paradigms.* New York: Routledge.

Goodwin, J. (Ed.). (2012). *SAGE secondary data analysis.* London: Sage.

Granovetter, M. S. (1973). The strength of weak ties. *American Journal of Sociology, 78*(6), 1360–1380.

Guadamuz, A. (2001). Habeas data vs. the European data protection directive. *Journal of Information, Law and Technology* (3). Retrieved from https://warwick.ac.uk/fac/soc/law/elj/jilt/.

Gunkel, D. J. (2020). *An introduction to communication and artificial intelligence.* Cambridge: Polity.

Habermas, J. (1971). *Knowledge and human interests.* Boston, MA: Beacon Press. (Original work published 1968).

Habermas, J. (1973). A postscript to Knowledge and human interests. *Philosophy of the Social Sciences, 3*(1), 157–189.

Habermas, J. (1989). *The structural transformation of the public sphere.* Cambridge, MA: MIT Press. (Original work published 1962).

Hacking, I. (1983). *Representing and intervening: Introductory topics in the philosophy of natural science.* Cambridge: Cambridge University Press.

Hagenaars, J. A., & Halman, L. C. (2019). Searching for ideal types. *European Sociological Review, 5*(1), 81–96.

Halford, S., & Savage, M. (2010). Reconceptualizing digital social inequality. *Information, Communication and Society, 13*(7), 937–955.

Hall, E. T. (1959). *The silent language.* New York: Doubleday.

Hall, S. (1983). The problem of ideology – Marxism without guarantees. In B. Matthews (Ed.), *Marx: A hundred years on* (pp. 57–85). London: Lawrence & Wishart.

Hallin, D. C. (2020). Comparative research, system change, and the complexity of media systems. *International Journal of Communication, 14*, 5775–5786.

Hallin, D. C., & Mancini, P. (2004). *Comparing media systems: Three models of media and politics.* Cambridge: Cambridge University Press.

Hallin, D. C., & Mancini, P. (Eds.). (2012). *Comparing media systems beyond the western world.* Cambridge: Cambridge University Press.

Hallin, D. C., & Mancini, P. (2017). Ten years after Comparing media systems: What have we learned? *Political Communication, 34*(2), 155–171.

Hargittai, E. (2002). Second-level digital divide: Differences in people's online skills. *First Monday, 7*(4). Retrieved from http://firstmonday.org/issues/issue7_4/hargittai/index.html.

Hasebrink, U., & Domeyer, H. (2012). Media repertoires as patterns of behaviour and as meaningful practices: A multimethod approach to media use in converging media environments. *Participations: Journal of Audience and Reception Studies, 9*(2), 757–779.

Hasebrink, U., & Popp, J. (2006). Media repertoires as a result of selective media use: A conceptual approach to the analysis of patterns of exposure. *Communications: The European Journal of Communication Research, 31*(3), 369–387.

Haythornthwaite, C. (2005). Social networks and internet connectivity effects. *Information, Communication and Society, 8*(2), 125–147.

Helles, R. (2021). Digital methods for media and communication research. In K. B. Jensen (Ed.), *A handbook of media and communication research: Qualitative and quantitative methodologies* (pp. 307–327). London and New York: Routledge.

Helles, R., Lomborg, S., & Lai, S. S. (2020). Infrastructures of tracking: Mapping the ecology of third-party services across top sites in the EU. *New Media and Society, 22*(11), 1957–1975.

Helles, R., Ørmen, J., Radil, C., & Jensen, K. B. (2015). The media landscapes of European audiences. *International Journal of Communication, 9*, 299–320.

Herrmann-Pillath, C. (2017). *China's economic culture: The ritual order of state and markets.* London and New York: Routledge.

Hesmondhalgh, D. (2017). Capitalism and the media: Moral economy, well-being and capabilities. *Media, Culture and Society, 39*(2), 202–218.

Hindman, M. (2018). *The internet trap: How the digital economy builds monopolies and undermines democracy.* Princeton, NJ: Princeton University Press.

Hosseinmardi, H., Ghasemian, A., Clauset, A., Mobius, M., Rothschild, D. M., & Watts, D. J. (2021). Examining the consumption of radical content on YouTube. *PNAS – Proceedings of the National Academy of Sciences, 118*(32), e2101967118.

Howard, P. N. (2010). *The digital origins of dictatorship and democracy: Information technology and political Islam.* Oxford: Oxford University Press.

Howard, P. N. (2015). *Pax Technica: How the internet of things may set us free or lock us up.* New Haven, CT: Yale University Press.

Høyer, S., Lauk, E., & Vihalemm, P. (Eds.). (1993). *Towards a civic society: The Baltic media's long road to freedom.* Tartu: Nota Baltica.

Hsieh, Y. P. (2012). Online social networking skills: The social affordances approach to digital inequality. *First Monday, 17*(4). Retrieved from https://firstmonday.org/ojs/index.php/fm/article/view/3893.

Hughes, T. P. (1983). *Networks of power: Electrification in Western society 1880–1930.* Baltimore, MD: The Johns Hopkins University Press.

Hughes, T. P. (1994). Technological momentum. In M. R. Smith & L. Marx (Eds.), *Does technology drive history? The dilemma of technological determinism* (pp. 101–113). Cambridge, MA: MIT Press.

Husson, F., Lê, S., & Pagès, J. (2017). *Exploratory multivariate analysis by example using R* (2nd ed.). Boca Raton, FL: CRC Press.

Hutchby, I. (2001). *Conversation and technology: From the telephone to the internet.* Cambridge: Polity.

Ignatow, G., & Robinson, L. (2017). Pierre Bourdieu: Theorizing the digital. *Information, Communication and Society, 20*(7), 950–966.

Inglehart, R. (1990). *Culture shift in advanced industrial society.* Princeton, NJ: Princeton University Press.

ITU. (2005). The internet of things: Executive summary. Retrieved from http://www.itu.int/dms_pub/itu-s/opb/pol/S-POL-IR.IT-2005-SUM-PDF-E.pdf.

ITU. (2019). Percentage of individuals using the internet. International Telecommunications Union. Retrieved from https://www.itu.int/en/ITU-D/Statistics/Documents/statistics/2019/Individuals_Internet_2000-2018_Dec2019.xls.

ICA. (2019). ICA code of ethics. Retrieved from https://cdn.ymaws.com/www.icahdq.org/resource/resmgr/governance_documents/ica.code.of.ethics.may2019.pdf.

Jacobson, T. L. (2016). Amartya Sen's capabilities approach and communication for development and social change. *Journal of Communication, 66*(5), 789–810.

Jakobson, R. (1960). Closing statement: Linguistics and poetics. In T. A. Sebeok (Ed.), *Style in language* (pp. 350–377). Cambridge, MA: MIT Press.

James, W. (2013). *Pragmatism: A new name for some old ways of thinking.* Retrieved from http://www.gutenberg.org/ebooks/5116 (Original work published 1907).

Jenkins, H. (2006). *Convergence culture: Where old and new media collide.* New York: New York University Press.

Jensen, K. B. (2008a). Intermediality. In W. Donsbach (Ed.), *International encyclopedia of communication* (Vol. 6, pp. 2385–2387). Malden, MA: Blackwell.

Jensen, K. B. (2008b). Text and intertextuality. In W. Donsbach (Ed.), *International encyclopedia of communication* (Vol. 11, pp. 5126–5130). Malden, MA: Blackwell.

Jensen, K. B. (2009). Three-step flow. *Journalism – Theory, Practice, and Criticism*, *10*(3), 335–337.

Jensen, K. B. (2012). Lost, found, and made: Qualitative data in the study of three-step flows of communication. In I. Volkmer (Ed.), *Handbook of global media research* (pp. 435–450). Malden, MA: Wiley-Blackwell.

Jensen, K. B. (2013). How to do things with data: Meta-data, meta-media, and meta-communication. *First Monday*, *18*(10). Retrieved from https://firstmonday.org/ojs/index.php/fm/article/view/4870.

Jensen, K. B. (2021). *A theory of communication and justice*. London and New York: Routledge.

Jensen, K. B. (2021a). Media effects: Quantitative traditions. In K. B. Jensen (Ed.), *A handbook of media and communication research: Qualitative and quantitative methodologies* (3rd ed., pp. 156–176). London and New York: Routledge.

Jensen, K. B. (2021b). The qualitative research process. In K. B. Jensen (Ed.), *A handbook of media and communication research: Qualitative and quantitative methodologies* (pp. 286–306). London and New York: Routledge.

Jensen, K. B. (Ed.). (2021c). *A handbook of media and communication research: Qualitative and quantitative methodologies* (3rd ed.). London and New York: Routledge.

Jensen, K. B. (2022). *Media convergence: The three degrees of network, mass, and interpersonal communication* (2nd ed.). London and New York: Routledge.

Jensen, K. B., & Helles, R. (2011). The internet as a cultural forum: Implications for research. *New Media and Society*, *13*(4), 517–533.

Jensen, K. B., & Helles, R. (2017). Speaking into the system: Social media and many-to-one communication. *European Journal of Communication*, *32*(1), 16–25.

Jolliffe, I. T., & Cadima, J. (2016). Principal component analysis: A review and recent developments. *Philosophical Transactions of the Royal Society A: Mathematical, Physical and Engineering Sciences*, *374*(2065), 20150202.

Kaminski, M. E. (2017). Intellectual and social freedom. In D. Gray & S. E. Henderson (Eds.), *The Cambridge handbook of surveillance law* (pp. 470–490). Cambridge: Cambridge University Press.

Kapantai, E., Christopoulou, A., Berberidis, C., & Peristeras, V. (2021). A systematic literature review on disinformation: Toward a unified taxonomical framework. *New Media and Society*, *23*(5), 1301–1326.

Kaplan, D. (2021). Public intimacy in social media: The mass audience as a third party. *Media, Culture and Society*, *43*(4), 595–612.

Katz, E. (1959). Mass communication research and the study of popular culture: An editorial note on a possible future for this journal. *Studies in Public Communication*, *2*, 1–6.

Katz, E., & Lazarsfeld, P. F. (1955). *Personal influence*. Glencoe, IL: The Free Press.

Katz, J. E., & Aakhus, M. (Eds.). (2002). *Perpetual contact: Mobile communication, private talk, public performance*. Cambridge: Cambridge University Press.

Kay, A., & Goldberg, A. (1999). Personal dynamic media. In P. A. Mayer (Ed.), *Computer media and communication: A reader* (pp. 111–119). Oxford: Oxford University Press. (Original work published 1977).

Keane, J. (2009). *The life and death of democracy*. London: Simon & Schuster.

Kim, S. J. (2016). A repertoire approach to cross-platform media use behavior. *New Media and Society*, *18*(3), 353–372.

Kim, Y. Y. (Ed.). (2018). *The international encyclopedia of intercultural communication*. Hoboken, NJ: Wiley-Blackwell.

Kincaid, D. L. (Ed.). (1987). *Communication theory: Eastern and western perspectives*. San Diego, CA: Academic Press.

King, G., Pan, J., & Roberts, M. E. (2014). Reverse-engineering censorship in China: Randomized experimentation and participant observation. *Science, 345*(6199), 1251722–1251722.

Kleine, D. (2013). *Technologies of choice: ICTs, development, and the capabilities approach*. Cambridge, MA: MIT Press.

Kleingeld, P., & Brown, E. (2013). Cosmopolitanism. Retrieved from https://plato .stanford.edu/entries/cosmopolitanism/.

Krämer, N. C., Sauer, V., & Ellison, N. (2021). The strength of weak ties revisited: Further evidence of the role of strong ties in the provision of social support. *Social Media & Society*, (April–June), 1–19.

Kurbalija, J. (2016). *An introduction to internet governance* (7th ed.). Geneva: DiploFoundation.

Labinger, J. A., & Collins, H. (Eds.). (2001). *The one culture? A conversation about science*. Chicago, IL: University of Chicago Press.

Lai, S. S. (2021). *Human capabilities in a datafied society. Empirical approaches to studying the interplay between digital communication and internet infrastructures*. PhD dissertation. University of Copenhagen.

Lai, S. S., Pagh, J., & Zeng, F. H. (2019). Tracing communicative patterns: A comparative ethnography across platforms, media, and contexts. *Nordicom Review, 40*(1), 141–157.

Lakoff, G., & Johnson, M. (1980). *Metaphors we live by*. Chicago, IL: University of Chicago Press.

Lampe, C., Ellison, N., & Steinfield, C. (2006). A Face (book) in the crowd: Social searching vs. social browsing. In *Proceedings of the 2006 20th anniversary conference on computer-supported cooperative work* (pp. 167–170). New York: Association for Computing Machinery.

Lasswell, H. D. (1948). The structure and function of communication in society. In L. Bryson (Ed.), *The communication of ideas* (pp. 32–51). New York: Harper.

Lazarsfeld, P. F., Berelson, B., & Gaudet, H. (1944). *The people's choice*. New York: Duell, Sloan, and Pearce.

Lazer, D. M. J., Baum, M. A., Benkler, Y., Berinsky, A. J., Greenhill, K. M., Menczer, F., ... Zittrain, J. L. (2018). The science of fake news: Addressing fake news requires a multidisciplinary effort. *Science, 359*(6380), 1094–1096.

Le Roux, B., & Rouanet, H. (2004). *Geometric data analysis – From correspondence analysis to structured data analysis*. Berlin: Springer.

Lê, S., Josse, J., & Husson, F. (2008). FactoMineR: An R package for multivariate analysis. *Journal of Statistical Software, 25*(1), 1–18.

Leguina, A., & Downey, J. (2021). Getting things done: Inequalities, internet use and everyday life. *New Media and Society, 23*(7), 1824–1849.

Lerner, D. (1958). *The passing of traditional society*. New York: Free Press.

Leskovec, J., & Horvitz, E. (2007). Planetary-scale views on an instant-messaging network. Retrieved from https://arxiv.org/abs/0803.0939.

Lessig, L. (1999). *Code and other laws of cyberspace*. New York: Basic Books.

Lessig, L. (2006). *Code version 2.0*. New York: Basic Books.

Lewin, K. (1945). The research center for group dynamics at Massachusetts Institute of Technology. *Sociometry, 8*(2), 126–136.

Li, Y. (2013). Social class and social capital in China and Britain: A comparative study. *Social Inclusion, 1*(1), 59–71.

Li, Y., Bernard, J.-G., & Luczak-Roesch, M. (2021). Beyond clicktivism: What makes digitally native activism effective? An exploration of the Sleeping Giants movement. *Social Media + Society, 7*(3), 1–22.

Libert, T. (2015). Exposing the hidden web: An analysis of third-party HTTP requests on 1 million websites. *International Journal of Communication, 9*, 3544–3561.

Lindell, J. (2017). Distinction recapped: Digital news repertoires in the class structure. *New Media and Society, 20*(8), 3029–3049.

Lindlof, T. R., & Taylor, B. C. (2019). *Qualitative communication research methods* (4th ed.). Los Angeles, CA: Sage.

Ling, R. (2012). *Taken for grantedness: The embedding of mobile communication into society.* Cambridge, MA: MIT Press.

Ling, R., Goggin, G., Fortunati, L., Lim, S. S., & Li, Y. (Eds.). (2020). *The Oxford handbook of mobile communication and society.* New York: Oxford University Press.

Ling, R., & Yttri, B. (2002). Hyper-coordination via mobile phones in Norway. In J. E. Katz & M. Aakhus (Eds.), *Perpetual contact: Mobile communication, private talk, public performance* (pp. 139–169). Cambridge: Cambridge University Press.

Liu, P., & Chao, W. (2020). *Computational advertising: Market and technologies for internet commercial monetization* (2nd ed.). London and New York: Routledge.

Livingstone, S. (2003). On the challenges of cross-national comparative media research. *European Journal of Communication, 18*(4), 477–500.

Lobkowicz, N. (1967). *Theory and practice: History of a concept from Aristotle to Marx.* Notre Dame, IN: University of Notre Dame Press.

Lomborg, S., & Frandsen, K. (2016). Self-tracking as communication. *Information, Communication and Society, 19*(7), 1015–1027.

Lührmann, A., Tannenberg, M., & Lindberg, S. I. (2018). Regimes of the world (RoW): Opening new avenues for the comparative study of political regimes. *Politics and Governance, 6*(1), 60–77.

Lynd, R. S., & Lynd, H. M. (1929). *Middletown: A study in American culture.* London: Constable.

Lyon, D. (2010). Surveillance, power, and everyday life. In P. Kalantzis-Cope & K. Gherab-Martin (Eds.), *Emerging digital spaces in contemporary society: Properties of technology* (pp. 107–120). London: Palgrave Macmillan.

MacKinnon, R. (2011). Liberation technology: China's "networked authoritarianism". *Journal of Democracy, 2*, 32–46.

Magidson, J. (2002). Latent class models for clustering: A comparison with K-means. *Canadian Journal of Marketing Research, 20*, 37–44.

Magidson, J., & Vermunt, J. K. (2004). Latent class models. In D. Kaplan (Ed.), *The Sage handbook of quantitative methodology for the social sciences* (pp. 175–198). Thousand Oaks, CA: Sage.

Malinowski, B. (1922). *Argonauts of the Western Pacific.* London: Routledge.

Mancini, P. (2020). Comparing media systems and the digital age. *International Journal of Communication, 14*, 5761–5774.

Mann, M. (2012). *The sources of social power (volume 1: A history of power from the beginning to AD 1760).* Cambridge: Cambridge University Press.

Mansell, R. (2002). From digital divides to digital entitlements in knowledge societies. *Current Sociology, 50*(3), 407–426.

Mansell, R., & Ang, P. H. (Eds.). (2015). *The international encyclopedia of digital communication and society.* Hoboken, NJ: Wiley-Blackwell.

Marcus, G. E. (1995). Ethnography in/of the world system: The emergence of multi-sited ethnography. *Annual Review of Anthropology, 24*(1), 95–117.

Mayer-Schönberger, V., & Cukier, K. (2013). *Big data: A revolution that will transform how we live, work, and think.* Boston, MA: Houghton Mifflin Harcourt.

Mazzucato, M. (2018). *The entrepreneurial state: Debunking public vs. private sector myths.* London: Penguin.

McCombs, M. E., & Shaw, D. L. (1972). The agenda-setting function of mass media. *Public Opinion Quarterly, 36*(2), 176–187.

McLuhan, M. (1964). *Understanding media: The extensions of man.* New York: McGraw-Hill.

McQuail, D. (1983). *Mass communication theory: An introduction.* London: Sage.

McQuail, D., & Deuze, M. (2020). *McQuail's media and mass communication theory* (7th ed.). Los Angeles, CA: Sage.

Mead, G. H. (1934). *Mind, self, and society.* Chicago, IL: University of Chicago Press.

Merton, R. K. (1968). *Social theory and social structure* (Enlarged ed.). New York: The Free Press.

Meyen, M., Pfaff-Rüdiger, S., Dudenhöffer, K., & Huss, J. (2010). The internet in everyday life: A typology of internet users. *Media, Culture and Society, 32*(5), 873–882.

Meyrowitz, J. (1994). Medium theory. In D. Crowley & D. Mitchell (Eds.), *Communication theory today* (pp. 50–77). Cambridge: Polity Press.

Mihelj, S., Leguina, A., & Downey, J. (2019). Culture is digital: Cultural participation, diversity, and the digital divide. *New Media and Society, 21*(7), 1465–1485.

Miller, D., Costa, E., Haynes, N., McDonald, T., Nicolescu, R., Sinanan, J., … Wang, X. (2016). *How the world changed social media.* London: UCL Press.

Mills, A. (2019). Now you see me – Now you don't: Journalists' experiences with surveillance. *Journalism Practice, 13*(6), 690–707.

Moore, M., & Tambini, D. (2018). *Digital dominance: The power of Google, Amazon, Facebook, and Apple.* Oxford: Oxford University Press.

Moss, G. (2018). Media, capabilities, and justification. *Media, Culture and Society, 40*(1), 94–109.

Mowbray, J., Hall, H., Raeside, R., & Robertson, P. J. (2018). Job search information behaviours: An ego-net study of networking amongst young job-seekers. *Journal of Librarianship and Information Science, 50*(3), 239–253.

Mueller, M. (2017). *Will the internet fragment? Sovereignty, globalization and cyberspace.* Hoboken, NJ: Wiley-Blackwell.

Myovella, G., Karaçuka, M., & Haucap, J. (2019). Digitalization and economic growth: A comparative analysis of sub-Saharan Africa and OECD economies. *Telecommunications Policy, 44*, 101856.

Nagy, V. (2017). How to silence the lambs? Constructing authoritarian governance in post-transitional Hungary. *Surveillance and Society, 15*(3/4), 447–455.

National Radio and Television Administration. (2021). *The national radio listening report for 2016.* Retrieved from http://www.nrta.gov.cn/art/2017/10/20/art_2178_39206.html.

NTIA. (1995). Falling through the net: A survey of the "have nots" in rural and urban America. Retrieved from https://www.ntia.doc.gov/ntiahome/fallingthru.html.

Negroponte, N. (1995). *Being digital.* New York: Alfred A. Knopf.

Negt, O. (1973). Massenmedien: Herrschaftsmittel oder Instrumente der Befreiung? [Mass media: Means of domination or instruments of liberation?]. In D. Prokop (Ed.), *Kritische Kommunikationsforschung [Critical communication research]* (pp. I–XXVIII). Munich: Carl Hanser Verlag.

Newcomb, H., & Hirsch, P. (1983). Television as a cultural forum: Implications for research. *Quarterly Review of Film Studies, 8*(3), 45–55.

Ng, Y. M. M., & Taneja, H. (2019). Mapping user-centric internet geographies: How similar are countries in their web use patterns? *Journal of Communication, 69*(5), 467–489.

Nimrod, G. (2019). Selective motion: Media displacement among older Internet users. *Information, Communication and Society, 22*(9), 1269–1280.

Nordenstreng, K., & Thussu, D. (Eds.). (2015). *Mapping BRICS media*. New York: Routledge.

Norman, D. A. (1990). *The design of everyday things*. New York: Doubleday.

Nussbaum, M. C. (2011). *Creating capabilities: The human development approach*. Cambridge, MA: Belknap Press.

O'Hara, K., & Hall, W. (2018). *Four internets: The geopolitics of digital governance*. Waterloo: Centre for International Governance Innovation.

Oblak Črnič, T., & Luthar, B. (2017). Media repertoires and discursive communities: Studying audiences in the multimedia age. *Communications, 42*(4), 415–439.

OECD. (2020). *Population with tertiary education (indicator)* [Data Set]. Retrieved from https://doi.org/10.1787/0b8f90e9-en.

Pagh, J. (2020). *Exploring everyday uses of the internet in the United States*. PhD dissertation. University of Copenhagen.

Pagh, J., Zeng Skovhøj, F. H., & Lai, S. S. (2021). A good way to talk: A comparative analysis of communication choices in China, Denmark and the US. *Information, Communication and Society*, Online First, 1–16.

Papacharissi, Z. (2010). *A private sphere: Democracy in a digital age*. Cambridge: Polity.

Pariser, E. (2011). *The filter bubble: What the internet is hiding from you*. London: Penguin.

Park, D. W., & Pooley, J. (Eds.). (2008). *The history of media and communication research: Contested memories*. New York: Peter Lang.

Pearce, K. E., & Rice, R. E. (2017). Somewhat separate and unequal: Digital divides, social networking sites, and capital-enhancing activities. *Social Media + Society, 3*(2), 1–16.

Peck, J. (2021). History, communication, and media. In K. B. Jensen (Ed.), *A handbook of media and communication research: Qualitative and quantitative methodologies* (3rd ed., pp. 232–251). London and New York: Routledge.

Peters, J. D. (1999). *Speaking into the air: A history of the idea of communication*. Chicago, IL: University of Chicago Press.

Peters, J. D. (2001). Witnessing. *Media, Culture and Society, 23*(6), 707–723.

Picone, I., Kleut, J., Pavlíčková, T., Romic, B., Hartlety, J. M., & De Redder, S. (2019). Small acts of engagement: Reconnecting productive audience practices with everyday agency. *New Media and Society, 21*(9), 2010–2028.

Piketty, T. (2020). *Capital and ideology*. Cambridge, MA: The Belknap Press.

Plantin, J.-C., Lagoze, C., Edwards, P. N., & Sandvig, C. (2018). Infrastructure studies meet platform studies in the age of Google and Facebook. *New Media and Society, 20*(1), 293–310.

Polyakova, A., & Meserole, C. (2019). *Exporting digital authoritarianism: The Russian and Chinese models: Policy brief, democracy and disorder series on democracy in Asia*. Washington, DC: Brookings Institution. Retrieved from https://www.brookings.edu/research/exporting-digital-authoritarianism.

Pomeranz, K. (2000). *The great divergence: China, Europe, and the making of the modern world economy*. Princeton, NJ: Princeton University Press.

Porat, M. (1977). *The information economy: Definition and measurement*. Washington, DC: Government Printing Office.

Powell, B. B. (2009). *Writing: Theory and history of the technology of civilization*. Malden, MA: Wiley-Blackwell.

Prensky, M. (2001). Digital natives, digital immigrants part 1. *On the Horizon, 9*(5), 1–6.

Putnam, R. D. (2000). *Bowling alone: The collapse and revival of American community*. New York: Simon & Schuster.

Qi, X. (2013). Guanxi, social capital theory and beyond: Toward a globalized social science. *British Journal of Sociology, 64*(2), 308–324.

Quinn, K. (2016a). Contextual social capital: Linking the contexts of social media use to its outcomes. *Information, Communication and Society, 19*(5), 582–600.

Quinn, K. (2016b). Why we share: A uses and gratifications approach to privacy regulation in social media use. *Journal of Broadcasting and Electronic Media, 60*(1), 61–86.

Radu, R. (2019). *Negotiating internet governance*. Oxford: Oxford University Press.

Ragnedda, M., & Ruiu, M. L. (2020). *Digital capital: A Bourdieusian perspective on the digital divide*. Bingley: Emerald Publishing Limited.

Rainie, L., & Wellman, B. (2012). *Networked: The new social operating system*. Cambridge, MA: MIT Press.

Rheingold, H. (1994). *The virtual community*. London: Minerva.

Roberts, M. E. (2018). *Censored: Distraction and diversion inside China's great firewall*. Princeton, NJ: Princeton University Press.

Robinson, L. (2011). Information channel preferences and information opportunity structures. *Information, Communication and Society, 14*(4), 472–494.

Rocher, L., Hendrickx, J. M., & de Montjoye, Y.-A. (2019). Estimating the success of re-identifications in incomplete datasets using generative models. *Nature Communications*, 1–9. Retrieved from https://www.nature.com/articles/s41467-019-10933-3.

Roesner, F., Kohno, T., & Wetherall, D. (2012). Detecting and defending against third-party tracking on the web. *Proceedings of the 9th USENIX conference on networked systems design and implementation*. Retrieved from https://www.usenix.org/conference/nsdi12/technical-sessions/presentation/roesner.

Rogers, E. M. (1962). *The diffusion of innovations*. Glencoe, IL: Free Press.

Rogers, E. M. (1999). Anatomy of two subdisciplines of communication study. *Human Communication Research, 25*(4), 618–631.

Rogers, E. M. (2003). *Diffusion of innovations* (5th ed.). New York: Free Press.

Rogers, R. (2019). *Doing digital methods*. Los Angeles, CA: Sage.

Rojszczak, M. (2021). Surveillance, legal restraints and dismantling democracy: Lessons from Poland. *Democracy and Security, 17*(1), 1–29.

Rosengren, K. E., Wenner, L., & Palmgreen, P. (Eds.). (1985). *Media gratifications research: Current perspectives*. Beverly Hills, CA: Sage.

Ryan, M.-L. (1991). *Possible worlds, artificial intelligence, and narrative theory*. Bloomington, IN: Indiana University Press.

Salganik, M. J. (2018). *Bit by bit: Social research in the digital age*. Princeton, NJ: Princeton University Press.

Sargsyan, T. (2016). Data localization and the role of infrastructure for surveillance, privacy, and security. *International Journal of Communication, 10*, 2221–2237.

Savolainen, R. (1995). Everyday life information seeking: Approaching information seeking in the context of 'way of life'. *Library and Information Science Research, 17*(3), 259–294.

Savolainen, R. (2016). Approaches to socio-cultural barriers to information seeking. *Library and Information Science Research, 38*(1), 52–59.

Scheerder, A., van Deursen, A., & van Dijk, J. (2017). Determinants of internet skills, uses, and outcomes: A systematic review of the second- and third-level digital divide. *Telematics and Informatics, 34*(8), 1607–1624.

Schramm, W. (1964). *Mass media and national development*. Stanford, CA: Stanford University Press.

Schroeder, R. (2010). Mobile phones and the inexorable advance of multimodal connectedness. *New Media and Society, 12*(1), 75–90.

Schroeder, R. (2016). Big data business models: Challenges and opportunities. *Cogent Social Sciences*, *2*(1), 1166924.

Schroeder, R. (2018). *Social theory after the internet*. London: University of Central London.

Schudson, M. (1991). Historical approaches to communication studies. In K. B. Jensen & N. W. Jankowski (Eds.), *A handbook of qualitative methodologies for mass communication research* (pp. 175–190). London: Routledge.

Schudson, M. (1998). *The good citizen: A history of American civic life*. Cambridge, MA: Harvard University Press.

Scott, J. C. (1998). *Seeing like a state: How certain schemes to improve the human condition have failed*. New Haven, CT: Yale University Press.

Sen, A. (1999). *Development as freedom*. New York: Random House.

Sen, A. (2009). *The idea of justice*. Cambridge, MA: The Belknap Press of Harvard University Press.

Shannon, C. E., & Weaver, W. (1949). *The mathematical theory of communication*. Urbana, IL: University of Illinois Press.

Siebert, F., Peterson, T., & Schramm, W. (1956). *Four theories of the press*. Urbana, IL: University of Illinois Press.

Silver, C., & Lewins, A. (2014). *Using software in qualitative research: A step-by-step guide* (2nd ed.). Los Angeles, CA: Sage.

Silverstone, R. (2006). Domesticating domestication: Reflections on the life of a concept. In T. Berker, M. Hartmann, Y. Punie, & K. J. Ward (Eds.), *Domestication of media and technology* (pp. 229–248). Maidenhead: Open University Press.

Simonson, P., Peck, J., Craig, R. T., & Jackson, J. P. (Eds.). (2013). *The handbook of communication history*. New York: Routledge.

Sin, S.-C. J., & Vakkari, P. (2017). Information repertoires: Media use patterns in various gratification contexts. *Journal of Documentation*, *73*(6), 1102–1118.

Small, M. L. (2017). *Someone to talk to*. London: Oxford University Press.

Statista. (2022a). Market share of leading web analytics technologies worldwide in 2021. Retrieved from https://www.statista.com/statistics/1258557/web-analytics-market -share-technology-worldwide/.

Statista. (2022b). Mobile operating systems' market share worldwide from January 2012 to January 2022. Retrieved from https://www.statista.com/statistics/272698/global -market-share-held-by-mobile-operating-systems-since-2009/.

Stockmann, D. (2013). *Media commercialization and authoritarian rule in China*. Cambridge: Cambridge University Press.

Strate, L. (2016). Media ecology. In K. B. Jensen & R. T. Craig (Eds.), *International encyclopedia of communication theory and philosophy* (Vol. 3, pp. 1159–1167). Hoboken, NJ: Wiley-Blackwell.

Sunstein, C. R. (2007). *Republic.com 2.0*. Princeton, NJ: Princeton University Press.

Taneja, H., & Webster, J. G. (2016). How do global audiences take shape? The role of institutions and culture in patterns of web use. *Journal of Communication*, *66*(1), 161–182.

Tefertiller, A. (2018). Media substitution in cable cord-cutting: The adoption of web-streaming television. *Journal of Broadcasting and Electronic Media*, *62*(3), 390–407.

The Buggles. (1979). *Video killed the radio star*. London: Island Records.

Thompson, J. B. (1995). *The media and modernity*. Cambridge: Polity Press.

Thorhauge, A. M., & Lomborg, S. (2016). Cross-media communication in context: A mixed-methods approach. *MedieKultur: Journal of Media and Communication Research*, *60*, 70–86.

Travers, J., & Milgram, S. (1969). An experimental study of the small world problem. *Sociometry, 32*(4), 425–443.

Trepte, S., Reinecke, L., Ellison, N. B., Quiring, O., Yao, M. Z., & Ziegele, M. (2017). A cross-cultural perspective on the privacy calculus. *Social Media + Society, 3*(1), 1–13.

Tworek, H. J. S. (2019). *News from Germany: The competition to control world communications, 1900–1945.* Cambridge, MA: Harvard University Press.

United Nations. (1948). The universal declaration of human rights. Retrieved from http://www.un.org/en/universal-declaration-human-rights/.

United Nations. (2019). Demographic yearbook – 2018. United Nations, Statistical Division. Retrieved from https://unstats.un.org/unsd/demographic-social/products/dyb/dyb_2018/.

Uprichard, E. (2009). Introducing cluster analysis: What can it teach us about the case? In D. Byrne & C. Ragin (Eds.), *The SAGE handbook of case-based methods* (pp. 132–147). London: Sage.

Vallina, P., Feal, Á., Gamba, J., Vallina-Rodriguez, N., & Anta, A. F. (2019). Tales from the porn: A comprehensive privacy analysis of the web porn ecosystem. *Proceedings of the internet measurement conference.* Retrieved from https://dl.acm.org/doi/10.1145/3355369.3355583.

van Deursen, A. J., & Helsper, E. J. (2017). Collateral benefits of internet use: Explaining the diverse outcomes of engaging with the internet. *New Media and Society, 20*(7), 2333–2351.

van Dijck, J., Poell, T., & de Waal, M. (Eds.). (2018). *The platform society: Public values in a connective world.* Oxford: Oxford University Press.

van Dijk, J. (2017). Digital divide: Impact of access. In P. Rössler (Ed.), *The international encyclopedia of media effects* (pp. 1–11). London: Wiley.

van Rees, K., & van Eijck, K. (2003). Media repertoires of selective audiences: The impact of status, gender, and age on media use. *Poetics, 31*(5–6), 465–490.

Veale, M., & Borgesius, F. Z. (2022). Adtech and real-time bidding under European data protection law. *German Law Journal, 23*(2), 226–256.

Vermunt, J. K., & Magidson, J. M. (2002). Latent class cluster analysis. In J. A. Hagenaars & A. L. McCutcheon (Eds.), *Applied latent class analysis* (pp. 89–106). Cambridge: Cambridge University Press.

Ververis, V., Marguel, S., & Fabian, B. (2020). Cross-country comparison of internet censorship: A literature review. *Policy and Internet, 12*(4), 450–473.

Vihalemm, P. (Ed.). (2002). *Baltic media in transition.* Tartu: Tartu University Press.

Vitak, J., & Ellison, N. B. (2013). "There's a network out there you might as well tap": Exploring the benefits of and barriers to exchanging informational and support-based resources on Facebook. *New Media and Society, 15*(2), 243–259.

Wallerstein, I. (1974). *The modern world-system* (Vol. 1). New York: Academic Press.

Wang, G. (Ed.). (2011). *De-westernizing communication research: Altering questions and changing frameworks.* London: Routledge.

Watzlawick, P., Beavin, J. H., & Jackson, D. D. (1967). *Pragmatics of human communication: A study of interactional patterns, pathologies, and paradoxes.* New York: Norton.

Webster, J. G. (2014). *The marketplace of attention: How audiences take shape in a digital age.* Cambridge, MA: MIT Press.

Weiss, L. (2006). Infrastructural power, economic transformation, and globalization. In J. A. Hall & R. Schroeder (Eds.), *An anatomy of power: The social theory of Michael Mann* (pp. 167–186). Cambridge: Cambridge University Press.

Wellman, B., & Haythornthwaite, C. (2008). *The internet in everyday life.* London: Wiley.

Westlund, O., & Bjur, J. (2014). Media life of the young. *Young, 22*(1), 21–41.

Williams, R. (1974). *Television: Technology and cultural form*. London: Fontana.

Williams, R. (1975). *Culture and society 1780–1950*. Harmondsworth: Penguin. (Original work published 1958).

Winner, L. (1980). Do artifacts have politics? *Dædalus, 109*(1), 121–136.

Winseck, D. (2017). The geopolitical economy of the global internet infrastructure. *Journal of Information Policy, 7*(1), 228–267.

Winston, B. (1998). *Media, technology, and society – A history: From the telegraph to the internet*. London: Routledge.

Wittgenstein, L. (1953). *Philosophical investigations*. London: Macmillan.

Woolley, S. C., & Howard, P. N. (Eds.). (2019). *Computational propaganda: Political parties, politicians, and political manipulation on social media*. Oxford: Oxford University Press.

World Bank. (2021). Rural population (% of total population) – China. Retrieved from https://data.worldbank.org/indicator/SP.RUR.TOTL.ZS?locations=CN.

Wu, A. X., & Taneja, H. (2019). How did the data extraction business model come to dominate? Changes in the web use ecosystem before mobiles surpassed personal computers. *Information Society, 35*(5), 272–285.

Wu, X. (2019). Inequality and social stratification in postsocialist China. *Annual Review of Sociology, 45*(1), 363–382.

Yang, M. M.-H. (1994). *Gifts, favors, and banquets: The art of social relationships in China*. Ithaca, NY: Cornell University Press.

Zeng Skovhøj, F. H. (2020). *"I cannot go through a day without the internet": Exploring the dynamics of everyday uses of the internet in China*. PhD dissertation. University of Copenhagen.

Zhao, Y. (2012). Understanding China's media system in a world historical context. In D. C. Hallin & P. Mancini (Eds.), *Comparing media systems beyond the western world* (pp. 143–174). Cambridge: Cambridge University Press.

Zillen, N., & Hargittai, E. (2009). Digital distinction: Status-specific types of internet usage. *Social Science Quarterly, 90*(2), 274–291.

Zimmer, J. C., & Henry, R. M. (2017). The role of social capital in selecting interpersonal information sources. *Journal of the Association for Information Science and Technology, 68*(1), 5–21.

Zimmerman, D. H., & Wieder, D. L. (1977). The diary: diary–interview method. *Urban Life, 5*(4), 479–498.

Zou, M. (2015). Employment relations and social stratification in contemporary urban China: Does Goldthorpe's class theory still work? *Sociology, 49*(6), 1133–1150.

Zuboff, S. (2019). *The age of surveillance capitalism: The fight for a human future at the new frontier of power*. New York: Public Affairs.

INDEX

Note: Page numbers in **bold** reference tables. Page numbers in *italics* reference figures.

For Product Safety Concerns and Information please contact our EU
representative GPSR@taylorandfrancis.com
Taylor & Francis Verlag GmbH, Kaufingerstraße 24, 80331 München, Germany

www.ingramcontent.com/pod-product-compliance
Lightning Source LLC
Chambersburg PA
CBHW050352270326
41926CB00016B/3703